Frank Swinnerton, one of the true literary men of the twentieth century, is a novelist, critic, reviewer, journalist, essayist, literary historian and broadcaster. For more than fifty years a dominating figure in the world of letters, Mr. Swinnerton began his career at an English publishing house, where he met such authors as H. G. Wells, W. H. Hudson, and G. K. Chesterton. Among his more than fifty published works are *The Grace Divorce, A Tigress in Prothero, Figures in the Foreground, Death of a Highbrow,* and *Quadrille.* Born in London, Mr. Swinnerton makes his home in Surrey, England.

By the same author

DEATH OF A HIGHBROW
THE GRACE DIVORCE
A TIGRESS IN PROTHERO
THE WOMAN FROM SICILY
QUADRILLE
THE SUMNER INTRIGUE
A MONTH IN GORDON SQUARE
MASTER JIM PROBITY
A FLOWER FOR CATHERINE
THE DOCTOR'S WIFE COMES TO STAY
FAITHFUL COMPANY
ENGLISH MAIDEN
A WOMAN IN SUNSHINE
THANKLESS CHILD
THE FORTUNATE LADY
THE TWO WIVES
HARVEST COMEDY

ELIZABETH
THE GEORGIAN HOUSE
SKETCH OF A SINNER
A BROOD OF DUCKLINGS
SUMMER STORM
THE ELDER SISTER
YOUNG FELIX
THE THREE LOVERS
COQUETTE
SEPTEMBER
SHOPS AND HOUSES
NOCTURNE
THE CHASTE WIFE
ON THE STAIRCASE
THE HAPPY FAMILY
THE CASEMENT
THE YOUNG IDEA
THE MERRY HEART

FIGURES IN THE FOREGROUND
BACKGROUND WITH CHORUS
SWINNERTON: AN AUTOBIOGRAPHY
THE BOOKMAN'S LONDON
LONDONER'S POST
AUTHORS AND THE BOOK TRADE

THE GEORGIAN LITERARY SCENE
TOKEFIELD PAPERS
A LONDON BOOKMAN
GEORGE GISSING: A CRITICAL STUDY
R. L. STEVENSON: A CRITICAL STUDY
THE REVIEWING AND CRITICISM OF BOOKS
(J. M. Dent Memorial Lecture)
THE CATS AND ROSEMARY: A BOOK FOR CHILDREN

FRANK SWINNERTON
A Galaxy of Fathers

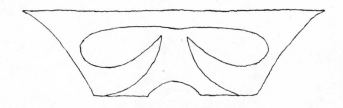

The fundamental defect of fathers
is that they want their children
to be a credit to them.

Bertrand Russell *Sceptical Essays*

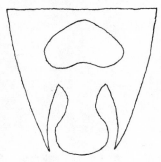

1966

DOUBLEDAY & COMPANY, INC., GARDEN CITY, NEW YORK

Library of Congress Catalog Card Number 66-17236
Copyright © 1966 by Frank Swinnerton
All Rights Reserved
Printed in the United States of America
First Edition in the United States of America

To my daughter
OLIVIA
and the
memory of
her sister
JANE

Contents

1	Fathers and Sons	11
2	Fathers and Daughters	18
3	The Social Background I	21
4	The Social Background II	27
5	The Social Background III	32
6	Thomas Seward	35
7	George Crabbe	48
8	The Arts in the Eighteenth Century	59
9	Burney's Early Years	65
10	Burney's Married Life	73
11	Burney and the Children	78
12	Two Authors in the Family	88
13	'Thou Shalt Live with Me for Ever'	94
14	Mrs Thrale	99
15	*Evelina*	103
16	Fanny as a Prodigy	109
17	The Burneys Move Upward	117
18	Burney Goes to Court	124

CONTENTS

19   Servitude   133

20   Liberation   142

21   Madame D'Arblay   148

22   Edgeworth of Edgeworthstown   154

23   Richard's Wife and Friends   162

24   Philosopher Day   169

25   Richard is Free   174

26   The Edgworth Family is Supervised   181

27   Maria   191

28   Danger at Home   198

29   The Visit to France   204

30   Farewell to Richard   213

31   A Jovial Doctor   219

32   Wolf at the Door   226

33   A Writer is Made   233

34   The Last Flickers   240

     Epilogue   245

     Index   249

The Author Explains

My dislike of footnotes, and the modern habit of peppering the text with tiny numerals which refer to masses of unilluminating detail at the end of a book or chapter, is so intense that the reader will find neither of these distractions in *A Galaxy of Fathers*. Wherever possible, sources are mentioned in the narrative; if they are not, fellow-students of the eighteenth century will recognize them, and those who read for entertainment will I hope thank me for an absence of parade. The book is one result of sixty years' pleasurable reading and rumination. I hope I have not been wasting my time in writing it.

F.S.

Old Tokefield
Cranleigh
Surrey

ONE

Fathers and Sons

I BEGIN, apologetically, by paraphrasing the summary of Jaques, in *As You Like It*. First a man is an infant; then, if normal, he becomes a schoolboy, an adolescent, a lover and husband, a father, and a grandfather—or slippered pantaloon. That is the limit of his progress. Beyond it, he dissolves into something called an ancestor, who, to Anglo-Saxons, is interesting only if one of his descendants does something remarkable.

In greater rôles he can be studied and re-studied as an influence upon his age, an artist, poet, or philosopher. In those less renowned he may represent material for the psychologists or genealogist, who, if he returns to an ungovernable self or revives an idiosyncrasy first noted in an older member of his family, will smack their lips as prospectors do when they discover a vein of gold. He is that fascinating specimen, an abnormality.

I am not concerned in the present book with abnormalities, or with the future or distant past. I seek only to portray a number of men as fathers. In various respects they were typical, in others exceptional; as fathers they conform, it seems to me, to a single interesting pattern; and as individuals they have one thing in common, which is that all have been made familiar to us by certain extant writings which show them as they would wish to be seen and as they would wish not to be seen. The writings, in part, are autobiographies which they did not live to complete, and in part the letters, diaries, and memorials of their children. All lived to be old; all illustrated different aspects of a century which, for some of us, has deep and inexhaustible interest.

Some have argued that while the child is father of the man, the man himself, having become father to a male child, develops a new personality. Over-simplifying, they tell us of crazed jealousy of a usurper; whereas, in reality, the father's emotions include excitement, pride, dreams of triumphs for his offspring in sport and career, and exasperation at the infant's helplessness and noisy egotism. These are simple reactions. Only if conflict among them produces a dangerous sense of insecurity in both father and son do they become complex.

As the boy learns to say 'me', and 'I want', and 'give, give!' the father becomes a child again. His love of juvenile sport revives. Pretending to show his son how to use new kites, cricket bats and balls, and miniature railways, he tends to appropriate them for his own use. When carried too far, his appropriations create lifelong resentments. Any boy wishes to play, however incompetently, with his own property.

He says: 'Let me! Let me!' The father, withholding the toy, replies: 'Yes, I know it's yours, boy; but you must do it like this. Watch me!' The chances between five feet ten and two or three feet are unequal; unseemly angers occur. If the mother intervenes, what is known as the eternal triangle rears its pointed apex. The psychiatrists are proved right after all.

Matters change when the boy goes to school and has other fights on his hands. He then needs a mature ally who can not only help with prep. but appreciate a stiff upper lip in hours of defeat. If the father responds with understanding, true friendship is forged. If he quibbles, or is cross, he is judged with tense severity.

This is a difficult time. Other schoolboys are boasting of their superhuman fathers, who score centuries at cricket, own gigantic cars, or receive decorations in the Birthday Honours. This son must have an effective retort. He develops an anxious loyalty to his own parent, who, perhaps, has done no more than write a book or shake hands with famous men at a reunion dinner. He wishes his father had been more lucky; he badly needs material for boasting.

Another element enters the relationship. This may be the boy's form-master, whose immediate and positive successes are apparent to all. He knows much, and demonstrates his knowledge. He bats like an Australian, crushes impudent juniors with rapier-like irony, bestows or withholds valuable marks, and is on view during many waking hours. Poor father, on the contrary, is unseen for days or months on end, grows miserly and querulous, or is preoccupied with boring affairs of his own.

His notions of mathematics are antediluvian, he slips over dates in history or the latitude of Juan Fernandez. His estimates of Buonaparte, popular song, popular comedians, and space fiction have not kept up with the seasons. Though still affectionate, the boy begins to think, first, that his master knows more than his father, and then that he himself does so. What a schoolmaster friend of mine calls 'the superiority complex' is bred.

He and the master are moderns; his father, sometimes obscurantist in other matters, but always irritable in face of a son's diminished respect, is seen to be old-fashioned. He may become even ridiculous; for children and adolescents share disdain of the fetish 'experience'. That is the real break between the generations.

If the break is not healed—and of course it is often healed by humour and intelligence, or by a common sorrow such as the loss of wife and mother—a sense of injury may remain with both father and son. 'I'm not a child any longer'; 'these youngsters are insufferably conceited.' Unfortunately fathers grow old before sons mature. Unless they retain elasticity of mind, and fight off painful illness or declining power, they develop a habit of grumbling. In that case they must be very wealthy indeed, with the weapon of disinheritance, to maintain any authority whatever.

Supposing the father to have attained a place in the world which distinguishes him from his fellows, he dies to an accompaniment of public lament. The question of a biography arises. Who is to write it? 'Why,' somebody asks the son, 'don't you do it yourself? You knew him better than anybody.'

Well, that seems to be true. None, except mother and wife, was ever so near; none saw him in the hours when that astonishing *persona* was not in the popular view; none has such command of family papers, old letters, the memory of, let us say, fifty years during which dignity has been added by success to deportment that was not always free from humbug.

'They don't know what he was like at home, in the early morning, when he sat in his dressing-gown, unshaven, dribbling tea down his chin, rowing with Mother, bellowing with tummy-ache, cursing the England Selectors, muttering foul oaths under his senile breath because he had been passed over in the choice for some honour he coveted . . . I do!'

The temptation is great. Such a book could exorcize the devils of indebtedness, humiliation, rebelliousness, conscious or implanted inferiority. 'I should do him justice, of course; anything else would be intolerable.'

In order to stimulate discussion, I have taken an extreme case. there are many pious biographies of their fathers by unreproached and unresentful sons, all of which show a determination to minimize faults. In Victorian days, especially, when blemishes were thought to be private faults, dutiful and respectable books were written by sons, as well as by other men, about teachers and philosophers and religious leaders; and not until Augustus Hare wrote *The Story of My Life* did innocent ladies and gentlemen guess what hypocrisies and horrors of domestic punishment could be inflicted by the supremely virtuous.

No glimpse of anything untoward was permitted by A. C. Benson, who celebrated his father, an Archbishop of Canterbury, with no hostility at all. One reason for this was probably that his mother, the Archbishop's devout wife, was still alive to censor his work. Another was the fact that A. C. Benson himself, whose platitudinous works of mild philosophy were so cruelly parodied by Max Beerbohm in *A Christmas Garland*, felt unsullied reverence for a great Churchman who had attained power without losing his convictions.

Benson's shorter biography of his brother, the dynamically Catholic Robert Hugh Benson, shows no such devotion. It abounds in dithyrambic passages, one of which describes trees and clouds mourning the death of that rather highly coloured novelist; but there is an undercurrent of brotherly dislike which the author was unaware of. In any case, Robert Hugh was only in a clerical sense a Father, and A.C. may well have suffered grievously from the candour of his younger and much cleverer brother.

The biography of the Archbishop is a different matter. It is in two large volumes, fully documented; and like others of its type is to be found in a dusty state in very large libraries, where it is read from time to time by ribalds who want to demonstrate that behind the lofty brows and monstrous whiskers of Victorian giants lie chinlessness and solemn ineptitude.

Lytton Strachey was not, as is commonly believed, the first person to write malicious biography. Debunking is an ancient sport, as, to go no farther back in history than the eighteenth century, J. T. Smith's *Nollekens and his Times* will prove; and it has been practised with irony or hatred for centuries. A few sons, while maintaining decorum, have laughed mischievously at the foibles of their great and good parents, diminishing them in size and with exquisite mockery adding destructive details for our amusement.

Of these, the familiar examples are Samuel Butler, son of another Archbishop, who, after producing an official biography, more candidly introduced his father into a novel, *The Way of All Flesh*, and Edmund Gosse, whose curious piece of self-betrayal, *Father and Son*, which also supplemented an official biography, has its own place in English literature. Dickens, too, while writing no formal biography of John, the Naval Pay-office clerk, laughed heartily at Mr Micawber; and I think there can be no doubt that H. G. Wells, while writing *Mr Polly*, had his own father, and perhaps his brothers, very much in mind.

Other men, not sons, but intimate or domesticated juniors, have been less genial than Wells and Dickens or less deliberately malicious than Gosse or Butler; but with son-like hostility have left their heroes tarnished. John Gibson Lockhart, beginning to write the life of his father-in-law with some indebtedness to the early chapters of *Redgauntlet*, proceeded to make Walter Scott a dull snob who romanticized the Highlander, grasped at estates and social standing, meddled illegitimately for the sake of money in business which he took no trouble to understand and which he overloaded with impracticable commitments, and at last became a hack in order to satisfy his creditors. Lockhart was often malignant as a party journalist; his biography of Scott is really a destructive portrait, needing at its best the corrective of Scott's own '*Gurnal.*'

Similarly, John Forster, who was Landor's literary executor, produced a Life of his benefactor which Mrs Lyn Linton, ardently defensive of her 'Father', calls 'disgraceful'; and James Anthony

Froude saw no harm in justifying Jane Welsh by means of a ruthlessly unpleasant picture of Thomas Carlyle in the home and as a private critic of his contemporaries. Forster ('treacherous and disloyal as he was egotistic and jealous'), Froude, and Lockhart were all responsible for a fall in the prestige of men for whom they professed the greatest admiration. They were probably unaware of their animus; but in spirit they were true sons.

In Carlyle's case, the fall was hastened by our discovery that apart from rhetorical lamentation he had little to say: the brilliance of his dramatic descriptions is now ignored. In Landor's case, the very aloofness of the original, and for many readers the remoteness of his themes, made him an easy candidate for oblivion. In Scott's case, the originality of his contribution, in its day, to the craft and richness of the Novel is discounted. I blame Lockhart, one of those dull, clever parasites who cut a figure while alive, and then sink into the shadows, for carrying Scott into limbo along with him.

Scott's decline in reputation as a man began with the appearance of Lockhart's book; that his decline in reputation as a writer was helped by the fact that he wrote too much after his vein was exhausted confirms, but does not justify, Lockhart's portrait. As to John Forster, 'cold, carping and unsympathetic', as Mrs Lynn Linton calls him, he aimed at greatness by magnitude, and is now remembered only as the satellite of Dickens.

Quite different are two men who have had sly fun with their fathers' characters. I refer to George Crabbe, junior, who had proposed to read aloud to George senior the affectionately demure record he had begun, and Osbert Sitwell, through whose barbed brilliance Sir George Sitwell has been made a delightful figure for succeeding generations.

These instances will suggest the reason why a man who wishes to be lauded after death should arrange that neither a son, nor a son-in-law, nor a disciple should write his biography. Unless he very circumspectly does this he may be held up to ridicule, or have his less attractive peccadilloes cruelly exposed. If naturally a hypocrite, he should write the book himself, insisting upon his virtues. If over-fond of women or wine, or given to homo-sexual practices, he should outlive his contemporaries, after freely threatening all gossips with the laws of libel, and destroying all evidence of his sins. He will not escape, if he is a writer, the ghoulish disclosures of those who psychoanalyse his writings; but he will have taken a simple precaution.

Alternatively, and best of all, he should beget a literary daughter.

TWO

Fathers and Daughters

THE literary daughter can be an encumbrance to a literary father during his lifetime, as a corpse is to one who has just committed murder; there is no getting rid of her. But when once the father is dead she can be relied upon as the acme of loyalty. Even if her father has not been an admirable character, she will defend him. If he has been less distinguished than herself, she will exaggerate his distinction. If, from vanity, he has left in her hands notes or records of his earlier days, she will expand them with hundreds of undeserved compliments. She will extol his scholarship and his verse, his inventive genius, parental wisdom, social gifts, and lovable character, leaving it to men to say that he was a criticaster, boaster, sot, bore, liar, or gambler. She does this, not from a strained sense of duty, but because she really believes that the man she saw first from her cradle has god-like qualities.

Nowadays, perhaps, the spell is less potent. Fathers and mothers are discarded earlier as their offspring taste freedom and find others doing the same. In the eighteenth century, which was the century of Men, daughters were kept in awe of superior beings. For the most part they did as they were told. No careers were open to them; they were bred for marriage, sewing, and housewifery; especially for marriage:

'Why must women be *driven to the necessity* of marrying?' Mrs Delany wrote in 1750 to her sister Ann, 'a state that should always be a matter of choice! and if a young woman has not fortune sufficient to maintain her in the position she has been bred to, what can she do but marry? and to avoid living either very obscurely or running into debt, she accepts of a match with no other view than that of interest.

Has not this made matrimony an irksome prison to many, and prevented its being that happy union of hearts where mutual choice and mutual obligations make it the most perfect state of friendship?'

She was speaking of young women in her own class, which was that of impoverished aristocracy, and she had suffered herself from dictated marriage; but her words have a wider application. Outside matrimony or some kind of domestic situation either with her own family or in some genteel household, there were no situations vacant.

Nor was liberty of action or comment allowed to these same young women. In a more majestic mood this same Mrs Delany insisted upon discipline in the nursery:

'I am glad you have got our little god-daughter, Sally; I hope she will improve from your advice, and *by all means curb her* if she is *too forward in giving her opinions*: a conceited man or woman is *abominable*, but a conceited girl is *insupportable.*'

So daughters were to be seen, not heard; corrected if they spoke out of turn; kept in a state of subordination to their parents, especially to their fathers. The effect of this discipline, a paradox which has been seen through the ages, was to make girls adore their fathers.

I have emphasized this point because it is of certain fathers who were adored that I write hereafter. They include Thomas Seward, Canon Residentiary of Lichfield Cathedral, Charles Burney, the historian of Music, Dr Mitford, a medical practitioner who did not practise, and Richard Lovell Edgeworth, inventor, educationalist, and Utilitarian. They do not include the Rev. George Austen, Rector of two neighbouring parishes in Hampshire, those of Deane and Steventon.

Jane Austen was in a different category from the other daughters I have indicated. Like her own Elizabeth Bennet, she hoped 'never to ridicule what is wise and good.' 'Follies and nonsense,' she said, '*do* divert me, I own, and I laugh at them whenever I can.' She could criticize Elizabeth Bennet's eccentric and fundamentally irresponsible father, scathingly expose the snobbery of Sir Walter Elliott, and make exquisite fun of Mr Woodhouse; but except for some affectionate amusement at Mr Austen's enthusiasm for pigs she showed for him nothing but loving respect. She did not write his biography; he would not have wished it.

He was a modest scholar. 'His tenderness as a Father, who can do justice to? . . . The Serenity of the Corpse [for the Rev. George Austen was just dead when she reported the fact to her brother, Captain Francis Austen] is most delightful!—It preserves the sweet, benevolent smile which always distinguished him.' But then, unlike my other Fathers, he had never striven to impose his will upon his children; and Jane was the indulged younger daughter in a family of intelligent, high-spirited, and resourceful boys. Laughter was prevalent in her home; laughter and unstinted, unsentimental love.

She was encouraged from an early age in the use of her pen, which produced sometimes delicious burlesques of her favourite reading, the 'horrid' romance of Mrs Radclyffe and others. Such freedom was allowed her that she ran lightly through the Parish Register in her father's church at Steventon, and in the space at the beginning of the Register which provides an 'example' of the forms to be used she recorded her own banns and imaginary marriages. Nobody forbade; nobody objected to her sportive fancy.

'On a date unspecified,' she wrote, 'the banns of marriage were published between Henry Frederic Howard Fitzwilliam of London and Jane Austen of Steventon,' while just below this she announced that 'Edward Arthur William Mortimer of London and Jane Austen of Steventon were married, on a date also unspecified.' To fill still-unused lines she added: 'Marriage was solemnized between us, Jack Smith, Jane Smith late Austen.'

This will show the latitude permitted by her father, whose predecessor at Steventon had been Dr Russell, Mary Mitford's maternal grandfather. None of the other Fathers in my Galaxy would have been similarly complaisant. None of them could have allowed his daughter the 'open pleasantry' nourished in a genius by those who were neither disciplinarians nor possessive egotists nor gambling snobs who used their children as a principal source of income or fame. But then Mr Austen was unworldly. He was, strictly speaking, a private man. His letters were destroyed; he left no memorials of his life; he died lamented by his family, and would now be forgotten if Jane had not written those merry novels which yield new delights at every re-reading.

She was a fortunate woman. Her life was free from interference.

THREE

The Social Background

I

ALL these fathers belonged to the eighteenth century. We think of that century as a clearly defined period with a character of its own; an age of reason in which thought and poetry were uninspired by ecstasy. But was it as uniform as the common notion assumes? The eldest man in my Galaxy was born, one year before that epitome of Englishness Samuel Johnson, in 1708, when Queen Anne was on the throne and Marlborough was almost a king; the youngest was born in 1760, the year in which George III succeeded his grandfather. All lived to read of the tragic events in France in which a king lost his life and a tyrant was carried by events to supreme power. Almost all witnessed the upsurge of a new lyricism in English poetry, conducted by men born before the century ended.

G. M. Trevelyan, seeking to define the eighteenth century as a period, ingeniously traced its beginning to the year in which Daniel Defoe began, at Harley's command, to make that 'tour through the whole island of Great Britain' which enabled him to describe conditions prior to 1724. Its end, he thought, was shown in the years 1821–1832, when William Cobbett, in the *Rural Rides*, set down characteristically energetic views of wrongs and wickednesses as he saw them at the end of the age. It is an illuminating and very helpful suggestion.

It is especially so to those of us who have been bewildered by more formal efforts to focus the century from 1701 to 1820. Those efforts have carefully and earnestly concentrated upon the importance of a single aspect of the complex and ever-changing pattern. To one historian, for example, only a Utilitarianism which began with Locke and ended with Bentham is to be seen. To another, on the contrary, the key is to be found in John Wesley, who substituted for the rational a passionate assurance that salvation could be won only by the most abject faith. Both views are credible; both are partial.

To a third historian the political struggles were all-important; first, those between Marlborough and the Tories led by Harley and Boling-broke, those between Robert Walpole and his enemies, then, onward, between the elder Pitt and a crowd of knaves, between Burke and Fox, between Pitt the younger and men who, groaning under new taxes, thought his wars would destroy England.

A fourth has argued for many pages the question whether the power of the Crown was, or was not, an ever-increasing menace to liberty; and Sir Lewis Namier, who pooh-poohed the whole affair, had much sport in showing how one constitutionalist after another elaborated a single paragraph in Horace Walpole's letters to prove a danger which, he said, never existed. I must admit an inability to recognize this sinister force in the old buffer who could never understand how the apple got into the dumpling, and who thought some of Shakespeare's work 'sad stuff'; but I am not a historian.

A fifth worthy member of this class concentrates upon the growth of Empire and the immense wealth and corruption of Warren Hastings and the Nabobs. A sixth, consisting of professors such as George Saintsbury, who wrote a book with the strange title *The Peace of the Augustans*, is absorbed in the problem of literary fashion as it passed from classicism, via the baroque, to the romantic, or emotional. To a seventh it was a century in which common land was ruthlessly stolen from the freemen of England by racketeers who enclosed it and reduced the freemen to broken pauperism. And to an eighth, who traced the development of aesthetic, as well as political, theory to the Continent and as far back as the Renaissance, it was a time when men everywhere were stirred into profounder thought by military humiliation. All these views must be remembered as we follow a less sweeping course; the facts on which they are based will be incidentally glimpsed. I seek only, in the present book, to sketch the life of the community as background to the lives of individuals representing their age in a single capacity—as Fathers.

     .   .   .   .   .

Some of these men, taking advantage of social conditions favourable to their class, did a great deal, out of doors, of coursing, fishing, and bird-shooting. At home they sat very comfortably at leisure, reading, talking, dining amply with large parties of friends as their guests, and playing the card games of commerce, loo, quadrille, cribbage, and whist or whisk. Others braved the abominable roads on horseback or in their own usually springless carriages, and crossed stormy waters at the risk of their lives in ships no bigger than fishing smacks. If they went to Ireland they were in constant danger from human enemies as well as the elements.

They lodged in great discomfort. John Byng, fifth earl of Torrington, said in 1781: 'The imposition in travelling is abominable; the innkeepers are insolent, the hostlers are sulky, the chambermaids are pert, and the waiters are impertinent; the meat is tough, the wine is foul, the beer is hard, the sheets are wet, the linnen is dirty, and the knives are never clean'd.'

Nor was this all. The Rev. James Woodforde (1740–1803), immortal as the keeper of the *Diary of a Country Parson*, was for some time in the habit, when he visited London, of staying at the Belle Sauvage on Ludgate Hill. He commended the landlord and landlady, and handsomely tipped the servants; but he was so much bitten by bugs that his face and hands were 'terribly swelled', and he preferred at last to sleep ('tolerably well') in his clothes in an armchair.

If they were rich, men had their own chariots, drawn by four or six horses. The less rich were content with smaller chaises or phaetons, with in some case only one horse. If, possessing none of these conveniences, they travelled in haste, they went post, which meant that they hired vehicles from point to point in their journey; or at the very worst they rumbled and jolted along in what were called stage-wagons such as those in which Swift travelled from Moor Park when he visited his mother in Leicestershire.

Superior to these wagons were the stage-coaches, or what Wesley, who was not used to them, called 'machines', which journeyed between London and certain provincial cities at stated hours, and held four or six inside passengers; and if a stranger fat woman with many bandboxes intruded upon the others, or if children were sick *en route*, the consequences were almost insupportable. Servants, and those who needed to economize, had outside places at lower fares.

The coaches often left, like modern aeroplanes, in the dead of night. They travelled blindly along the turnpike roads with only side-lights to signal their approach.

The man who tells us most about the costs and hazards of travelling by coach and hired chaise in the eighteenth century is that same obscure country parson, James Woodforde. He kept a record of the exact time taken by his journeys, the food eaten at the inns at which he and his niece Nancy alighted, and the methods by which year after year he returned from his Norfolk rectory at Weston Longueville to his family home in Somerset, with diversions to Oxford and Bath (where the innkeeper's name was Pickwick). And he never grumbled.

He set out from Weston Longueville, using his own little 'cart' or curricle, which cost nine guineas when new, or a hired chaise, which cost ten shillings for a single one-way journey; and he later caught 'the heavy Coach for London'. The fare between Norwich and London or Bath and London was thirty shillings a head, plus a surcharge for the exceess luggage which Woodforde, prepared for a four-months stay away from home, always carried. After travelling all night from 7 p.m. his party from Norwich reached London at three o'clock the following afternoon, when they drank, as a reviver, some rum and water, which cost him, for two persons, sixpence.

By private four-horse coach, or by express chaise, spanking along main turnpike roads, it was possible to cover a hundred miles in a day. On horseback, unless one were Nicks (or Dick Turpin), flying to York in pursuit of an alibi, sixty miles in a day seems to have been found a comfortable stint. There was little occasion for haste; the ease of upholstery lay in the future. Nothing discouraged whole middle-class families from setting out on long journeys and reaching the homes of their friends and relations, where they stayed for weeks at a time, sure of their welcome, and all 'very low' at parting again.

Throughout the century men made great journeys on horseback. Defoe did this in the seventeen-twenties; Wesley did it in mid-century, until his health failed; Byng did it later on; Dr Darwin, Richard Lovell Edgeworth, and Dr Mitford did it at all times in their lives. No other power than that of the horse was available; and the ladies of the family, when there were no carriages to be had, rode alongside or behind the men.

Arriving at their destinations, they found that with a little contrivance houses could be made to hold a number of guests. There were no queues for baths; servants were plentiful and able to provide meals which would make a modern dietician shudder ('We had a very good dinner,' says James Woodforde, after visiting a cousin in 1789. 'A fine Piece of fresh Salmon, a leg of mutton rosted, fricasseed Rabit, a Couple of Ducks rosted and Peas, a currant Pye and Syllabub, Ec. A good Desert of Fruit after Dinner, Strawberries, Cherries and Currants'); and in Ireland, according to Mrs Delany, 'High living is too much the fashion. You are not invited to dinner to any private gentleman of £1000 a year or less, that does not give you seven *dishes* at one course; and Burgundy and Champagne; and these dinners they give once or twice a-week, [so] that provision is now as dear as in London'; and while the men fished and coursed, rode, smoked, and drank, the women bore children, visited, cooked, bottled fruit, made and mended clothes, drank tea, chatted, and of course joined the men at cards after dinner. They played for money; but sometimes females of the family were excused payment of their losses.

When friends dined at each other's houses, and stayed late over wine and cards or discussion, they did so on moonlight nights. This fact gave its name to the Lunar Society founded by Erasmus Darwin and composed, with him, of Samuel Galton, James Keir, Matthew Boulton, Joseph Priestley, James Watt, and other seeking spirits, the meetings of which took place at different houses when the moon was at its full.

The reason for this choice was the darkness and ill-condition of the roads. When men had drunk deeply—and some of them, not the Lunatics, would drink all afternoon and evening—they were apt, like Parson Woodforde's convivial brother John, to be thrown from their horses into ditches, where they might die from exposure. Erasmus Darwin once carried home a man whom he had chanced to see lying unconscious at the side of the road; and was amused rather than amazed to find that he had saved the life of his normally sober brother-in-law. One of James Woodforde's servants, stunned by his fall, and subsequently sobered, spent the whole night looking for his horse, which had been found by somebody else and taken to a convenient stables.

These were the travels and occupations, not of the labouring poor, who never left their cottages after dark, but of those who, while not belonging to the aristocracy, were little pinched for money, and maintained a social life with which it seems they were rarely bored.

FOUR

The Social Background

II

GREAT FOLK, involved in politics, provided their relations with sinecures, or 'patent places under the Crown' which supplied luxury without labour. They were held by men of birth who drew the salaries attached to them and employed drudges to do the work for very inferior pay. Horace Walpole, for example, was made, first, Inspector of Imports and Exports in the Custom House, and, later, successively, Usher of the Exchequer, Comptroller of the Pipe and Clerk of the Estreats. These places brought him, it is said by his biographer, R. W. Ketton-Cremer, an income of over three thousand pounds a year, and allowed him to become the arch dilettante, gossip, and letter-writer extraordinary which we know him to have been. When attacked by political opponents as an idle placeman, he indignantly defended his rights, on the ground that his father, the giver of these good things, had rendered immeasurable service to the State, and was entitled to provide for his children.

Horace Walpole was far from being alone in the possession of sinecures. The eighteenth century, in England and on the Continent, where princes and rich nobles abounded, was an era of patronage. Until the middle of the century, when Johnson told Boswell that the system was dead, authors and artists and musicians were obsequious to possible patrons. The owners of great estates, being a class apart, ruled the country—abroad, their own principalities and dukedoms—and regulated all culture. In England, they nominated Members of Parliament and distributed clerical livings among their sons or dependants. Until the merchants and Nabobs forced their way into power by money, the possession of land was the one great source of wealth and influence. Hence the enclosures; hence the subservience to rank of those who were not genteelly born; hence the eagerness for royal and noble approbation.

This last explains Johnson's acceptance of his pension. He was no lickspittle; but when told that the King himself had offered him three hundred pounds a year as a mark of royal favour he did not hesitate to accept. It explains why Burke was among those who encouraged, or were said to have encouraged, Charles Burney's joy in his daughter Fanny's Court post. It explains George Crabbe's little snobberies and his devotion to the Duke and Duchess of Rutland. It also explains, while the spirit of the century lingered, Walter Scott's land-hunger, eagerness to please 'my fat friend' King George the Fourth, and pride in the friendship of the head of his Clan, the Duke of Buccleugh.

Having undisputed greatness, relics of which can be seen today in the indifference to censorious public opinion of persons born to rank (while the middle classes cling painfully to respectability, and will even commit murder to maintain its appearance), the nobles of the eighteenth century did as they chose. They gambled heavily, giving a ruinous lead to their imitative social inferiors, the squires; they were sometimes guilty of political jobs which today would be exposed at once by the popular newspapers; and they ignored with ease the squalor in which debtors, thieves, and the London gin-making and gin-sousing poor lived.

The best of them, however, followed the course advocated by Sir Winston Churchill and his father, Lord Randolph: they 'trusted the people', and looked after their welfare. Though mighty, they were not tyrannical. As a consequence they were not hated; and if the words 'levellers' and 'subordination' crop up throughout the century, the one being used by Johnson with scorn, and the other with approval as a highly proper rule of life, the general view of the French Revolution, when it came, was that such bloody deeds as were done in Paris were not to be copied here.

The nobility might be supreme, especially at Court and in Governments; but those who gambled were often ruined by reckless wagers, by cards, by betting on horses. Inheriting rich estates, the rents from which seemed inexhaustible, they constantly found themselves in monetary difficulties. They also had upstart rivals. Merchants, even before Queen Anne's day, were acquiring the mansions of greater men who had been forced to give them up, or mansions which they built for themselves. Such merchants traded with the Continent in wool and manufactured goods; they sold corn abroad; they grew so rich that they could afford to bribe electors on a grand scale (it was always done) and acquire political influence.

They wanted power; and as a means to prestige they wanted estates. Since original landlords wanted money, there could be only one end. Labourers who had worked contentedly for their masters on farms and in fields and gardens, and had made steady, if uneconomic, use of land held in common by villagers everywhere, found their ancient liberty threatened. They had already, by the end of the seventeenth century, been forced according to Defoe, to defend their rights against unscrupulous attempts to exclude them from the common land. Now, as the eighteenth century progressed, they were compelled to fight even harder as rapacious landlords seized more and more of what they had previously enjoyed. The so-called 'enclosures' of common land became one of the scandals of the age.

They have long been the subject of bitter discussion, largely arising from the indignant assembly of details by J. L. and Barbara Hammond. These details have been re-interpreted by other writers who claim that the enclosures were of value to what is called the National Economy; but they were not made from patriotism. They were made from greed, or from the desperation of gamblers; and the effect of them was to turn husbandmen into paupers.

Defoe tells of an episode as early as the reign of King William the Third. 'At Tring,' says he, 'is a most delicious house, built *à la moderne*, as the French call it, by the late Mr Grey, who was for many years Secretary of the Treasury . . . There was an eminent contest rose between Mr Grey, and the poor of the parish, about his enclosing part of the common to make him a park; Mr Grey presumed upon his power, set up his pales, and took a large parcel of open land, call'd Wiggington-Common; the cottagers and farmers oppos'd it, by their complaints a great while; but finding he went on with his work, and resolv'd to do it, they rose upon him, pull'd down his banks, and forced up his pales, and carried away the wood, or set it in a heap and burnt it; and this they did several times, till he was oblig'd to desist; after some time he began again, offering to treat with the people, and to give them any equivalent for it. But that not being satisfactory, they mobb'd him again. How they accommodated it at last, I know not; but I see that Mr Gore [Mr Grey's successor in ownership of the delicious house] has a park, and a very good one but not large: I mention this as an instance of the popular claim in England; which we call right of commonage, which the poor take to be as much their property, as a rich man's land is his own.'

Those were early days in a struggle which lasted throughout the century. What happened in many instances was that the gamblers, at their wits' ends for some means of averting ruin, introduced Bills into Parliament, which were passed by means of conspiracy among their friends, entitling them to enclose the land and rob the commoners. This is clearly shown by a quotation given in Mr. Hammond's book, *The Village Labourer*, from George Selwyn, Chairman of the relevant Parliamentary Committee. He said of Bolingbroke (not St John, but his brother): 'Bully has a scheme of enclosure which, if it succeeds, I am told will free him from all his difficulties.' The scheme was intended to put a noble and already-landed but largely insolvent debtor 'once more on his legs' at the expense of his humble neighbours.

And the consequences? John Byng, riding about England in 1781, found that the neighbourhood of Burford, in Oxfordshire, 'is now spoilt by enclosures . . . As a sportsman I hate enclosures, and, as a citizen, I look on them as the greedy tyrannies of the wealthy few, to oppress the indigent many, and an iniquitous purchase of invaluable rights.' Eight years later, riding in the Midlands, he stayed at a wretched inn in Meriden, near Coventry, and there conversed with a woman cottager:

'[Byng] "Has Meriden Common been long enclosed?" [Woman] "Ah, lackaday, Sr, that was a sad job; and ruin'd all us poor volk: and those who then gave into it, now repent it." [Byng] "Why so?" [Woman] "Because, we had our garden, our bees, our share of a flock of sheep, the feeding of our geese; and could cut turf for our fuel. Now all that is gone! Our cottage, as good a one as this, we gave but 50 shillings a year for; and for this we are obliged to pay £9 10s.; and without any ground: and coals are risen upon us from 7d. to 9d. the hundred. My cottage with many others is pull'd down;

and the poor are sadly put to it to get a house to put their heads in!!!
Heigh ho!" '

The poor who were to be trusted by the true nobility, and robbed
of their rights by the gamblers or the acquisitive, were not always
the honest creatures we should like to think them. They were mostly
illiterate and very dirty; the footmen who arrogantly sent non-
tipping visitors from their masters' doors were worse than those
lines of Continental hotel-servants which we all remember with
hostility; the easily-obtainable cookmaids had often to be sent away
from a house when the consequences of forbidden amours became
too evident; and as part of the general festivity celebrated in comic
fiction they drank, quarrelled, and fought in a way greatly embarrassing to those in real life who were dependent on their service.

Highwaymen were a menace on certain roads or heaths; wandering
pedlars or beggars by arts escaped the Vagrancy Laws and collected
largesse or property from householders; pickpockets abounded in the
cities. Country girls, arriving in London and asking for direction to
the homes of the ladies who had engaged them as servants, were
pounced upon by harpies who converted them at once into prosti-
tutes. Prostitution was unchecked in the dark streets; so that prowling
lechers such as the young Boswell were easily accommodated. And
when Wesley gathered multitudes to hear his promise of damnation
to sinners he aroused such conviction of evil in his congregations that
devils were heard to howl in quite mediaeval fashion and were even
seen as they escaped from those who writhed in torment under his
exorcisms.

FIVE

The Social Background

III

MOST of the clergy lacked Wesley's salvationist energy. They had a horror of what they called 'enthusiasm', which was the contemporary name for fanaticism; and they could not approve his habit of riding from county to county and holding meetings which stirred crowds for a day into paroxysms of faith or terror. They did not exorcize. They read their sermons, visited the devout sick, baptized children, churched women, sometimes—under the Squire—managed their villages; but they did not wrestle fiercely with sin. Some of them, like the unattractive parsons in *Tom Jones*, guzzled, rode to hounds, and looked like pigs.

Oliver Goldsmith, of course, painted from his warm heart the portraits of two delightful characters, the one Primrose, the other that beloved cleric in *The Deserted Village*:

> Now yonder copse, where once the garden smiled,
> And still where many a garden flower grows wild,
> There, where a few torn shrubs the place disclose,
> The village preacher's modest mansion rose.
> A man he was to all the country dear,
> And passing rich with forty pounds a year,
> Remote from towns he ran his godly race,
> Nor e'er had chang'd, nor wish'd to change, his place
> . . . .
> But in his duty prompt, at every call,
> He watch'd and wept, he prayed and felt for all.

The preacher, however, had been lucky to receive forty pounds a year for tending his village flock. Obscure clergy were often no better off than their poorest neighbours. Particulars are given in Mrs Delany's *Autobiography and Correspondence* of an unfortunate curate named Robert Walker. He and his wife, after losing one child, had still eight others to rear. His total annual income was made up of

£5 from the Governors of Queen Anne's Bounty;

£2 from the Lord of the Manor;

£3 from the several inhabitants of his village, Seathwaite, settled upon their tenements as a rent charge;

£3 from surplice fees and voluntary contributions; He had £40 for his wife's fortune; no real estate of his own (he was the youngest of twelve, and the progeny of obscure parents);

£4 was the value he set on his house and garden.

We are not told how this wretched man and his family subsisted on £17 a year; but they must have represented the lowest possible state among the clergy.

By contrast, such men as the scholarly father of Jane Austen, and the not particularly scholarly Parson Woodforde, were wealthy. George Austen, indeed, although early orphaned, was very generously treated in youth by an uncle who, with the help of a cousin, enabled him to minister to a pair of Hampshire villages with a joint population of under three hundred. Parson Woodforde's living, which was in the gift of New College, Oxford, carried him to a Norfolk village of which the population was 360. His stipend was £300 a year. He seems always to have been able to find a useful curate to work while he took long holidays in Somerset, and at least one of them refused all payment for the help he had rendered.

Woodforde was always at home to receive his tithes; and he gave those who paid them a merry evening at the rectory, with quantities of food and liquor. He interfered very little with the morals of his parishioners; he gardened and farmed, killed hundreds of superfluous toads, fished giant pike from his 'great pond', and read almost nothing at all. *Tom Jones, Roderick Random,* and *Evelina* were lent to him, the last of which, by a Miss Burney, he found 'very cleaver and sensible.' In addition he baptized and buried his parishioners, and in times of great hardship for the poor actively helped in the distribution of bread among them. On certain days of the year he presented the old men of his village with a shilling each, and the children a penny apiece; he dined with the Squire, preached two or three times, much against his will, in Norwich Cathedral; and was a humane man who noted down in his diary the immense meals eaten at home and abroad and, very meticulously, his winnings and losings at cribbage, loo, and quadrille, which games he played with his niece Nancy, winning or losing sixpence a time, or, in his own words, 'neither won or lost.'

Other clergymen rose to wealth, rank, chariots, and bishoprics. They belonged by birth to the nobility or the near-gentry. If they had money, or sinecures, they found the eighteenth century an ideal period to live in. The majority dwelt remote from intrusive urbanization; they idled through long days of ease, taking excursions of pleasure whenever so inclined. Untroubled by theological subtleties, they became at last invalids who enjoyed virtuous consideration from children or relations, and said their prayers with perfect equanimity. It is not surprising that they bestirred themselves to no revolutionary thought or aspiration. As long as they kept quiet, all, for them, was for the best in this best of possible worlds.

SIX

Thomas Seward

ONE who kept quiet until he reached senility was Thomas Seward. There was no clear reason why the story of his uneventful life should be written by anybody; and even Anna, his literary daughter, 'the Swan of Lichfield', who composed a memoir of Erasmus Darwin, did no more than contribute some brief notes on her father to the Press. Like Seward himself, she was a strange mixture of timidity and arrogance; but she was a much more respectworthy person than he. She had a busy, affected pen; he had only an obsessive concern with his own health and comfort.

'Sir,' remarked Samuel Johnson, 'his ambition is to be a fine talker; so he goes to Buxton, and such places, where he may find companions to listen to him. And, sir, he is a valetudinarian, one of those who are always mending themselves. I do not know a more disagreeable character than a valetudinarian: . . . Sir, he brings himself to the state of a hog in a stye.'

Johnson's impatience can be explained. Seward was one year older than himself, and had missed all the adversity against which he struggled in boyhood. Born when his mother was forty-four, Seward spent his younger days at ease, attended Westminster School, and went to Cambridge, where he became a Fellow of St John's College and made grand acquaintances. One who met him at that time—she became Mrs Delany—found him at the age of twenty-six 'civil and sensible, but a little *affected in his expressions,* which is the University air.' She thought the affectation would be cured as he saw more of the world.

Although he saw more of the world, it was a very small world, and he showed no curiosity for anything larger. After being for two years domestic chaplain to the Duke of Grafton he became travelling tutor, or governor, to Lord Charles Fitzroy; but the travels of that young man were quickly ended at Genoa by a malignant fever, and the tour ended. Horace Walpole tells a characteristically amusing and malicious story of what happened. 'Lord Charles Fitzroy . . . being saved (as Mentor thought) by Dr Shadwell, the governor whipped up to his chamber, and began a complimentary ode to the physician, but was called down before it was finished on his pupil's relapse, who DID die. However, the bard was too much pleased with the *début* of his poem to throw it away, and so finished it, though his gratitude had been still-born.'

At some time subsequent to this calamity, Seward was made rector of Eyam, a village in the high peak of Derbyshire; and his elder daughter, who was to be admired during her lifetime and ridiculed ever afterwards, was born at Eyam on December 12th, 1742. As far as I can tell, Seward retained this living, under the free-and-easy clerical system of the eighteenth century, for many years, long after his appointment in 1747 as Canon Residentiary of Lichfield Cathedral. From 1753 until his death in 1790 he was allowed through the courtesy of an absentee bishop to live very enviably in the Bishop's Palace in Lichfield, entertaining selected guests from the neighbourhood and indulging his taste for conversation. Johnson, when he occasionally visited the city of his birth, had the annoyance of finding an interloper enjoying undeserved sovereignty there.

Seward's immediate predecessor in the Bishop's Palace was Gilbert Walmsley, whom Boswell describes as Registrar of the Ecclesiastical Court. Walmsley had been young Sam Johnson's benefactor. He was a man of whom Johnson always spoke with respect. Indeed, he is praised in *The Lives of the Poets* as 'one of the first friends that literature procured me, and I hope that at least my gratitude made me worthy of his notice . . . He was of an advanced age, and I was only not a boy, yet he never received my notions with contempt . . . I honoured him, and he endured me.'

This testimony to one who invited to 'his elegant table' a genius whom Anna Seward—a typically genteel person—called 'the low-born squalid youth' was exceptional; but Johnson met at Walmsley's table (he admitted) 'companions such as are not often found.' No such acknowledgement was ever made to another benefactor, Mr Hunter, headmaster of the free-school at Lichfield, who introduced him to Walmsley.

Now Hunter was father to the girl who became Mrs Thomas Seward. Boswell simply calls him Johnson's earliest teacher; and Anna Seward, resenting this affront to her grandfather, never forgave it. Though she modelled her prose style, to its detriment, on Johnson's she lost no opportunity of decrying the man, his criticism, and his failure to appreciate her own idols, Milton and Gray. He was hateful to her. He respected neither her father nor herself.

There was a further incompatibility. Thomas Seward (he pronounced the name See-ward) was a Whig. He consorted, when he could do so, with Dr Parr, the lisping political libertarian, who sought to rival Johnson as a talker, and whose affectations moved Thomas de Quincey to brilliant destructiveness. And until they quarrelled he was on terms of intimacy with another of Johnson's antipathies, Erasmus Darwin, then resident in Lichfield.

The antipathy in this case was returned. Darwin and Johnson could never agree; and Darwin, in spite of a very tiresome stammer, insisted upon being heard. He was afraid of nobody; as a scientist and very peculiar poet he could not be crushed by the loudest of opposition. Seward, Parr, Darwin: what an unpleasant trio! How different from Burke, Boswell, Reynolds, Lord Monboddo, and the rest of the Johnsonian circle! Only duty to his step-daughter brought Johnson to a city where so much was known to his detriment that he was incessantly humiliated.

Anna Seward extolled her mediocre parent (as Mary Russell Mitford extolled the loud-voiced Dr Mitford) in fervent letters. She thus made his valetudinarian longevity much more amusing to our irreverence than his supposed scholarship, and converted a dull man into a character resembling Jane Austen's Mr Woodhouse. This was a feat for which she should be given credit.

Sniggering ridicule has been her lot for a century and a half. Commentators have sneered at the coynesses and pomposities natural to a literary lady of restricted experience. They have found her easy game. Yet she had merits even as a critic; some of her letters contain wit, others humour; while as the portrait-painter of her father—she cannot have been such a fool as to miss the fact that he was an old humbug, and the further fact that she enjoyed the exhibition of herself as a beloved and ever-attentive daughter—she rises far beyond pedantry.

As a daughter she was bound to pretend that Seward had talents. She was deeply hurt when no reference was made to him in Dr Parr's list of the literary characters of Cambridge. She spoke highly of his verses, a few of which were printed—'by mistake, his name was not inserted'—in Dodsley's Miscellany; and she explained the absence of any formal publication by saying that her father, although 'an elegant poet', was 'too much devoted to society to give up much time to poetic composition; while, like his daughter, he shrunk from the trouble of publishing what he had written, and, with more carelessness, lost the copies'.

He suffered, too, even in Dodsley, from the printers' improvements. Lines *On Seeing Shakespeare's Monument at Stratford upon Avon*, which compare our poet with Virgil, were given correctly in the first edition; but subsequently appeared, for the sake of rhyme, as:

> Nor yet unrivall'd the Meonian strain,
> The British eagle and the Mantuan swain
> Tower equal heights.

'Swain', explains Anna, should be 'Swan'.

There was also an edition of Beaumont and Fletcher, in which Seward collaborated with one Simpson. 'The large collection of notes in that work,' Anna says, 'is almost exclusively my father's, and also the excellent preface. They abound in highly ingenious emendation, and in just criticism.' The work is forgotten. Erasmus Darwin, quite as disrespectful towards Seward as towards Johnson, linked the two men in an epigram:

> From Lichfield famed two giant critics come,
> Tremble, ye Poets! fear them! Fee, Fo, Fum!
> By Seward's arms the mangled Beaumont bled,
> And Johnson grinds poor Shakespeare's bones for bread.

Full of admiration for her father and his tepid gifts, Anna began as a young girl to write imitative poetry. Her mother, the schoolmaster's daughter, 'good literal being' as Anna calls her, felt that one bad poet in the family was enough. She therefore tried to wean the child from a repellent hobby. In vain. Anna wrote on.

Seward himself did not object. He presumably thought himself complimented. Erasmus Darwin, however, who had a mischievous mind, and who resented a little quip of Seward's about his family motto, whispered to his friends that Anna was the best poet in the family. 'This', said Anna, 'was a piece of arch injustice to my father's muse which disgusted him with mine.' From that moment Seward supported his wife in discouraging a pernicious habit.

Dismayed but dutiful, Anna temporarily forsook poetry. She joined in 'the gay amusements of her juvenile companions,' and for a time was as frivolous as they. Her complexion was 'clear, glowing, and animated'; her features 'agreeable though not regular.' And, as she told a friend in later life, 'I have no charm, no grace, no elegance of form or deportment . . . I wish to be obliging; yet, if my manners are not rustic, there is about me an hereditary absence, which always did, and always must prevent their taking the polish of perfect good breeding; and, to balance my tolerable properties, there is frequent indiscretion from an excess of frankness, and from native and yet unconquered impetuosity of temper;—and fortitude, alas! I almost wholly want.'

The want of fortitude prevented her from risking the candours of those brutes, the eighteenth-century reviewers. She pretended to despise, even to ignore them; but she could not face their bludgeons. As a consequence, she found flattering correspondence with flatterers the chief outlet for her emotions. Elaborate compliments, literary advice and recommendation *ex cathedra*, and attempts at noble scenic description sometimes give her letters a ludicrous pom-posity.

Seward played his part in all this, and more. His valetudinarianism increased; the narrowness of his interests confined hers. She was at least twice in love, first with a hypersentive young soldier who after-wards became a Colonel, and second with a young Cornet who jilted her and married money. The second affair gave Seward no trouble; but 'discovering' the first, he 'disapproved and dissolved it.' The suitor was sent away to nurse his passion. He did this so persistently that although marrying somebody else he could never forget his Anna. In middle-life, his spouse revealed, he visited Lichfield and ventured to call at the Palace; but on being asked to wait while Anna prepared herself for the interview he lost courage, and fled without seeing her.

Once her engagement to the hypersensitive gentleman had been 'dissolved', Anna became absorbed in a sentimental attachment to a beautiful girl, the friend of her younger sister Sally (who died while combating parental opposition to her own betrothal), long resident with the Sewards. This girl had all the virtues: intelligence, affectionateness, and gratitude for Miss Seward's cultivation of her mind. Her name was Honora Sneyd; and we shall hear more of her hereafter.

At the same time Anna was inspired by a friendship approaching infatuation with William Hayley, the intimate of Blake and Cowper, of whom Southey said 'everything about that man is good, except his poetry.' Anna thought even the poetry was good; and only belated discovery that Hayley had disingenuously concealed his paternity of a young son brought a general disillusion. Under the influence of these attachments she flowered as a poet, writing odes in honour of soldiers dead and alive (including the lamented Major André, whose enlistment and dreadful fate in America Anna attributed to a blighted love for Honora), and attempting other pieces in which she thought she captured what her father called 'the Meonian strain.'

She extended her correspondence to Mrs Thrale and the Ladies of Llangollen, the latter of whom had everything that appealed to her, from rank to solitude and a taste for poetry, and, among men, to Southey, Scott, and a brilliant boy, long afterwards famous as a translator of Dante—Henry Cary. Such was her admiration for Scott that she left him as an embarrassing legacy copies of all her letters, demanding that they should be collected and published by himself.

.　　　.　　　.　　　.　　　.

Domestically, she concentrated loving care upon her father, who until he was altogether overcome by lethargy managed to visit various great persons, in the hope, if Johnson's account is accepted, of finding listeners. One such person was Lady Hertford, at whose house Seward was astonished in 1758 by the strange behaviour of another guest, to whom he seems not to have been introduced. The guest, whose name was Horace Walpole, gave his friend George Montague a sketch of Seward. 'Strolling about the house,' wrote Walpole, 'he saw me first sitting on the pavement of the lumber room with Louis, all over cobwebs and dirt and mortar; then found me in his own room on a ladder writing on a picture; and half an hour afterwards lying on the grass in the court with the dogs and the children, in my slippers and without my hat. He had had some doubts whether I was the painter or the factotum of the family; but you would have died at his surprise when he saw me walk into dinner and sit by Lady Hertford. Lord Lyttleton was there, and the conversation turned on literature: finding me not quite ignorant added to the parson's wonder, but he could not contain himself any longer when after dinner he saw me go to romps and jumping with the two boys; he broke out to my Lady Hertford, and begged to know who and what sort of man I really was, for he had never met with anything of the kind.'

Lichfield had no such carefree aristocrats, and the meeting had no sequel. Walpole, whose feeling of superiority to a parson is shown in his letter, dismissed Seward as 'learned' but ridiculous; Seward concluded that he was happier in the company of those he was used to. He did not like to be treated with indifference. As Anna said to a correspondent nearly fifty years later, 'without parity of rank and of station, something to me always appears wanting to the perfect freedom and comfort of society on the part of the inferior. Even superior talents must be content to find themselves in the background . . . as if genius, learning, and knowledge of human character, were not equally to be found in the middle as in the higher classes of society.'

So to Dr Seward and Anna it had to be Buxton for a change of air, and otherwise Lichfield, and the Bishop's Palace, where they were buttressed by familiar things, and where they had unquestioned standing. 'It is to the circle where such powers of mind diffuse themselves,' remarked Anna, rather defiantly, 'that the title of best company belongs.'

Seward's wife, 'good literal being', died; it made no difference to his ways. He still had his Nancy to be alert for his comfort and apprehensive for his health. It pleased him to be the subject of so much concern, and he yielded to the pleasure, dividing his time between armchair and bed, with minute excursions and in summer a seat in the garden. For the greater aeration of his terrace he caused some dense trees which had been there for many years to be felled in the Dean's Walk; but air was no substitute for agreeable shade, and he afterwards experienced fruitless regret for his tampering with Nature. He had guests as often as possible for tea and dinner and conversation, and when Boswell visited Lichfield, with or without Johnson, he was cordially received at the Palace, once in Seward's bedroom, where 'I found him dressed in his black gown, with a white flannel night-gown above it; so that he looked like a Dominican friar.'

This was when Seward had one of his colds, and he was 'mending himself'; but he could not bear to miss the entertainment afforded by a visitor. Indeed, his normal day must sometimes have lacked variety. He read, poetry as a rule; and his favourite poets were Shakespeare, Milton, and Gray. Anna says that in poetry 'he was an unprejudiced and generous enthusiast,' although he found Thomson's *Seasons* 'frequently turgid and obscure.' I do not think he can have read much fiction; for that was little favoured by his daughter: 'I read not, neither doubtless do you, the Novel trash of the day. Hours are too precious for such frivolous waste, when the mind has in itself any valuable resources.' And if we discount the general valetudinarianism, and occasional bouts of violent coughing, his one trouble in old age was that 'his failing memory about his property, made him perpetually fancying that he had none, and was become poor.' This fretted him very much.

When he was seventy-eight, Seward gave Anna a tremendous fright. Readers of Richardson's novels who have ceased to wonder how it happened that the heroines of these endlessly fascinating works could immediately sit down to record sensational events will be unsurprised by her letter to a friend named Newton. It is in her finest style.

'Yet too agitated,' she says, 'to employ my pen on indifferent subjects, it is to such friends as yourself only that I am capable of writing. You who have long known and loved my poor father; you who are so kindly interested in my feelings, and in my destiny; it is you whom I wish to address in hours like this, when my mind is, as the subsiding seas, still trembling from the storm.

'You are aware of how slight a thread the life of my aged nursling has been long suspended. His drop into the grave is an event which, I fear, will baffle any resolution to sustain with the cheerful resignation which reason and religion dictate. That entire dependence upon my love and attention, resulting from the decay of his corporeal and intellectual faculties, has doubled our bond of union, and grafted the maternal upon filial tenderness. He seems at once my parent and my child; nor shall I suffer less, perhaps even more, from the loss of him, than if he had died while power, and authority, and exertion were in his hands.

'He has been several weeks exempt from these sudden seizures of apparently mortal torpidity, which often put his existence into the extremest peril. Last Sunday morning, I was roused from my slumbers, between seven and eight, by these alarming words from my servant: "Madam, my master is very ill. He was seized, a few minutes ago, in a different way from what he used to be, with a dreadful fit. You had better not go to him. We have sent for Dr Jones."

'You will suppose I was not to be restrained from a sight which, God knows, I was not able to endure without agony. That dear feeble frame, and venerable face, which I had often seen sunk in the stupor of apoplectic palsy, torn and distorted by convulsive and apparently agonized struggles!

'Ere I had been ten minutes in the room, his physician entered, and pronounced the seizure epileptic. He said he should blood him copiously, not with the least hope that he could now be rescued from death; but to prevent the continuance of the fits, and render his expiring moments calm and easy; adding, he has not the strength to bear the loss of blood, which is necessary to subdue these convulsed struggles; but if not subdued they would be immediately fatal.

'The loss of blood *did* subdue the fits, of which he had no return;

but sank into cold, damp, and, in appearance, deadly slumber. The physician said he would pass away in these slumbers; and assured me that he had little more to suffer.

'I asked why it might not be hoped that he, who had survived apoplexy and palsy so often, might survive this new and more terrible attack? It was replied, that when epilepsy seizes, after a succession of other dangerous diseases, and after years of previous debility, there had been scarce an instance where it had not been speedily fatal; that it would, however, be right to make every effort to save while breath remained; that a coffee-cup of madeira should be poured down his throat every half hour, the capability of swalloing being lost; that nothing more could be done, that medicine was useless; that he might expire in a few minutes, or might continue some hours; but I was instructed not to entertain a certainly fallacious hope. Dr Jones added, "I am obliged to go out of town directly, nor can I be of any further use." '

Valetudinarianism was at an end. One might have thought that Anna, being a clergyman's daughter, would send for the only person whose service could be of use to her dying father, a priest of his own Church. She did not do so. Whether she had no faith in prayer, or whether she believed her father would die most easily, as he had lived, in the placidity of coma, we do not know. In an ecstasy of literary accomplishment, she continued, still addressing her correspondent with the greatest relish:

'Alas! what a day of desponding anguish did I pass by his bed-side! that bed on which he lay stretched out, his legs, and feet, and hands, icy cold; his eyes closed;—the damp of death on his sunk temples;— a breathing corpse!—but he had no struggles; that was some comfort. The wine we punctually administered each half hour, without his seeming sensible of its being poured down. I expected every breath would be his last. In this state he remained from the time of his being bled, between eight and nine in the morning, till two hours after midnight.

'Totally exhausted by the ceaseless tears I had shed, I was persuaded by my servants to go to bed, upon their promise of giving the wine at the appointed intervals.

'With all the sorrow which, I think, filial affection knows to feel,

I took what I believed my everlasting leave; kissing repeatedly his cold lips and hands. Assured by everybody around me, that he could not live till day-break, I bid them avoid coming to me till I rung, and desired that when they saw me, I might learn the event rather from their silence, than their words.

'So many hours weeping procured a friendly stupor on pressing my pillow. I fell into a heavy slumber, nor awoke till the clock struck six. Then, with a deep sense of woe, did I open my swoln eyelids. Darkness and silence were around me, and the sense of deprivation sat heavy on my heart. Never more! said I aloud, never more!'

What else Anna thought at this time she did not tell her correspondent. She was too intent upon her dramatic story to indulge in self-analysis; and we do, I think, understand why, in the later years of her life, she consigned to Scott for posthumous publication so many packages of her letters. This was one of her masterpieces.

'During an whole hour,' she continued, 'I had not resolution to ring my bell for the fatal information. At length, and without summons, I heard the sound of quick steps approaching my door. Strange, thought I, and unfeeling speed!—they have surely forgotten my injunctions. I lifted the drop-bolt. "Madam, my master is alive, and much better—he has spoken—he has asked for you, and for his breakfast."

'Up I started, and, huddling on a slight covering, hastened down to his apartment, my heart bounding in my very throat. O Friend,

> "Not thro' the arch so hurries the blown tide
>   As I, recomforted, did pass that door."

The door, which I never again expected to open with the gladness of filial hope,—Yes, I beheld that beloved father, sitting nearly upright in his bed, supported by a back-chair, his eyes open, and a portion of intelligence, with a look of tender affection, lighting them up once more.

' "My dear Nancy," said he, in a faint voice. "I am glad you are come to give me my breakfast. I feel hungry." ' . . .

'When he had eaten his breakfast with liking and appetite, and was laid down again to doze, I learnt the particulars of this miraculous revival. His attendants said that he remained in the state in which I left him, till between five and six, when, on giving him the wine, they perceived he swallowed it, though without moving his limbs, or opening his eyes. On repeating it, the next half hour, he expressed unwillingness to take it, and, lifting up his hand, tried to push it from him. However they persuaded, or rather half-forced him to take it. On the next attempt of that sort he opened his eyes, and said, with tolerable distinctness,—"No, no, not wine—tea, and bread and butter." . . .

'He has continued slowly to mend from that time. His appetite is returned, and he sits up some hours every day in his arm-chair, and can converse a little himself, with some wanderings, that show impaired memory rather than deranged intellect. He attends with pleasure to what we say, and read, to amuse him.'

Seward lived for another three-and-a-half years, receiving what Anna called her 'filial attentions.' 'Too passionate was my affection,' she continued, 'to have had any merit in devoting myself to its duties. All was irresistible impulse. I made no sacrifices, for pleasure lost its nature and its name, when I was absent from him. I studied his ease and comfort, because I delighted to see him cheerful; and, when every energy of spirit was sunk in languor, to see him tranquil. It was my assiduous endeavour to guard him from every pain, and every danger, because his sufferings gave me misery, and the thought of losing him anguish.'

Her reward? 'The pleasure he took in my attendance and caresses, survived till within the last three months, amidst the general wreck of sensibility. His reply to my inquiries after his health, was always "Pretty well, my darling"; and when I gave him his food and his wine,—"That's my darling," with a smile of comfort and delight, inexpressibly dear to my heart. I often used to ask him if he loved me, his almost constant answer,—"Do I love my own eyes?" '

He loved not only his own eyes but his own comfort. He did not bring himself absolutely to 'the state of a hog in a stye'; he brought himself to the state of a self-indulgent old idler who lodged comfortably in his Bishop's Palace and was content to witness his daughter's enslavement to his whims. He was thus an eighteenth-centucy father; while Anna was an eighteenth century daughter, so romantir that, having nobody else to live for, she deliberately saw herself as a ministering angel, and gloried in her ruin.

SEVEN

George Crabbe

IF WE turn from this sketch to that of another clerical poet, drawn at length by his son in a standard biography, we shall find an amusing contrast. George Crabbe, by far the most gifted of all my Fathers, and referred to here solely for a few parallels and differences, was born more than forty years later than Thomas Seward. He was survived by two sons, his three daughters (any one of whom might have been condemned to a task of piety) having died in infancy; and between himself and his eldest son and biographer, who was also named George after his father, grandfather and great-grandfather, there was such simple understanding that the son, who began his work while the poet was alive, admits that some readers may accuse him of 'unfilial levity.' No daughter, in that masculine century, could have risked such a charge.

Young George Crabbe based his book, he tells us, upon fireside anecdotes told by his father while they sat together in snug conference. There was no valetudinarianism in the father, who refrained from any expression of a wish that his son should publish memoirs of his life. George simply thought the story worth telling, and 'I pleased myself with the fond anticipation, that when I should have completed my manuscript he himself might be its first critic, and take the trouble to correct it wherever I had fallen into any mistakes of importance.' And, on his father's death before the book was finished, instead of indulging Sewardian grief at the irreparable loss of a parent, he candidly admits that 'when the blow fell, it had many alleviations.'

True, George, having reached the end of his task, was snubbed by Samuel Rogers and Tom Moore, who demanded strict revision by a more literary hand. True, the more literary hand chosen by the publisher's ill-judgment was that of John Gibson Lockhart, who took it upon himself to revise Crabbe's own letters. Yet even Lockhart could not spoil the portrait. For all the book's small inaccuracies and suppressions, and perhaps failure to show enthusiasm for the poet's work, which Fitzgerald believed young George never to have read, it gives us a real Crabbe; and what follows is almost entirely derived from George's work.

Crabbe the poet was the eldest child of a man who, having been schoolmaster and parish clerk at Norton, in Norfolk, later became, in need, a warehouse-keeper and collector of salt duties in the town of Aldeburgh, in Suffolk. There the boy was born on the first of January, 1755. He was brought up amid a dreary landscape and a dreary society which he described from close and unsentimental observation in a number of his poems; and as his father was poor, and in later years inflamed by fatal inebriety, there was considerable hardship and unhappy conflict in the home. Crabbe's life was hazardous, and his education spasmodic. At times he conducted it himself; at other times he was subjected to brutality and ridicule which left him self-distrustful in the midst of pride.

He did, however, go to a school in Stowmarket, where he showed a gift for mathematics, and he was able, later, to gain a knowledge of Latin which in an hour of urgent need proved a life-line. It was resolved that he should become a doctor; but there was no money for effective training, and what he discovered of medicine was, even for that age of bolus and blood-letting, insignificant. Nor had he the temperament to fight less scrupulous and more aggressive rivals. In young manhood he was considered by all, including his father, to be an instance of futility. Discouragement followed every effort he made. His preoccupations were with poetry and love for an attractive girl named Sarah Elmy, to which he added a devotion to botany and the butterfly, and, with less ardour, geology. At last, he was forced, in defeat, to work for his father in a quayside warehouse at Aldeburgh, where he was bitterly reproached by a one-time fellow-student for treachery to the ideals of learning.

The humiliation inflicted by this work, and the reproach, was great; but attempts to get cheap experience of surgery in London were failures, as were several efforts to live by medicine in his home county. He was in despair. At last, raising a loan of five pounds for use in yet another attack upon London, he tried vainly while there to sell his poems. The booksellers would have none of them. He published one, *The Candidate*, at his own expense; and when that produced neither fame nor protection from three great men, Lords North, Thurlow, and Shelburne, to whom he applied, he reached a state of near starvation.

At this point, turned from noble doors, and vainly roaming the London streets, where he was shocked by the violence of crowds during the Gordon Riots, he had the inspiration to approach Edmund Burke with a statement of his affairs, a selection of his verses, and a desperate appeal for assistance.

Burke, in spite of every preoccupation, granted the young man an interview, took him to live very near his own house, persuaded Dodsley to publish *The Library*, introduced him to Fox, Reynolds, Johnson, and other friends, and after many long conversations in which Crabbe expressed a desire for such a future, took steps which led to his admission to holy orders. These events (it should be noted that Burke had followed a similar course of kindness with the painter Barry, who found him 'father, brother, friend, everything') produced in Crabbe a lifelong gratitude; and testify to Burke's extraordinary benevolence to the unlucky.

They were followed by the unexpected present from Thurlow, the Lord Chancellor, who had previously been adamant, of a hundred pounds, ordination as a priest—in which Crabbe's knowledge of Latin played its part—and his appointment as curate to Mr James Benet, the rector of Aldeburgh. Very soon afterwards, still through the active advocacy of Burke, the young poet was made domestic chaplain to the Duke of Rutland at Belvoir Castle; and from that point he was moved to various parishes in England, always with opportunities for literary composition, and eventually with fame as a poet greatly exceeding his youthful dreams.

Crabbe had received many humiliations at Aldeburgh, where the people regarded him as a ne'er-do-well. Young George reports that when his father turned up again there, not, as before, under a heavy cloud of failure, but as one appointed to direct their spiritual life, he was looked upon with suspicion.

'The whisper ran through the town, that a man who had failed in one calling, was not very likely to make a great figure in a new one. Others revived, most unjustly, old stories, in which my father did not appear with quite clerical decorum; and others again bruited about a most.groundless rumour that he had been, when in London, a preacher among the Methodists . . . But perhaps the most common, as well as unworthy, of all the rumours afloat, was, that he had been spoiled by the notice of fine folks in town, and would now be too proud to be bearable among his own equals.'

Pride of another kind was Crabbe's defect. It was a poet's over-weening pride in his own spiritual superiority; and at all times in his life it bred resentment at any slight, even though that slight was unintentional. 'When I asked him,' says young George, 'how he felt when he entered the pulpit at Aldeburgh for the first time, he answered, "I had been unkindly received in the place—I saw unfriendly countenances about me, and, I am sorry to say, I had too much indignation,—though mingled, I hope, with better feelings,—to care what they thought of me or my sermon." '

This was the reaction of a man of sensitive and critical mind. The mind, sometimes harsh, sometimes resentful, can be seen at work in all his major poems, coupled with a simplicity of expression which it has baffled critics to define; but his early reaction to experience had been extraordinarily acute, so that every aspect of the sea and the social order was before him as he wrote. He repaid past suffering with astringent portraits; he pictured in his verses almost exclusively what had been before his eyes, and the local types he had known, from childhood. He was a realist in metre as Mrs Inchbold, whom he admired, was a realist in prose. And like another poet of great mildness of manners, Cowper, he could occasionally astonish by severity, by intolerance.

These traits are shown in the condemnation of Methodists interpolated in a preface to one part of *The Borough*. He there disclaims a wish to censure 'the religious opinions of any society or individual'; but he shows detestation of the spirit and manners of 'the enthusiast and the bigot, their folly and their craft'. In their tenets 'there is yet that imagined contention with the powers of darkness, that is at once so lamentable and so ludicrous: there is the same offensive familiarity with the Deity, with a full trust and confidence both in the immediate efficacy of their miserably delivered supplications, and in the reality of numberless small miracles wrought at their request and for their convenience; ... and there still remains the same wretched jargon, composed of scriptural language, debased by vulgar expressions, which has a kind of mystic influence on the minds of the ignorant.'

This was the way he wrote in prose. In poetry he sacrificed nothing of truth to charm of style; yet he produced his own charm by means of continuous accuracy and interestingness. His publisher spoke of his conversation as the saying of 'uncommon' things in so natural and easy a way that he often lost the credit of them. Young George, that kindly man who was praised by Edward FitzGerald as 'noble, courageous, generous,' supplements this comment with a verification of his own. He says:

'Perhaps no man with an appearance so prepossessing was ever more distrustful of his power to please. Coldness and reserve would benumb them; and he would be abstracted, and even distressed. ... Argument he sustained with great impatience; he neither kept close to his point, nor preserved his temper. This dislike of controversial discourse arose, in part, probably from a consciousness that he had not cultivated the faculty of close logical reasoning; but partly, also, from an opinion, or rather feeling, that he had, against all pretence of colloquial equality. He had seen the submission paid to the opinions of Johnson and Burke; and he always readily followed the lead of anyone whom he thought skilled on the topic in question; but when he ventured an assertion himself, he expected similar deference. And, to be candid, though what he said was pretty sure to be just, yet there was an unfair and aristocratic principle in this expectation, which I never could think quite in harmony with the general modesty of his nature.'

Once settled at Belvoir, Crabbe felt himself free to marry; and his Sarah, who had previously been cautious with the unselfishness of a good woman, agreed that it would now be safe to set up house. A suite of rooms in the Castle was set aside for their use; a life of tranquil marital comfort, they believed, was beginning.

Unfortunately the Duke of Rutland was at this moment appointed Lord-Lieutenant of Ireland, which meant that for the present he would be absent from home. His kindness to Crabbe was such that while he apparently did not think of taking his domestic chaplain to Dublin, and while he could not immediately find him appropriate preferment, he suggested the retention of the suite until such time as another arrangement could be made. Young George never learned the truth about this separation from his father, and his own doubts of Crabbe's fitness as chaplain, or as a potential dignitary of the Church, are such as would not have occurred to a devout daughter. He even suggests that Crabbe's manners when in noble company were not uniformly good.

'The aristocracy of genius,' he says, 'approaches too near the aristocracy of station: superiority of talent is apt, without intention, to betray occasional presumption ... Mr Crabbe could never conceal his feelings, and he felt strongly ... Nor, perhaps, did he at all times put a bridle on his tongue, for he might feel the riches of his intellect more than the poverty of his status. It is also probable that, brought up in the warehouse of Slaughden, and among the uneducated, though nature had given him the disposition of a gentleman—the politeness of a mild and Christian spirit—he may at that early period have retained some repulsive marks of the degree from whence he had so lately risen; he could hardly have acquired all at once the ease and self-possession for which he was afterwards distinguished.'

At any rate, he did not go to Dublin, and in fact he never again saw his kind patron, the Duke. Nevertheless, in December, 1783, he married Sarah Elmy; and in due course he became a Father.

Young George, growing meditative, writes on the subject of childhood the most impressive passage in his book, and proceeds to picture his own first memories in a way to give the happiest impression of a father to be found in any of the filial writings I have found while composing the present study.

'What a pity it seems,' he says, 'that the poignant feelings of early youth should ever be blunted, and, as it were, absorbed in the interests of manhood; that they cannot remain, together with the stronger stimuli of mature passions—passions so liable to make the heart ultimately selfish and cold. It is true, no one could endure the thoughts of remaining a child for ever; but with all that we gain, as we advance, some of the finer and better spirit of the mind appears to evaporate;—seldom do we again feel those acute and innocent impressions, which recalling for a moment, one could almost cry to retain. Now and then, under peculiar circumstances, this youthful tenderness of feeling does return, when the spirits are depressed either by fatigue or illness, or some other softening circumstance; and then, especially if we should happen to hear some pleasing melody, even chimes or distant bells, a flood of early remembrances and warm affections flows into the mind, and we dwell on the past with the fondest regret; for such scenes are never to return: yet though painful, these impressions are ever mingled with delight; we are tenacious of their duration, and feel the better for the transient susceptibility;—indeed transient; for soon the music ceases, the fatigue yields to rest, the mind recovers its strength, and straightway all is (to such salutary sensations) cold and insensible as marble . . .

'How delightful it is to recall the innocent feelings of unbounded love, confidence, and respect, associated with my earliest visions of my parents. They appeared to their children not only good, but free from any taint of the corruption common to our nature; and such was the strength of the impressions then received, that hardly could subsequent experience ever enable our judgments to modify them . . .

'Always visibly happy in the happiness of others, especially of children, our father entered into all our pleasures, and soothed and cheered us in all our little griefs with such overflowing tenderness, that it was no wonder we almost worshipped him. My first recollection of him is of his carrying me up to his private room to prayers, in the summer evenings, about sunset, and rewarding my silence and attention afterwards with a view of the flower-garden through his prism. Then I recall the delight it was to me to be permitted to sleep with him during a confinement of my mother's,—how I longed for the morning, because then he would be sure to tell me some fairy tale, of his own invention, all sparkling with gold and diamonds, magic fountains and enchanted princesses. In the eyes of memory I can still see him as he was at that period of his life,—his fatherly countenance, unmixed with any of the less loveable expressions that, in too many faces, obscure the character—but pre-eminently *fatherly*; conveying the ideas of kindness, intellect, and purity; his manner grave, manly and cheerful, in unison with his high and open forehead; his very attitudes, whether as he sat absorbed in the arrangement of his minerals, shells, and insects—or as he laboured in his garden until his naturally pale complexion acquired a tinge of fresh healthy red; or as, coming lightly towards us with some unexpected present, his smile of indescribable benevolence spoke exultation in the foretaste of our raptures.'

Crabbe's life from the time of his first fatherhood until many years later was a series of trials. He moved from one parish to another, sometimes affected by the discomforts of situation or the hostility of his congregations (unlike Parson Woodforde he experienced great difficulty in collecting his tithes), sometimes plunged into woe by the deaths of children and the mental illness of his wife; but always punctual in the preparation and delivering of sermons, and usually busy with his hobbies and the children who remained to him.

Although Thurlow explosively compared him, after an interview, to Parson Adams he had an austerity of manner in the pulpit, and a rigidity of moral doctrine which hearers who were used to the *bonhomie* of his predecessors found exasperating. One passage from *Tales of the Hall* is quoted by young George in illustration of his father's insistence upon good works:

> 'A moral teacher!' some contemptuous cried;
> He smiled, but nothing of the fact denied;
> Nor, save by his fair life, to charge so strong replied.
> Still, though he bade them not on aught rely
> That was their own, but all their worth deny,
> They called his pure advice his cold morality.
> 'Heathens', they said, 'can tell us right from wrong,
> But to a Christian higher points belong.'

Crabbe did not change. He persisted in his opposition to rage and ill-conduct. He disarmed through mere courage one furious bailiff who threatened him with a knife, and then thundered the man into flight. He calmly faced a violent election mob and insisted upon voting for an unpopular candidate. He protected dissenters; he lectured in the midst of almsgiving; and in defiance of what was expected of his cloth he attended concerts, balls, and plays, highly praising Liston and Mrs Siddons for their performances in contrasted roles. Only his innate simplicity, which as he grew older sweetened his manners yet further, gave him at last moral authority and a claim to the love, as well as the respect, of his parishioners.

During these years he wrote intermittently—there were several exercises in a literary form he loved, the Novel; but these were burned when Mrs Crabbe told him he was better in verse;—and as he published no poetry he was in a fair way to be forgotten as a poet. He had also much financial trouble as his boys became old enough to go to Cambridge University. He was resolved that they should go, whatever the cost, because he was resolved that both should enter the Church.

Probably this trouble drove him to renewed poetic composition; for in the earliest years of the nineteenth century he published, after four years of labour, *The Parish Register*. It has been remarked that the year 1807 was especially favourable to this production, since of the poets who had succeeded his old contemporaries, Burns and Cowper, only Scott and Byron (perhaps also Campbell) were in any large measure attracting popular and critical attention. Consequently he soon became one of the most admired poets of the time.

Hazlitt, in *The Spirit of the Age*, confessed to this, although personally he found much of what he read repulsive, and said of the author's Muse that it 'is not one of *the Daughters of Memory*, but the old toothless mumbling dame herself, doling out gossip and scandal of the neighbourhood . . . and fastening always on the worst as the most palatable morsels.'

This was the cry of a romantic, a member of that band of writers who were bringing emotional standards, and a re-discovery of Elizabethan riches, to their judgments of contemporary poetry. It was at the same time an admission that Crabbe, as an original force, could not be gainsaid. Crabbe's preoccupation was with the actual as he had seen it with his own eyes. Nevertheless, as soon as he read *The Lay of the Last Minstrel* he exclaimed: 'A new and great poet has appeared';

and while at first ridiculing Wordsworth's apparent artlessness he allowed it to make its impression upon him and proceeded to reflective admiration of the new school.

As a cleric he had never resisted pluralism, and he gathered to himself livings in Leicestershire which were served by curates—'respectable and diligent clergymen'—during his absences for years at a time in Suffolk and elsewhere. In this course he was concerned less with his own advantage, although of course the salaries he drew were a calculable necessity, than with his duty as a father. Both young George and his brother John had obediently taken orders: and it was Crabbe's aim to bring them under his immediate and local protection. He succeeded. Both boys were settled, George as his own curate, John as curate to a parish twenty miles away; and George, with full knowledge of what had been done for them, approvingly quotes an often-repeated and grateful exclamation of his mother's: 'What a father you have.'

The affection between George and his father, indeed, was full of intelligence. George was sensible of Crabbe's foibles—the sentimental attachment in old age to 'females', whose society and correspondence he greatly relished; the complacent pleasure in fashionable London society at the homes of Samuel Rogers and the Hollands, little snobberies at encounters with great folk, and even curiosity at a glimpse of Lady Caroline Lamb (to whom he was not introduced); and the ancient's preference for muddle in his study. This was 'a scene of unparalleled confusion—windows rattling, paint in great request, books in every direction but the right—the table—but no, I cannot find terms to describe it . . . Once, when we were staying at Trowbridge, in his absence for a few days at Bath, my eldest girl thought she should surprise and please him by putting every book in perfect order, making the best bound the most prominent; but, on his return, thanking her for her good intention, he replaced every volume in its former state;' 'for,' said he, "my dear, grandpapa understands his own confusion better than your order and neatness." '

This speech summarizes Crabbe's attitude. He was kind, thoughtful of others, lovingly exemplary as a father; but he would not submit to the smallest interference with his way of life. Once he had been raised by Burke and the Duke of Rutland from the misery of conscious defeat, he made a fetish of independence which he maintained until the end of his life. Within a few weeks of his death at the age of seventy-seven he preached at both young George's churches 'in a voice so firm and loud, and a manner so impressive, that I was congratulated on the power he manifested at that advanced stage of life . . .

'I said, "Why, Sir, I will venture a good sum that you will be assisting me ten years hence."

' "Ten weeks," was his answer—and that was almost literally the period when he ceased to assist any one.'

He was thus uncompromising to the last; limited, accurate, and fearless. We hardly need to be told that on the day of his funeral the shutters of the shops in Trowbridge were half-closed, and ninety-two of the principal inhabitants, including all the dissenting ministers, assembled of their own accord, followed him to the grave. The streets were crowded; the choir was in mourning, and the church was full. The effect, says young George, who never forgot this day, was appalling. In the course of a speech to children on the following Sunday, the master of the Free and Sunday School told his hearers that their beloved friend's last words to his two sons had been: 'Be good, and come to me.'

EIGHT

The Arts
in the Eighteenth Century

OWING to the preference of our latest historians for a metaphysical approach to life, which has caused them to find more congenial the devotional poets and neo-Platonists of the seventeenth century, we have been led to believe that for a hundred years dulness reigned in England. This, in my opinion, arises from incapacity to look in more than one direction at a time. It is easier to maintain that excellence lies only here, or there, than to allow that, in the arts especially, something different may have qualities no less important. As Bernard Shaw once observed, 'The Golden Rule is that there is no Golden Rule.'

The colour and splendour of Tudor and Stuart costume, the grand piracies of Drake and Raleigh, the beauty of a language used by men to whom all words were new-minted, and the exquisite reveries of Vaughan, Herbert, and Traherne among poets and Sir Thomas Browne among prose-writers do indeed delight the senses. They tell us, as Robert Louis Stevenson expressly insisted, that the finest deed is the better for a bit of purple.

The seventeenth century was not entirely mystical. It was the time when Puritanism had its first power. It was the time when wit and satire pierced all nobler motives with ridicule. From Ben Jonson to Dryden, and from Congreve to that great critic of chicane, Jonathan Swift, it carried the heroic and the devotional alike into what was not so much reason as scepticism. This was where the eighteenth century took over, as an age when everything was to be questioned, and when new knowledges were to be perceived and developed with enthusiasm.

Increasing wealth in the middle classes sent men abroad for the sake of previously unshared treasure. Sir Robert Walpole's celebrated art collection was a sign of the times. The delight in gardens, already cultivated by Sir William Temple and John Evelyn, increased until Capability Brown was in constant demand, and the great gardens now thrown open every summer to the general public were established. Artistic wonders of antiquity, including the Elgin Marbles, the acquisition of which in 1803 had been anticipated in many smaller enterprises, were brought to England. Artists and connoisseurs alike made pilgrimages to Rome and Florence; a remarkable trade began in restored fragments of classic statuary.

Italy, indeed, was rightly considered as a storehouse of beauty; and excavations at Pompeii stirred the imagination of British archaeologists as they had not been stirred for many a year. And, finally, it was a time when many young men, eager to excel in the Arts, came boldly to London to make their fortunes. That, in a land where, according to Hazlitt, people saw with the mind's eye and felt at the heart's core, but did not embody their perceptions in visible images, was something which had not happened before.

Many painters arrived, generally from the West Country. Thornhill, a Dorset man, taught Hogarth, a Londoner; and Hogarth, marrying Thornhill's daughter, drew and painted the London scene in such a way that if we want to see in imagination what the vulgar population of England looked like we turn inevitably to his work.

Jonathan Richardson, whose treatise, *A Theory of Painting*, opened Johnson's eyes to the existence of an art previously unknown to him, taught Hudson, a Devonian; and Hudson, marrying Richardson's daughter, became the wealthiest painter in England, and took Joshua Reynolds (also from Devonshire) as his unbiddable pupil.

Reynolds in turn, quarrelling with Hudson, hurried back to Devonshire, learned his painting from yet another Devonian, William Gandy, set off to Italy to study the Masters; and when he returned captured first London and then the entire world of art. One of his pupils was Hazlitt's friend James Northcote, who was born in Plymouth and stole to town, against his father's command, to do what his predecessors from the West had done. He, too, made a fortune.

As the century grew older, Reynolds established the Royal Academy, thereby giving painters what in another walk of life would be called a platform. He had grasped the fact that while one man may sink, his strength is multiplied if he belongs to a body of men engaged in similar work. By his tact and delightful manners Reynolds gave his fellows social importance; and having this unity and social importance they were enabled to exhibit glories of portraiture and landscape which in spite of the vicissitudes of fashion remain as a monument to English craftsmanship.

In the same way a little, dirty, illiterate starveling also went in youth (using for his trip certain monies received as prizes) to Rome, and before he became famous was guilty of faking antiques and smuggling dutiable canvases and lace from their country of origin. This was Joseph Nollekens. He owed much to a meeting in Rome with David Garrick, who not only sat to him for a bust but with splendid consequences persuaded Laurence Sterne to do the same; and as he matured he became unquestionably the greatest of all English sculptors. Roubiliac, a Frenchman, might produce warmer and more familiar likenesses—his Cibber seems to show the very man;—but in the grand style Nollekens was unsurpassed.

He was a character, as well as a genius: and this helped his fame. Fanny Burney called him 'a jolly, fat, lisping, laughing, underbred, good-humoured man as lives.' Being a prude, she felt bound to add: 'His language is as vulgar as his works are elegant.' And, on his art, Johnson remarked: 'Well, Sir, I think my friend Joe Nollekens can chop out a head with any of them.'

Johnson had an extraordinary appreciation of merit in others; and while he was himself the typical literary figure of the century (Horace Walpole called him 'the representative in epitome of all the contradictions in human nature'), while Garrick was the universal actor, and Burke, for all his passions and the shadiness of his financial dealings, was the most eloquent orator, political theorist, and talker of the age, Nollekens and Reynolds, the one in marble, the other on canvas, gave the age colour enough to confute all who would try to persuade us that the eighteenth century was condemned to dreary materialism. It was, on the contrary, a century of eager thought and experiment in nearly every direction.

Only in Music had the English no genius. Many great men of the century were tone-deaf. Crabbe, according to his son, and Garrick, according to Charlotte Burney, had no musical ear at all; Burke, Fox, Pitt, and Johnson, said Burke's biographer James Prior, were in the same condition. Whereas, in the sixteenth and seventeenth centuries, there had been English composers whose work still enchants us, the eighteenth had almost no native music at all.

Addison explained this in an early number of *The Spectator* by saying 'at present our notions of music are so very uncertain, that we do not know what it is we like; only, in general, we are transported with anything that is not English: so it be of a foreign growth, let it be Italian, French, or High Dutch, it is the same thing. In short, our English music is quite rooted out, and nothing yet planted in its stead.' This being so, musicians as a class were despised.

Ballads were sung, and in some cases, fortunately, preserved. Thomas Arne, who wrote *Rule, Britannia*, composed forgotten operas and oratorios and delightfully set some lovely words to equally lovely airs. Otherwise the only composer widely known in England, though not always admired there, was Handel, a German from Saxony. He was unique, inexhaustible, and deeply admired by the wise; but it was Italian music, and especially the Italian opera, spasmodically brought to London by those who sought to improve national taste, which enjoyed the vogue.

Few people in the country knew so much as the name of Johan Sebastian Bach. If they heard any of his music they were repelled by its coagulation and confusion. While, therefore, Bach continued in general neglect to compose oratorios, fugues, and concertos of a quality peculiarly agreeable to modern minds, and German princelings kept their own purveyors of serenades, symphonies and operas for State occasions, Italians alone were held, all over Europe, but particularly in England, to be the only models worthy of admiration.

Thomas Gray, for example, the most admired poet of his day, who loved to sing to his own accompaniment on the harpsichord and, after its introduction, the pianoforte, formed his taste exclusively on the study of Palestrina, Marcello, and Pergolesi. To him, Pergolesi was 'all divinity.' C. P. E. Bach's 'lessons for the pianoforte', in spite of their 'passion', were 'charming, and in the best Italian style,' though 'the old musicians do not like them.' Apparently he knew nothing of the greater father of C. P. E. and J. S. (or 'Opera') Bach.

I have said the Italian opera was often performed in London.

There was what Mrs Delany called 'the opera party', which condemned Handel. And when the enthusiasm of this party waned there was a particular reason. This was that operas were always vehicles for what are now called star singers. If these singers were absent, interest ceased. The operas, dealing for the most part with personages in Greek or Roman history who were indistinguishable from each other, were so full of declamatory recitative, and so boring, that only the singers kept them alive.

As was natural, the admired singers exploited their power. They made the operas still more ridiculous by indulging in every vocal trick they could think of. They warbled and embellished, shook their notes, held their notes, and continued to exhibit virtuosity until uncritical audiences burst into applause. The critical remained silent. Grétry, the French composer, who wrote *Memoires* towards the end of the century, said that even in Italy, when a favourite singer was no longer on the stage, 'every one retired into his box to play cards and eat ices, while the pit yawned.'

In London the pit did not yawn. If displeased, as Gray recalled, it threw lighted candles, broken bottles, and penknives at the stage, tore up the benches, and removed and burned entire scenes in the street. Only enthusiasm for a particular young singer, who pleased by her appearance and purity of tone, on one occasion prevented a tumult.

Musical taste, although more national, was no better in Paris, where the *opéra comique*, in which a libretto of spoken verse, decorated with songs, had grown from ballet and miscellaneous entertainment into a distinguishable *genre*. Here the singing, to other ears than those of the French, was execrable. Gray and Horace Walpole, making a grand tour in 1739, could hardly endure what they heard at the Opera. Walpole said the music resembled a gooseberry tart as much as it did harmony; and Gray, after speaking of a chorus 'that screams, past all power of simile to represent,' observed that scenes from the classics were 'transacted by cracked voices, trilling diversions upon two notes and a half, accompanied by an orchestra of humstrums ... Our astonishment at their absurdity you can never conceive; we had enough to do to express it by screaming an hour louder than the whole *dramatis personae*.'

The French, it must be admitted, liked their own opera. Rousseau, in *La Nouvelle Heloise*, says, 'you can have no idea of the frightful cries, the long roars with which the theatre resounds during the performance. One sees the actresses, almost in convulsions, violently tear the yelps out of their lungs, their fists clenched against their chests, their heads thrown back, their faces inflamed, their veins swollen, their stomachs heaving, . . . and the astonishing thing is that the spectators applaud hardly anything but these howlings. By the way they beat their hands together one would take them for deaf people, delighted to catch a piercing tone here and there.'

French opera was not brought to England; English opera could not hold its own against the Italian, which, however inane, was maintained by its performers. Therefore the only vocal music to appeal to serious-minded persons in the country was oratorio. When Handel's *Semele* was performed in London at least one very intelligent man, Dr Delany, felt that he could not attend so secular a piece. Fortunately Handel excelled in oratorio: even that religious zealot, John Wesley, attended with an approval which exceeded his expectations the performance of *Messiah* given in Bristol Cathedral in 1758.

This being the state of affairs it is proper that I should pass to my next Father, who was destined to be one of the two men (his rival was Sir John Hawkins, executor and first biographer of Johnson, and harsh father of novelist-memorialist daughter, Laetitia Hawkins) determined to make the art and history of music understood by their fellow-countrymen. I refer to Charles Burney.

NINE

Burney's Early Years

HE WAS a small, lively, over-worked music-teacher; and one of Handel's greatest admirers. His first momentous encounter with the composer might well have been his last; for Handel made a fetish of sight-reading, and Burney, following music thrust into his hand, sang a wrong note. Being furiously rebuked, he was paralysed with fear. Recovering, however, after a moment, he found courage enough to point out that the error had been, not his, but that of Handel's copyist. Handel examined the score; found Burney to be in the right; and at once apologized, in a peculiar lingo for the phonetic rendering of which Burney must bear the responsibility. 'I pec your barton—I am a very odd tog.'

There is more in this incident than its proof of a great man's power to admit impulsive injustice. Burney's musical scrupulousness, congenital diffidence, and remarkable charm are also illustrated. They, with the addition of industry, were his dominant characteristics. Because of them everybody, even Johnson, even George the Third, was delighted with his ingratiating tact.

'My life,' he wrote at the beginning of the note with which his daughter Fanny opened the much-condemned *Memoirs of Doctor Burney*, 'though it has been frequently a tissue of toil, sickness, and sorrow, has yet been, upon the whole, so much more pleasant and prosperous than I had a title to expect, or than many others with higher claims have enjoyed, that its incidents, when related, may, perhaps, help to put mediocrity in good-humour, and to repress the pride and over-rated worth and expectations of insolence.

'Perhaps few have been better enabled to describe, from an actual survey, the manners and customs of the age in which he lived than myself; ascending from those of the most humble cottagers, and lowest mechanics, to the first nobility, and most elevated personages, with whom circumstances, situation, and accident, at different periods of my life, have rendered me familiar. Oppressed and laborious husbandmen; insolent and illiberal yeomanry; generous and hospitable merchants; men of business and men of pleasure; men of letters; men of science; artists; sportsmen and country 'squires'; dissipated and extravagant voluptuaries; gamesters; ambassadors; statesmen; and even sovereign princes, I have had opportunities of examining in almost every point of view.'

It was true. He had seen all these types at close quarters; not profoundly, because he was without profundity and his whole existence was hurried, but with a familiarity assured by those pleasantly deferential manners which endeared him to the vain. Johnson's face lighted up at sight of him; Burke was his true friend and benefactor; Garrick called him 'a First Rate Man' and would sometimes call on the Burney household as early as eight o'clock in the morning. Johnson in fact spoke for everybody when he said: 'I love Burney . . . [He] is a man for all the world to love.'

This paragon was born in Shrewsbury on April 12th, 1726, the male in a pair of twins who were the youngest fruits of their father's second marriage. At that time the family name was MacBurney, although Burney himself, after the 'Mac' had been dropped, said he was unable to trace any Irish or Scottish ancestry. He was put out to nurse with a good but illiterate woman, Dame Ball, in the neighbouring village of Condover; and he remained in Dame Ball's charge for twelve or thirteen years.

No explanation of this long exile from his family has ever been offered; perhaps Burney's father, having removed from Shrewsbury to Chester and chosen from the several crafts at his command that of portrait-painter, forgot all about him. The boy did very well, however, with his foster-mother, from whom when the time came he parted, according to his own heightened phrase, 'in an agony of grief'; and he also had the privilege at Condover of affectionate acquaintance with a man who had known Henry Purcell. It was his first important friendship. This man, the Reverend George Lluellyn, encouraged his musical talent.

Industry, accompanied by a determination to please, carried Burney from one employment to another. He did well at the Free School in Chester, studied further with his half-brother, a church-organist at Shrewsbury, met and captivated Thomas Augustine Arne, when that dissolute musician was returning to London after two years' residence in Ireland, and was adopted by Arne as pupil and amanuensis. In London, chiefly at the home in Scotland Yard of Arne's beautiful and gifted actress-sister, Mrs Colley Cibber, he found himself, while still in his teens, the modest associate of Handel, actors such as Quin and Garrick, men of title, laughing wits, and, among poets, Christopher Smart, James Thomson, and Gray's friend William Mason, who, in spite of meagre gifts, was a busy and kindly man.

Burney transcribed music by day, played by night in Arne's orchestra at Drury Lane Theatre, and when not otherwise engaged studied alone (Arne gave him no tuition) until he attained a fair knowledge of his craft. He also composed and published, anonymously, the music for a pantomime, *Queen Mab*, the success of which his daughter fondly believed to have been comparable to that of *The Beggar's Opera* or, in later years, Sheridan's *The Duenna*.

Queen Mab, being anonymous, brought the composer neither fame nor fortune; after its production and publication he transcribed and performed as before. His manners and musical skill, however, attracted more friends and well-wishers, one of whom was Jacob Kirchman, or Kirkman, a German maker of harpsichords; and it was to Kirkman's enthusiasm that Burney owed his next important conquest. It was of a singular wealthy dilettante whom Fanny Burney described as being, by reputation, 'the first gentleman about town.'

Fanny's life of her father has been generally dismissed as 'unreadable.' It is nothing of the kind. True, the author's language mingles pseudo-Johnsonian pomposity with idioms learned during long residence in France; but within a heavy veil of verbiage it shows admirable narrative power. The opening chapters are both selective and pointed; and they vividly summarize Burney's earliest years, his extraordinary luck in forming life-long friendships, and the excitements to which he was introduced by his new patron, 'the first gentleman about town.'

This very fine gentleman, who illustrates the eighteenth century's special gift to our century of eccentricity, love of the arts, and the use of wealth and privilege in the encouragement of artists, was Fulke Greville, the descendant, Fanny explains, of 'The Friend of Sir Philip Sydney.' She continues: 'His person, tall and well-proportioned, was commanding; his face, features, and complexion, were striking for masculine beauty; and his air and carriage were noble with conscious dignity . . . He excelled in all the fashionable exercises, riding, fencing, hunting, shooting at a mark, dancing, tennis, &c; and worked at every one of them with a fury for pre-eminence, not equalled, perhaps, in ardour for superiority, in personal accomplishments, since the days of the chivalrous Lord Herbert of Cherbury.

'His high birth, and higher expectation—for a coronet at that time, from some uncertain right of heritage, hung almost suspended above his head—with a splendid fortune, wholly unfettered, already in his hands, gave to him a consequence in the circles of modish dissipation that, at the clubs of St James's-street, and on the race ground at Newmarket, nearly crowned him as chief . . .

'This gentleman one morning, while trying a new instrument at the house of Kirkman, expressed a wish to receive musical instruction from some one who had mind and cultivation, as well as finger and ear; . . . and gravely [asked] Kirkman whether he knew any young musician who was fit company for a gentleman.'

Kirkman, with an artist's contempt for aristocratic insolence, replied that he knew many such men, but particularly one 'who had as much music in his tongue as in his hands, and who was as fit company for a prince as for an orchestra.' He meant, of course, Charles Burney.

A meeting was arranged, on the pretext that Greville, before choosing his new harpsichord, wished to listen to a number of those in Kirkman's stock. 'Young Burney,' says Burney's daughter, 'with no other idea than that of serving Kirkman, immediately seated himself at an instrument, and played various pieces of Geminiani,

Corelli, and Tartini, whose compositions were then most in fashion. But Mr Greville, secretly suspicious of some connivance, coldly and proudly walked about the room, took snuff from a finely-enamelled snuff-box, and looked at some prints, as if wholly without noticing the performance.'

The effect of this disdain upon Burney was such that he abandoned all effort to please an inattentive listener. He began therefore to play for his own amusement, in particular a sonata of Scarlatti's to which he gave all the brilliance intended by the composer. Greville was impressed. 'To be easily pleased, however, or to make acknowledgment of being pleased at all, seems derogatory to strong self-importance; and his only comment was that Burney appeared to be fond of Italian music. Without replying, Burney at once gave a magnificent rendering of Handel's Coronation Anthem.'

His speechless defiance was completely successful. Greville was capitivated, not only by the performance, but by Burney's spirit. He decided at once that the young man was the person he sought; and when he learned of the apprenticeship to Arne he had no hesitation in offering Arne a premium of three hundred pounds for the release of his drudge. It was accepted. Burney, receiving nothing, merely found himself removed from music-copying and playing in the orchestra, and installed as a sort of musical familiar in Greville's household.

This ready acceptance of servitude to a fine gentleman will explain what happened forty years later, when Fanny was offered a place at Court.

Greville took his *protégé* everywhere, to his several homes, the gaming clubs, Newmarket, and Bath (where Burney waited, almost entirely in vain, outside the door of the great Bolingbroke for a glimpse of near-divinity); showing off his musical gifts, introducing him to the feverish life of all these places, and watching with lofty amusement to see innocent wonder become confusion, and confusion a love of dangerous sport. He gave no warnings; he cynically, and in the end admiringly, observed. The young man, he found, was not all innocence, and was not seduced. Instead, Burney proved as nimble with his wits as with his fingers, and in his turn watched how the gamblers, from being at first gay and apparently carefree, became engrossed in their desperate activity, and were carried to misery by it. This, among the rich, like the addiction to gin among the squalid, was the vice of the century.

'By degrees,' writes Burney's daughter, 'the fever of doubt and anxiety broke forth all round, and every breath caught its infection. Every look then showed the contagion of lurking suspicion; all was contrast the most discordant; . . . for wherever the laughing brilliance of any countenance denote exulting victory, the glaring vacancy of some other, hard by, displayed incipient despair. Like the awe of death was next the muteness of taciturnity, from the absorption of agonizing attention while the last decisive strokes, upon which hung affluence or beggary, were impending. Every die, then, became a bliss or a blast . . . every fear whispered ruin with dishonour.'

Greville had no qualms. His one thought was amusement at the expense of others. Horses, cards, and carouse left him rich and indifferent as before. And at last he indulged himself with a secret marriage, to a formidable young Irish beauty of fascinating temperament whom he might easily have had with her father's consent. An elopement being more fun than a formal wedding, it was young Burney, not her father, who gave the bride away.

From time to time Greville and his spirited wife lived largely at Wilbury House, the family seat in Wiltshire, where Burney was fully domesticated with them and included in every social party of the district. He made, besides many light acquaintances, one true friend, a man twenty years older than himself named Samuel Crisp, who loved the Arts and was the best adviser the Burney family ever had. He also acted energetically in games and charades; and when the time arrived played a more serious part by representing the Duke of Beaufort as godfather to the Grevilles' first daughter.

And then, one day in his brother's house in Hatton Garden, London, Burney met and fell in love with a girl as charming as himself, named Esther Sleepe. She was uneducated, and her father is said to have been something of a rogue; but her mother, who was half-French, was angelic, and the girl revealed a delicious enthusiasm for music, flowers, and the stars. Burney confessed his love; but was forced to reveal what both he and Esther felt to be a fatal bar to happiness—his virtual enslavement to the Grevilles. Greville, in a sense, had bought him from Arne for three hundred pounds.

True, the purchase and the patronage were now coloured by friendship; but it was the friendship of an aristocrat for a dependant; and the whole history of music, in the eighteenth century, all over Europe, was dominated by the fact of patronage, royal, noble, or wealthy. Even a composer of Haydn's quality was forced to produce the kind of music his patrons wanted; how much more, then, was a youngster without genius at the mercy of a gentleman who thought solely of his own amusement. Burney, ever humble to the great, lacked the courage to claim his freedom from Greville.

Remembrance of his master's secret marriage put into his mind the thought that he and Esther might also marry secretly; but Esther would have nothing to do with this plan. She knew that by accepting Greville's favour, and living in Greville's household, Burney had lost his former expectations of employment elsewhere as a professional musician. She knew that if he now tried to leave Greville he must endure the cold displeasure of a fine gentleman with unlimited power to punish. And, although herself attracted to Burney, she could not guess how great his attractiveness appeared to those who, as it afterwards proved, needed only this occasion to run to his assistance. She decided that her lover must wait.

He did so, with great patience, although with visible signs of mental distress, until the Grevilles announced that they proposed to live abroad for several years, and assumed that as a matter of course he would go with them. Was he not a beloved chattel? Burney was horrified. He knew that if he went he must lose Esther; and if he lost Esther his heart would break. He was forced in his pain to tell his love to the Grevilles, who could not believe that marriage to some little waif whom they had never seen should be allowed to outweigh the attractions of travel in their company. They were not unkind; they simply thought him foolish. Burney, however, possessed a miniature, newly painted, of his beloved. He produced it from his bosom.

The miniature 'was instantly and eagerly snatched from hand to hand by the gay couple; and young Burney had the unspeakable relief of perceiving that this impulsive trial was successful. With expansive smiles they examined and discussed the charms of the complexion, the beauty of the features, and the sensibility and sweetness conveyed by their expression.' At last Greville laughed aloud.

'Why don't you marry her, Burney?' he exclaimed.

Burney was overjoyed.

'May I?' he asked, in all simplicity.

TEN

Burney's Married Life

SO THEY were married in 1748, when Burney was twenty-two; and influential friends in the City caused him to be elected organist of St Dionis's Backchurch (the donor being one Godwin Bac, who had become a monk at Canterbury) at a salary of thirty pounds a year. As he immediately began to take pupils, he was already, before the birth of his first child Esther, or Hetty, embarked upon the life of monumental overwork from which he suffered until his death long afterwards.

The overwork, and the City atmosphere, so affected Burney's health that within two years he was in a state of what Fanny calls 'premature decay', to which was added 'the seizure of a violent and dangerous fever,' followed by symptoms of consumption. Blister after blister was applied to his ailing body by a certain Dr Armstrong, who fortunately had the intelligence to supplement this murderous treatment with a command that the invalid should instantly leave London.

According to Percy Scholes, in *The Great Dr Burney*, Armstrong, like the celebrated Erasmus Darwin, was something of a poet; and the following lines from a long extract given by Scholes exhibit the good sense of one medically in advance of his age:

> While yet you breathe, away; the rural winds
> Invite; the mountains call you, and the vales;
> The woods, the streams, and each ambrosial breeze
> That fans the ever undulating sky . . .
> Find, then, some Woodland scene where nature smiles
> Benign . . .

He saved Burney's life. Perhaps, also, he prolonged Mrs Burney's;

for while still in the noisome atmosphere which was killing her husband she had borne a second and a third child, the first being James, who sailed with Captain Cook and after many adventures became Rear-Admiral Burney, and the second a Charles who died at the age of sixteen months. The family moved by instalments to King's Lynn, in Norfolk, where the fourth and best-remembered of Burney's offspring, Frances, was born in 1752, when her father was twenty-six.

Nor did the Grevilles withdraw their kindness to the Burneys. They remembered Charles while they were abroad, and Esther, who was full of intelligence, heightened the appeal made by her husband. This accounts for the fact that Mrs Greville willingly agreed to be godmother to Frances, who remembers to tell the readers of her biography of Burney that she, with her father and mother, often visited Wilbury, where they were welcomed and made to feel that, when gratitude for their kindness was displayed, great folk could be extremely complaisant.

This was so much the case that when both the Grevilles began to write, Fulke as an elegant philosopher, and his wife as a poet, they sent their work to Burney for his comment. Mrs Greville, to whom Sheridan dedicated *The Critic* 'with no other motive than the gratification of private friendship and esteem,' was the real talent. Her husband was nothing more than a dilettante, and in the end a wreck, but she had heart and quality. She had, said Sheridan, a 'particular reserve, and dislike to the reputation of critical taste,' and although, in his phrase, she might 'continue to deceive herself in the idea that she was known only . . . for the graceful talents that adorn conversation,' she was admired for at least one poem, included in Pearch's continuation of Dodsley, which was called *Prayer for Indifference*.

Readers who suppose that emotion was absent from eighteenth-century poetry should read the *Prayer*. They will find in it something not merely to betray her own unhappiness but also to account for her tenderness to another wife.

> I ask no kind return in love,
>   No tempting charm to please—
> Far from the heart such gifts remove
>   That sighs for peace and ease!

Nor ease nor peace that heart can know
That, like the needle true,
Turns at the touch of joy or woe—
But, turning, trembles too . . .

Half-pleased, contented will I be,
Contented—half to please.

King's Lynn, a great centre of the wine trade, at first made a bad
impression upon the new organist at St Margaret's Church. The
natives, besides being, as Wesley observed, 'sermon proof', were
totally ignorant about music; and the organ itself was 'execrably bad'.
However, the natives, as natives do, improved on further acquaintance, and very soon the Burney charm persuaded the churchwardens
to take down this execrable organ, and replace it with one specially
built by John Snetzler, a German settled in London. Snetzler had
already made an organ for Handel; his new organ was 'unreservedly
esteemed one of the finest instruments in England.' Burney, therefore, for whose wife and children stools were provided in the organ
loft, must have attained real esteem in King's Lynn by the time he
was twenty-eight.

He sent his boy James to the local Grammar School, where the
usher was a remarkable student of ancient dialects named Eugene
Aram; he had two other sons named Charles, the first of whom died
within a few months, while his later namesake became an eminent
Grecian; he gave subscription concerts not only in King's Lynn but
elsewhere in the county of Norfolk; he taught in all the great county
houses, from Holkham to the Walpole establishment at Houghton;
he was able every year to visit London and keep in touch with his
friends; and, having long been an ardent admirer of *The Rambler*,
for which he obtained many readers, he at last entered into correspondence with Samuel Johnson.

This was in 1755, when the first plan of Johnson's great Dictionary
was produced. Busy Burney hurried to collect advance orders for
the work; and having obtained half-a-dozen he wrote Johnson a
letter in the very style of *The Rambler*, a style which Johnson, in his
acknowledgment, commended for its elegance. Burney's flattery, and
the offer of an immediate draft for six copies of the Dictionary

five years before Johnson was relieved from drudgery by his pension, proved irresistible. 'I have too much pleasure,' he declared, 'in pleasing men like you, not to feel very sensibly the distinction which you have bestowed upon me.'

Johnson was in his forty-sixth year, Burney not yet thirty.

The two men did not meet immediately, because Burney was still busy in Norfolk; but after a time, hankering for London, wealth, and mentally active society, he listened to the advice of Samuel Crisp, who wrote urgently from abroad, and moved Esther and his family to town again. They set up house in Poland Street, south of Oxford Street, which 'was not then,' wrote Fanny, in 1832, with a small quiver of former wit, 'as it is now, a sort of street that, like the rest of its neighbourhood, appears to be left in the lurch. House-fanciers were not yet as fastidious as they are become at present, from the endless variety of new habitations.

'Oxford road . . . . had little on its farther side but fields, gardeners' grounds, or uncultivated suburbs. Portman, Manchester, Belgrave Squares, Portland-place, etc. etc, had not yet a single stone or brick laid, in signal of intended creation; while in plain Poland-street, Mr. Burney, then, held successively for neighbours, the Duke of Chandos, Lady Augusta Bridges, the Hon. John Smith and the Miss Barrys, Sir Willoughby and the Miss Astons; and, well noted by Mr Burney's little family, on the visit of his black majesty to England, sojourned almost immediately opposite to it, the Cherokee King.'

In some way never explained by his biographer, Burney became a fashionable teacher of music. Pupils so greatly desired his instruction at their own homes that he set up a coach and was kept busy from eight o'clock in the morning until late at night. At one time, according to Johnson, he gave fifty-seven lessons in a week; and Scholes assures us that the usual payment for each lesson was a guinea. When one lady wished to engage him, Burney tried to decline by saying that his day already began at eight o'clock. The lady's answer was: 'Then you must come to me at seven.'

At home he composed music, including exercises for the harpsi-chord. He also wrote poems; and, dashing about London in his coach, he carried books from which he voraciously gobbled knowledge as formerly he had learnt and read Italian while riding on horseback along the Norfolk lanes. Since those days his interests had broadened; they now ranged from physical science, general and musical history, and art, to astronomy. He was never still, never idle; there was not a man in London busier than he, nor one more ambitious to achieve success, to meet the great, and to display widespread knowledge in well-informed company. He felt everything to be in train for incessant activity and its rewards, which were to include, as the ultimate good, a Royal appointment.

And then his beloved wife Esther died. She had borne at least eight, and perhaps nine, children in thirteen years; and the exquisite complexion of her youth may well have been that of the consumption which then caused so many young beauties to collapse in early womanhood. Exhaustion followed the birth of her last child; an alarming cough and great bodily pain succeeded; a hurried trip to the Bristol Hot Wells proved vain.

She died on September 28th, 1761, bravely repeating prayers, passages from the Bible, and a sorrowful verse from Gray's *Elegy*:

> For who, to dumb Forgetfulness a prey,
>   This pleasing, anxious being e'er resigned,
> Left the warm precincts of the cheerful day,
>   Nor cast one longing ling'ring look behind?

These, apart from a brief conversation with her eldest daughter, Hetty, were her final occupations. When she had cried her husband's name once, 'O, Charles!' she was gone. The busy Burney, too assiduous in love as in professional duties, was left, with pupils, friends, and six living children between the ages of six weeks and twelve years, a widower. He was thirty-five.

ELEVEN

Burney and the Children

HE STILL whisked in and out of the house in Poland Street as the embodiment, for his children, of wonderful beloved coat-tails. His elder boy, James, was already at sea as a ten-year-old midshipman; the others were at home, untaught and, as Burney disliked the notion of a governess for them, seemingly unsuperintended. Hetty, the eldest, at twelve played the harpsichord to admiration; Susan, between six and seven, would presently become a willing but less sparkling performer, a wit, and the recipient of a sister's confidential letters; Fanny, nine years old, and always a shy sprite who did not know the alphabet until she was past eight, had aptitude for nothing but the mischievous observation of human foibles; of the juniors Charles was four and Charlotte a baby.

Who looked after them all we are not told. It may have been Burney's mother and sisters, who were also in London; but I do not think so. Fortunately their mother, when not engaged in producing children, had been a gentle and intelligent companion, and Hetty was old enough to keep the lead over her sisters. No rebelliousness disrupted a naturally good-humoured and good-mannered household. The family continued, somehow, to function without maternal care for a couple of years.

At the end of that period, perhaps prompted by considerate friends, Burney realised that he was not doing his duty as a father. He resolved in 1764 to take two of his daughters to Paris and put them to school there. It also occurred to him that, once in Paris, he could do some research into French music, of which the general English opinion was so poor that nothing was really known about it.

The journey was undertaken in June, 1764, and with assistance from the Embassy he found a good school, which was rather more expensive than he hoped for. After taking Hetty, at least, as far as Lyons, where there was an Anglo-Irish colony, he returned to Paris for a short period of hasty exploration. He went to the Opera, visited the museums, and hastened home again, to resume teaching.

Fanny, who was thought too delicate for travel, and too susceptible to be exposed to the infection of Romish doctrines (her Sleepe grandmother had been a Catholic), was left behind. She was very near-sighted, bashful, abnormally sensitive, subject to headache, something of a prude, and so tiny that in later years her father's friend Crisp wrote: 'What a slight piece of machinery is the terrestial part of thee, our Fannikin! A mere nothing, a blast, a vapour disorders the spring of thy watch; and the mechanism is so frail that it requires no common hand to set it right again.'

Hence her loneliness, precociousness, and that almost sly reserve which ultimately produced a charge of duplicity from Mrs Thrale and the jealous editor of Mrs Delany's correspondence. 'Merely and literally self-educated,' she says herself, 'her sole emulation for improvement, and sole spur for exertion, were her unbounded veneration for the character, and affection for the person, of her father; who, nevertheless, had not, at the time, a moment to spare for giving her any personal lessons; or even for directing her pursuits.'

Burney, in fact, could beget children; but once they were born they were neglected while he ran to his pupils or shut himself into his study. The Parisian trip was the first sign he gave of concern for their education. Afterwards, when they could assist in his work by transcription or in the entertainment of such of his visitors as showed interest in music or the latest London literary star, his pride was ostentatious.

His own part in the trip was a success. According to Fanny, he made himself, while in Paris, 'acquainted with its antiquities, curiosities, public buildings, public places, general laws, and peculiar customs; its politics, its resources, its festivities, its art and its artists; as well as with the arbitrary tyrannies, and degrading oppressions towards the lower classes, which at that epoch, were, to an English looker-on, incomprehensibly combined, not with murmurs nor discontent, but with the most lively animal spirits, and the greatest glee of natural gaiety.'

How long the acquisition of this scrambled wisdom took Burney we now have no means of knowing; but apparently he was home again before the end of the year, driven, it may be, by economic fears. His finances had suffered positively, not only by the temporary loss of pupils, but by the death in 1764 of a rich banker who had engaged him for dinner and talk every Sunday for a fee of £100 a year; and after an expensive stay in Paris the need for earning bread was paramount. He determined to become a writer.

He did not yet know what he wanted to write. Poetry, although he had strung many verses, was out of the question. Nevertheless he knew several famous authors, from Johnson to Arthur Murphy; he commanded the Johnsonian style of long words and studied antitheses; and his interests were so wide and various that there seemed to be hardly a subject beyond reach of his active mind and scribbling pen.

Before he could reduce his ambitions to order, Burney became involved in an even more advantageous enterprise. This was a second marriage.

As a young mother, Esther had found congenial associates in two ladies of King's Lynn. One was a Mrs Allen, the intellectual wife of a wealthy wine-merchant, whose beauty 'was high, commanding, and uncommon'; the other was Dolly Young, a sweet and affectionate but depressed maiden whose face 'had various unhappy defects'. Esther, whose beauty captivated all who saw it, loved Dolly very much; and when she knew herself to be dying she recommended this deformed and speckled friend to Burney as the person most likely to love his children and make himself happy in a second marriage.

She had a wife's insensitiveness at such a time to her husband's need of physical beauty in a mate; and subsequent events quite ruined Dolly Young's always doubtful prospects. The first of these was the death of Mrs Allen's wealthy husband. The second was the widow's decision to spend a winter in London. Her ostensible purpose was to introduce her elder daughter, Maria, to the capital; but she also made up her mind that Maria needed music lessons from

Burney, and in bringing the girl every week to Burney's house she heard the lessons with interest and remained afterwards to take lessons on her own account. Was not everything very natural? And was not the sequel easily to be foreseen, especially by Mrs Allen?

Under bad advice she had entrusted her personal moneys, amounting to five thousand pounds, to a Russian timber-merchant named Gomme who went bankrupt; but she had still, under some family control, the fortune her husband had left. She also, says Fanny, 'had wit at will; spirits the most vivacious and entertaining; and from a passionate fondness for reading, she had collected stores of knowledge which she was always able, and "nothing loath" to display.' Besides talking with great self-confidence (she had 'a passion for conversation and argument of the gay and brilliant sort') she saw herself as a person extremely fit to control her husband's neglected children.

Burney was not captivated by Mrs Allen as he had been captivated nearly twenty years before by the lovely Esther. He was probably awed by the high, commanding beauty, the stored and displayed knowledge, by the wit at will; and much too agreeable as a man to resist any determined assault. In 1766, when a marriage between them was under discussion, he was just forty; Mrs Allen, with three children by her first husband of about the same age as Burney's eldest, may have been slightly older. Their marriage, which took place very surreptitiously in September or October, 1767, held advantages rather than romance for both; and by their children, who had sportive associations of long standing, was at first rapturously received.

The rapture did not last. Fanny Burney and Maria Allen, a pair of merry gigglers, were always on delightful terms, and Maria's unkempt letters speak to us after two hundred years with the authentic voice of headlong girlhood; but the new Mrs Burney's temper was described by Fanny, long afterwards, as 'impracticable', and it was indulged at the children's expense. She made scenes. She was a disciplinarian. When Hetty and Fanny were both old, Fanny reminded her sister that when, with Maria, they were vivaciously disagreeing about the charms of life in King's Lyn, Hetty had hushed them, saying: 'Mama's in the next room—if she hears us we shall be whipt!'

Furthermore, the new Mrs Burney soon objected to sixteen-year-old Fanny's habit of scribbling; and insisted that it should be abandoned. Every prized manuscript was burned; and when, some time later, Fanny could not restrain her impulse to write, she hid what she was doing. Keyhole-listening became a habit in the family; the girls learned not to speak their thoughts aloud. Hetty, returning from Paris a 'finished' young woman of eighteen, found what Burney afterwards called his wife's 'family regulations' so intolerable that she resolved to escape those regulations at speed.

In 1770, therefore, while her father was abroad, she quietly married her cousin, Charles Rousseau Burney, who had neither money nor patronage but, like herself, was a particularly talented harpsichord player with a temper as sweet as her own. Whether he played the violin by himself or joined Hetty in harpsichord duets, young Charles Burney moved hearers to enthusiasm. The marriage was a success.

Nor were these the only significant items in the family history. Burney's eldest son remained at sea; his second son, yet another Charles, who became in time a respected classical scholar, was packed off to the Charterhouse; and Esther's youngest daughter, Charlotte, a very lively and affectionate little girl but 'no favourite' with her step-mother, was summarily despatched to a school in Norfolk. Charlotte, according to a letter addressed by Fanny to Samuel Crisp, was 'never spoke to, never noticed at all, except as an *errand runner*';and when afterwards taken to Wales by Mrs Burney, who had become a valetudinarian, went with such anguish that Fanny was seriously disturbed. Fanny and Susan, who were useful and outwardly docile, remained at home to tend and worship their father.

As to Mrs Burney's Allen daughters, both eloped as soon as opportunity offered; and while sooner or later everybody was forgiven it is clear that Mrs Burney was a strong and managing woman, tactless, assertive, vehement-tempered, and little loved. Even Burney, mild as he was, went out, visited Samuel Crisp at Chessington, in Surrey, or travelled abroad. When at home, he filled his house with company to which his wife could exhibit her conversational powers, but from which he could steal away to what he called his 'chaos' or study.

Mrs Burney did at least one good service to the household, by introducing to it her brother-in-law, Arthur Young. Young, whom we know as the serious author of the best picture extant of pre-Revolutionary France, was in 1768 a gay spark who teased the young ladies of Poland Street, wanted to read their journals, and had very rompingly to be turned out of their rooms. Since he was odd and facetious, and his wife had something of Mrs Burney's choler, the two were for ever quarrelling; and Fanny, who may have thought the same thing about her father and step-mother, remarks in her early Diary, 'I wonder he could ever marry her!'

'They have, however,' she adds, 'given over those violent dislikes and quarrels with which they used to entertain their friends, not that Mrs Young had any reason to congratulate herself upon it, quite the contrary, for the extreme violence of her overbearing temper has at length so entirely wearied Mr Young that he disdains any controversy with her, scarce ever contradicting her, and lives a life of calm, easy contempt.'

The Youngs had more than incompatibility to torment them. His successive failures in agricultural experiment, and the unpopularity of his theories among practical farmers, were a constant occasion of alarm in a conventional wife. But I have quoted Fanny's comment for two reasons; first to show that the argumentative Mrs Burney and her argumentative sister, being of one breed, could be very disagreeable in the home; second to show that Fanny, like other wits, found amusement, not distress, in the unhappy bickerings of others. Having been driven into secrecy by her step-mother, she had now the private satisfaction of observing, satirically, the follies of those whom she should have loved and respected.

Here is one such scene, among the earliest indications we have of her great gift for recording, with detachment, the follies of her fellow-creatures:

'Mr Young . . . called today. [He was most] absurdly dressed for a common visit, being in light blue, embroidered with silver, a bag and sword, and walking in the rain! . . . He bowed to the ground on entering, then swinging his hat the full extent of his arm,—"This is the most unfortunate shower," cried he, "or, rather, I am most unfortunate in being caught in it. Pray how does Mr Burney do? Where is he?" We, in return, enquired after Mrs Young. "She's very well, in the environs of Soho, I believe." . . . We retorted a second inquiry after Mrs Young. "We just now parted in a pet," said he, "but, I think, we were to meet here——"

'Soon after she came in a chair. After common salutations—"Pray how came you to leave me so, Mr Young?" cried she—"Only think," turning to us—"the fellow of a coachman drove the horses' heads towards a court in Soho Square, and pretended he could not move them; and Mr Young was fool enough to get out, and let the man have his way,—when he deserved to be horse-whipped." "Instead of which," returned he, "I gave him a shilling! Where's the difference?" "Who but you," cried she, "would not have made the man come on with us? or else not have paid him?—and so I was forced to run into a toyshop, where he politely left me to my fate—and where I chanced to meet with a chair." O rare Matrimony! thought I.'

For Young she felt a kindness denied to his wife. 'He is an enterprising genius,' she very shrewdly decided, when she was nineteen; 'too successful in his early life, he expected a constancy in fortune, that has cruelly disappointed him . . . I sincerely hope [he] will be able to struggle effectually with his bad fortune; but how I know not.'

Nor did Young. When he called nearly a year later he was 'almost destitute'. 'This is a dreadful trial for him; yet I am persuaded he will still find some means of extricating himself from his distresses; at least, if genius, spirit, and enterprize can avail. In defiance of the gloom his misfortunes have cast over him, some starts of his former, his native vivacity break out. Dr King has lately published a book, entitled, "The Rites, etc. of the Greek Church." Mr Young took it up, and opening at the Preface——"God, so! what's here?" cried he, and read aloud that he had undertaken this work to relieve his mind from amost severe affliction occasioned by the loss of a virtuous and affectionate—— But it would be impertinent to obtrude my private misfortunes on the public.

' "He means his wife," said I.'

' "It would serve as well for his mistress" answered he.

' "For my own part," added I (very good naturedly) "it appears ridiculous ostentation to me, as I am almost certain he had little regard for her, and he was never in his life more gay than since her death; for I have heard well-authenticated particulars of her marriage; and therefore it seems more——"

' "Well, God so!" cried he, "I honour a man who dares to be singular; I like to see a man's oddities in his works."

' "But, I think," said I, "you are no friend to *affectation*; which to us who know him, this appears.—Are *you* affected?"

' "Affected!" exclaimed he with all his wonted impetuosity. "I had rather be a murderer!" '

It is clear from the manner in which this conversation is recorded that Fanny had been reading *A Sentimental Journey*; but it is also clear that she was a born novelist, and that however shy in public she was not tongue-tied with a man she liked.

I said the marriage of Burney to Mrs Allen held advantages for both. In the wife's case, a small-town middle-class beauty, who had no position in any London society, became at once a metropolitan hostess rich in Burney's literary, musical, and occasionally aristocratic friends such as the Grevilles and Lord Holdernesse. She could, and did, indulge her 'passion for conversation and argument of the gay and brilliant sort' as she had not been able to do at this level in King's Lynn; and unless silenced as she once was by Mrs Greville when extolling 'Sterne's seducing sensibility,' or rebuked by Johnson for clothes she was proposing to wear to church one Sunday at the Thrales', she lived in a state of considerable self-approval.

For Burney the advantage must have been pecuniary. Apart from the hundred pounds a year from his rich banker friend, he was entirely dependent on his earnings as a music-teacher; and even if he received a guinea a lesson, as Scholes claims, there must have been many cancellations, and, when people were out of London, breaks in continuity. Although no fortune-hunter, but an industrious man whose highest ambition was a sinecure, he cannot have ignored Mrs Allen's financial circumstances. Indeed, it was because she feared to lose her first husband's estate by re-marrying that the lady at first lived in a separate house, and remained, nominally, 'Mrs Allen'.

The effects of the new marriage were quickly to be seen in Burney's enhanced ambition. He had hitherto been plain 'Mr' Burney. Now he aspired to a Doctorate of Music; and as a step towards this degree he offered to compose a setting for Gray's *Ode* on the installation of the Duke of Grafton to the Chancellorship of Cambridge University. His offer brought a truly painful snub from the Duke's representatives when they learned how much it would cost to hire the necessary instrumentalists. Told that he must cut the estimate by half, Burney withdrew in dudgeon.

Oxford was more amenable. When he had complied with the University's one condition, that an applicant should be the member of a College, Burney was allowed to compose a long 'anthem', and to perform it in the Oxford Music School with singer and orchestra of his own provision. Two degrees, those of Bachelor and Doctor of Music, were bestowed; and Burney, who had been accompanied to Oxford by his wife, wrote a jubilant letter, boasting of his triumphs to the girls who, less privileged, waited in Poland Street.

'I know it will please you,' he said, 'to hear that the performance of my Anthem is just very well over . . . I shall tomorrow have both my Degrees with great unanimity and reputation . . . I know not when I shall get home.'

By this time Fanny had begun to keep a diary, in defiance of her step-mother. We thus know the pleasure they did receive, and the loving delight she took in her father's success. 'How strongly,' she wrote, 'how forcibly do I feel to whom I owe all the earthly happiness I enjoy!—it is to my father! . . . It is his goodness to me which makes all appear so gay, it is his affection which makes *my* sun shine . . . What value can compare with its worth?—the *worth of such a* treasure? a parent who makes the happiness of his children!'

Burney now caught a glimpse of the master-work which he thought would be sure to bring him literary fame. He resolved to take a long trip abroad, without his new wife, and without his adoring daughters, to gather material for his book. Having so resolved, he started as soon as possible, mislaying his sword *en route*, but carrying a mass of impedimenta which included letters of introduction from Garrick and others, and even packets addressed from friend to friend in various parts of the Continent. While travelling, he kept a diary, not only for private satisfaction, and not only with an eye to his ultimate masterpiece, but for a book, which he afterwards published at his own or Mrs Burney's expense, called *The Present State of Music in France and Italy: or the Journal of a Tour through those countries undertaken to collect Materials for a General History of Music.* This was the book which Johnson said he admired so much that he made it the model for his own *Journey to the Western Islands of Scotland.*

Burney's tour lasted for six months. Unprotected by a retinue of servants, such as great travellers, from Horace Walpole to Greville and William Beckford, commanded, and dependent at all times and in all weathers upon ramshackle hired vehicles, he lodged at verminous hotels, ate rancid food, and was extortionately overcharged. In addition, he was so often ill, and even physically battered, that by the end of the tour his purse was empty and he was a wreck.

In spite of every hardship he ransacked French and Italian cities for material, met in Geneva a living skeleton named Voltaire, in Bologna the Mozart father and son whom he had previously seen in London, and, on his return to Paris, Rousseau. Weather conditions were even more appalling in Paris than they had been elsewhere; but the Doctor could not allow his enthusiasm to be checked. He attended the Opera, where his verdicts agreed with those expressed thirty years earlier by Thomas Gray. The singers were still 'screaming like tortured infernals'; the soprano parts continued to be 'squalled by cats in the shape of women.'

There were two surprises. In Rome he learned indirectly, and by accident, that his eldest daughter was married; on reaching London he found that he no longer lived in Poland Street. Mrs. Burney, displeased with a good-natured but officiously match-making neighbour, had forbidden her step-children all association with this neighbour, and had bought another house a mile away, in Queen Square, Bloomsbury.

TWELVE

Two Authors in the Family

WHAT the returned traveller thought of these two events we do not know. There was no break with the new-married Hetty; and it is always said that as a hero-worshipper he was entranced by news that the house in Queen Square had once been occupied by Swift's printer-friend John Barber. But after one rapt glance at hallowed walls, and what one hopes was a cordial welcome, he scampered as fast as he could to Crisp's home in Surrey. There, without his wife, he was nursed, cheered, and encouraged to write up his diary for publication.

Crisp, once wealthy and a great party-giver, was now, no longer rich, a recluse. Macaulay said he was sulking because he could not persuade Garrick to revive his only play (we are assured that it was a very bad play indeed), which was called *Virginia*; but although one or two references in his letters show a slight sense of grievance it is more likely that, having wasted too much money in feasting greedy and ungrateful guests, Crisp could not bear to become publicly impoverished, and found solitude a relief.

He rented part of a very old mansion standing so far from practicable roads as to be a fortress against invasion. Unwanted guests were escaped; only his kindred and the Burneys were welcomed; and his affection for Burney and the Burney girls overflowed into hospitality. The girls, indeed, spent holidays at Chessington with an eagerness which suggests passionate longing to escape from 'family regulations' at home. There were no regulations at Chessington, where fun, charades, and freedom lightened the hearts of all.

As far as I can tell, Mrs Burney was never included in Crisp's invitations. Fanny, his 'Fannikin', on the other hand, enjoyed free entry. She and Crisp became such intimate correspondents that her letters to him give vividly attractive pictures of the Burney family and its musical and other friends. 'Dash away whatever comes uppermost,' Crisp instructed; 'the sudden sallies of imagination, clap'd down on paper, just as they arise, are worth folios.' 'There is no fault in an epistolary correspondence like stiffness and study.'

This was the best advice any young writer could have received. Fanny took it.

When Burney went to Chessington he was given a special writing-room known as 'the Doctor's Conjuring Closet'. It was secluded from the rest of the house, which for the girls was a fascinating warren of small rooms, staircases, low ceilings, and carven cupboards. The visitors could see from the roof a picturesque landscape extending for sixteen miles in every direction; and within doors or in the garden freedom was so complete that, for Fanny the place had an air of Paradise.

'The ever charming, engaging, beloved Mr Crisp', she called her host in the early days of friendship, adding: 'The frankness—the sincerity with which he corrects and reproves us, is more grateful to me, than the most flattering professions could be, because it is far, far more seriously kind and friendly . . . He protests he will take no denial from Papa for Hetty and me to go to Chesington [so the name was then spelt] this summer, and told Papa to remember that he had bespoke us: I fancy he is weary of asking almost, and I am sure my dear Papa is tired of refusing—for what in the world can be more disagreeable, more painful to a mind generous and good as his?—I declare I am almost ashamed to hear Chesington mention'd before him, and cannot for my life join in intreaties to go, tho' my heart prompts me most *furiously*. . . .

'O dear, O dear, the kindest letter from Mr Crisp. If my Papa has not the most obdurate, barbarous and inhuman heart in the world, he *must* be moved by it to permit some of us to accept his invitation. We are all in agonies of fear and suspense . . . I shall be *so* happy to see that dearest of men again! and then Miss Cooke—the good Mrs Hamilton, too—in *short*, Chesington is all in all.'

Crisp became 'Daddy Crisp'; more selflessly devoted to his 'Fanni-kin' and her sisters than any other person, and Burney's truest and most perceptive friend.

This last fact was shown when Burney's book was finished. The author showed his manuscript to four friends, three of whom, the Earl of Holdernesse, William Mason, and Garrick, advised him to omit the racier and more characteristic descriptive comments, on the ground that readers everywhere were surfeited with travel sketches. Only Crisp, the fourth, wanted him to retain every idiosyncratic quirk, on the ground that such things made the book Burney's own. Crisp was right; the others wrong. *The Present State of Music in France and Italy* is what would now be called underwritten. It is a a cramped little daily record of people met and music heard, with hardly any flourishes of egotism or humour.

Burney, however, was 'too timid', says Fanny, to risk displeasing those on whom, at heart if not in fact, he fawned. They were great men; he the music-teacher. His timidity had already been shown in his care not to offend his Continental acquaintances; it now led him astray.

The book's popular reception was very cordial; so cordial that Burney made up his mind to follow it with another, on Germany, where he knew that there was instrumental music (as opposed to vocal music, in which Italy was supreme) of the highest class. He remembered his old friend Kirkman as a maker of superlative harpsichords, and the magnificent organ which Snetzler had built for his church in King's Lynn. Now he prepared himself to meet the composers of a nation whose instruments he valued.

He was lucky in his encounters; for while some of these were with Italians such as the poet Metastasio, one was with Gluck, who was revolutionizing opera and, as Burney says, 'simplifying music'. 'With unbounded invention and powers for creating capricious difficulties, and decking his melodies with meretricious ornaments, he tries all he can to keep his muse chaste and sober. His three operas of *Orfeo*, *Alceste*, and *Paride* are proofs of this, as they contain few difficulties of execution, though many of expression.' Other comments have less interest for modern readers than this, which was probably taken directly from Gluck himself: Burney was gathering opinions and information, and filling his notebooks. He had no great critical acumen.

Unfortunately the German tour was made in winter, when, according to his enthusiastic daughter, he was 'assaulted by the rudest fierceness of country elemental strife' culminating in one final mischance that became a family story.

'After travelling by day and by night,' writes Fanny in *The Memoirs of Dr Burney*, 'to expedite his return, over mountains, through marshes, by cross-roads; on horse-back, on mules, in carriages of any and every sort that could hurry him on, he reached Calais in a December so dreadfully stormy, that not a vessel of any kind could set sail for England. Repeatedly he secured his hammock, and went on board to take possession of it; but as repeatedly was driven back by fresh gales, during the space of nine fatiguing days and tempestuous nights. And when, at last, the passage was effected, so nearly annihilating had been his sufferings from seasickness, that it was vainly he was told he might now, at his pleasure, arise, go forth, and touch English ground; he had neither strength nor courage to move, and earnestly desired to be left awhile to himself.

'Exhaustion, then, with tranquillity of mind, cast him into a sound sleep.

'From this repose, when, much refreshed, he awoke, he called to the man who was in waiting, to help him up, that he might get out of the ship.

' "Get out of the ship, sir?" repeated the man. "Good lauk! You'll be drowned!"

' "Drowned?—What's to drown me? I want to go ashore."

' "Ashore, sir?" again repeated the man; "why you're in the middle of the sea! There ar'nt a bit of ground for your toe nail."

' "What do you mean?" cried the Doctor, starting up; "the sea? Did you not tell me we were safe in at Dover?"

' "O lauk! that's two good hours ago, sir! I could not get you up then, say what I would. You fell downright asleep, like a top. And so I told them. But that's all one. You may go, or you may stay, as you like; but them pilots never stop for nobody."

'Filled with alarm, the Doctor now rushed up to the deck, where he had the dismay to discover that he was half-way back to France.'

After these painful experiences Burney 'became a prey to the merciless pangs of the acutest spasmodic rheumatism; which barely suffered him to reach his home, ere, long and piteously, it confined him, a tortured prisoner, to his bed.'

There, 'exchanging the light wines of France, Italy, and Germany, for the black and loathsome potions of the Apothecaries' Hall; writhed by darting stitches, and burning with fiery fever,' he had the additional torment of wanting to write his new book in peace. Escaping from his wife's 'family regulations' and passion for talk, he rushed once more to Chessington.

It was necessary, however, for him to earn some money; and the only way in which he could earn money was by giving music lessons. He was therefore quickly back again to the overwork of the past, now increased by the fact that he stole every possible moment for literary composition. The consequences were seen by his friend Crisp as suicidal. 'As to that rogue your father,' Crisp wrote to Fanny, 'if I did not know him to be incorrigible, I should say something of that regular course of irregularity he persists in—two, three, four, five o'clock in the morning, sups at twelve!—is it impossible for him to get the better of his constitution? has he forgot the condition he was in the winter after his first return to England? . . .'

And in another letter: 'When I come to town (which I believe will not be very distant) I shall without ceremony send for Dr Monro, have a strait waistcoat immediately put on him, debar him the use of pen, ink, and paper and books, to which (if he is mutinous) shall be added a dark room—what does he mean? if he has no consideration for himself, has he no regard for his relatives? . . . The booby has nothing to do but to allow some repose to his thin carcase, to get well again . . . Devil take him!'

The devil had taken him already. Leisure, peace of mind, health, were all sacrificed to the determined assault upon lasting fame. He knew that Sir John Hawkins was writing a rival history. He knew that his flights through Continental cities and brief contacts at home and abroad were no real substitute for scholarship. He had not found answers to essential questions about the music of the ancients, about folk music, or even about the origins of counterpoint. All he could do was to press on with his compilation, heaping detail upon detail in desperate profusion, 'endeavouring to *divert* when I have not the least chance of *instructing*.'

This frenzy of work was hampered by incessant calls upon his energy. 'My father's History goes on very slowly indeed,' wrote Fanny, in April 1775. 'The town is very full. He teaches from nine to nine almost every day, and has scarce time to write a page a week.' His fingers were twisted with rheumatism ('not one straight finger have I on my right hand'), his body was in pain from what may have been an obstruction in the gall-bladder; but 'his mind refused all relaxation. So urgent grew now the spirit of his diligence for the progress of his work, that he not only declined all invitations to the hospitable boards of his friends, he even resisted the social hour of repast at his own table.'

Fanny barely refers in the *Memoirs*, in which the preceding words occur, to her own part in this turmoil; yet the truth is that but for her help Burney would never have completed his book. Her previously discouraged habit of scribbling was vindicated. With little time during the day to keep her Diary, and with her first novel, *Evelina*, a secret joy, set down upon scraps of paper or invented and remembered amid a thousand other occupations, she became her father's devoted amanuensis. Thus was her astonishing devotion to him exploited by one who in time was to ruin her literary style by his pernicious example.

THIRTEEN

'Thou Shalt Live with Me for Ever'

WHEN she was fifteen, Fanny had been described by a male visitor to Poland Street as 'the silent, observant Miss Fanny.' At home, and with family friends, she allowed her natural vivacity to shine; so attractively that certain young men amused themselves when they chanced to be alone with her by flying preposterous conversational kites. They did not guess that those kites, and her own rejoinders, were afterwards written down with great spirit in her Diary.

One young man, a Mr Thomas Barlow, whom she described as 'rather short, but handsome,' who had 'a great desire to please, but no elegance of manners' and in spite of worthiness was 'not at all agreeable,' showed no amusement. At their first meeting he fixed his attention upon her with 'a *seriousness* of attention much more expressive than complimenting.' Like other persons of great nervous gaiety, Fanny could not relish solemnity; and she took quite a dislike to the callow Mr Barlow.

She was then not quite twenty-three years of age, and the meeting took place at a party given by Hetty. Her presence was due to Hetty's entreaty that she would come to help entertain 'a very stupid family' of two old people named O'Connor and their deaf and dumb daughter. To these monsters were added Burney's mother and two of his sisters, Fanny's aunts, with Mr Barlow as makeweight. Whether Hetty had already seen him as a possible husband for Fanny we do not know; but when, in order to enliven the dullness, Fanny suggested the playing of a game called 'cross-questions' he sat next to her and, after long considering what question to ask, he finally chose 'what she thought most necessary in love.' She afterwards remembered with terror that her reply had been 'Constancy.'

The evening dragged very wearisomely; but at last 'the coach came for me about eleven. I rose to go. He earnestly entreated me to stay one or two minutes. I did not, however, think such compliance at all requisite, and therefore only offered to set my grandmother down in my way ... When we had all taken leave of our host and hostess, my grandmother, according to custom, gave me a kiss and her blessing. I would have fain eluded my aunts, as nothing can be so disagreeable as kissing before young men: however, they chose it should go round; and after them Mrs O'Connor also saluted me, as did her daughter, desiring to be better acquainted with me. This disagreeable ceremony over, Mr Barlow came up to me, and making an apology which, not suspecting his intention, I did not understand,—he gave me a most ardent salute!'

Nor was that the end of the matter. Four days later Fanny received a very fine letter, written in the best eighteenth-century style, to the effect that the feelings of the Evening were the most refined he had ever enjoyed, referring to his 'ardurous Pen', and venturing to declare that 'the Affability, Sweetness, and Sensibility, which shone in your every Action' led him irresistibly to Love and Admire the Mistress of them.' He spoke, as might have been expected, of CONSTANCY.

Fanny copied the letter into her Diary. It was her first proposal. She did not laugh at it; but knew instantly that she could never love Mr Barlow in return. 'However,' she told the 'Nobody' to whom the Diary was addressed, 'as I do not consider myself as an independent member of society, and as I knew I could depend upon my father's kindness, I thought it incumbent upon me to act with his concurrence. I therefore, at night, before I sent an answer showed him the letter.

'He asked me a great many questions. I assured him that forming a connection without attachment—(and that I was totally indifferent to the youth in question)—was what I could never think of. My father was all indulgence and goodness. He at first proposed that I should write him word that our acquaintance had been too short to authorise so high an opinion as he expressed for me, but I objected to that as seeming to infer that a *longer* acquaintance might be accept-able: he therefore concluded upon the whole that I should send no answer at all.'

This, obviously, was very bad advice. Whether Burney supposed that by giving it he should be saved any further interruption of his night's work, or whether he was already disposed to face the loss of Fanny to any suitor who offered, I do not know. He may have found Mr Barlow's epistolary style less grotesque than it now seems; long words were particularly in his line. But I do not think he wanted to be rid of Fanny. Quite apart from the affection he bore to all his children, he found her too useful as his amanuensis—'Secretary Fanny' he called her—for that. But he would not let her dismiss Mr Barlow out of hand, as she wished to do.

As has always been usual in such affairs, the entire family was informed, and the entire family was racked with discussions of the advantages to Fanny of such a marriage. Led by Hetty, who was happy with her husband, all took Mr Barlow's part. All, including her maiden aunts, warned Fanny against the distress of dying an old maid. Hetty went so far as to write to Fanny's own 'Daddy Crisp', 'representing in the strongest light the utility of my listening to Mr Barlow.'

'He has written me such a letter! God knows how I shall answer it. Everybody is against me but my beloved father . . . they all of them are kindly interested in my welfare; but they know not so well as myself what may make me happy or miserable. To unite myself for life to a man who is not *infinitely* dear to me is what I can never, never consent to, unless, indeed, I was strongly urged by my father. I thank God most gratefully he has not interfered.'

Fanny's days were spent in an agony of dread lest she should en-counter the unwelcome young man. She pretended, in order to run no risk of meeting him at the O'Connors', that she was too unwell to join the party. Mr Barlow called to commiserate, stammering, and seeming to be 'so confounded he scarce knew where he was.' It was a most embarrassing scene. She afterwards learned from her aunts that when they reached the O'Connors, and Mr Barlow handed them from the coach, 'he looked *ready to drop*' at discovering her absence. They met again. He wrote again—a finer letter than ever.

It was shown to Burney. 'My father looked grave, asked me for the letter, put it in his pocket unread, and wished me good night.'

'I was seized with a kind of *pannic*. I trembled at the idea of his espousing, however mildly, the cause of this young man. I passed a restless night, and in the morning dared not write without his permission, which I was now half afraid to ask.'

After a further interview with Mr Barlow, in the course of which, after vehemently refusing him, she advised her suitor to 'go and *ponder* upon this affair for about half an hour. Then say—what an odd, queer, strange creature she is—and then—think of something else.' He protested. He entreated her not to be severe. On a further rebuff he 'took his leave—returned back;—took leave;—and returned again. . . He would fain have taken a more *tender* leave of me,—but I repulsed him with great surprise and displeasure.'

Alas! More was to come. 'The next day, a day, the remembrance of which will be never erased from my memory,—my father first spoke to me *in favour* of Mr Barlow, and desired me not to be peremptory in the answer I was going to write . . . I scarce made any answer; I was terrified to death.'

Terrified? Yes, but perhaps the episode, which was so much in key with the novel she was secretly writing, had its enjoyments too. Moreover, when in the Diary Fanny graphically described her sensations she had already reached an emotional, and on her part a tearful, understanding with Burney. ' "Oh, Sir;" cried I, "I wish for nothing! only let me live with you." "My life!" cried he, kissing me kindly. "Thou shalt live with me for ever, if thee wilt!" '

The approved letter to Mr Barlow—of which Fanny kept a copy —was decisive:

'Sir, I am much concerned to find that my silence to the first letter with which you honoured me has not had the effect it was meant to produce, of preventing your giving yourself any further trouble upon my account.

'The good opinion you are pleased to express of me, however extraordinary upon so short an acquaintance, certainly claims my acknowledgments; but as I have no intention of changing my present situation, I can only assure you of my good wishes for your health and happiness, and request and desire that you will bestow no further thoughts, time, or trouble upon,

Sir, Your most humble servant. F. Burney.'

The episode was over.

FOURTEEN

Mrs Thrale

THE Burneys were now removed from Queen Square, Mrs Burney's purchase of that house having proved not quite valid. They lived in another house, also bought by that determined lady while her husband was abroad, in St Martin's Street, Leicester Fields. Sir Isaac Newton had spent the last two years of his life in it; and Burney persuaded himself mistakenly that Newton had superintended its erection. At the very top of the house was a sort of tower with a leaden roof, which had been Newton's observatory, a fact which gave Burney's astronomical study a tremendous fillip.

More entertaining was done in St Martin's Street. It was more central than Queen Square; and was convenient for Sir Joshua Reynolds, who lived on the eastern side of the Fields, near the end of Long Acre, and for Garrick, who had a new house in the Adelphi. Nollekens, the sculptor, also came from his home in Mortimer Street, beyond the Oxford road; the Grevilles did not forget their *protégé;* and once, at least, Johnson attended a party.

There were also musical acquaintances from abroad; and the Italian opera stars, then enjoying one of their London seasons of prosperity, were sometimes persuaded to play and sing, besides listening with applause to the performances of Hetty Burney and her husband. Fanny saw and heard all these people; and being a wonderful reporter, and perhaps improviser, with a lighter than Boswellian memory for words and phrases, she very brilliantly noted in her Diary their fantastic airs, broken English, sullen moods, and scandalous stories about absent friends. She missed nothing. Malice and admiration mingled with her relish in grown-up children.

Presently too, Burney was summoned to the Streatham mansion of a rich brewer named Henry Thrale, to teach the Thrales' eldest daughter, Queeney, how to play the harpsichord. Thrale—called by Johnson 'my Master'—was credited by his wife with a fine person and good manners; she, the celebrated Mrs Thrale, was an alert and vivacious hostess who loved to entertain odd characters for mutual diversion. She fed them well, and gave them all the sense of being important.

She did not, although she claimed aristocratic descent, belong to the *ton*. She had no associations with the Court. Her circle was composed, not of lords and ladies, but of two or three erudite females, who later included Anna Seward, and of such men as Johnson, Burke, Garrick, Arthur Murphy the dramatist, Johnson's friend Bennet Langton, a Seward who had no connection with Lichfield, Dr Beattie the author of a once-famous poem called *The Minstrel*, and a curious person name Baretti. Baretti had been introduced by Johnson as a teacher of Italian. He was domesticated with the Thrales for three years, and he became notorious by stabbing a man to death in Haymarket with a pocket-knife. He was acquitted through the staunch testimonies to his virtue of Johnson and others, and afterwards had the post of foreign secretary to the Royal Academy.

Burney was added to this circle. Having entered the house as music-teacher, he found Queeney's lessons, owing to Mrs Thrale's interruptions for gossip and discussions, unfruitful; but acquaintance with the mistress of the house so glowed and prospered that the music-teacher was almost entirely lost in the friend. There can be no doubt that entry into the Thrale circle, leading to the freer grandeur of the Johnson circle, was the greatest social delight Burney ever enjoyed. His contacts with Johnson had previously been slight; they now became, through assiduity on his side, and pleasure in flattery on Johnson's, extremely cordial; and so remained for the last eight years of Johnson's life.

It must also be said that although the Johnson circle was in a sense a *coterie* it was not a clique. Its members were free from snobbery and the lower forms of self-interest, and were ready to accept any fellow-professional as an equal. In joining it Burney may have been aware of intellectual inferiority; but he was not made aware of it by others.

This was an important fact. As a boy who had been nurtured by an illiterate foster-mother, and forced to placate his betters by quick tact and smiling deference, he had attracted Arne, Handel, Mrs Cibber, and above all the Grevilles. As a teacher of the harpsichord, receiving in great houses the kindly condescension of their owners, he kept his pupils and increased their number by means of humility and charming manners. A perception of the need for this deportment was ingrained.

Similar tact and smiling deference, similar attention to courtesy, was taken to Streatham. Whenever Burney dreamed of advancement it was through patronage and a sinecure. He was already a Musician in Ordinary to his sovereign, and he aspired—it was his lifelong dream —to the Mastership of the King's Band. Meanwhile, at the Thrales', and in the society of his greatest idol Johnson, he could be more nearly at ease in good company than ever before. He gratified everybody, including Mrs Thrale, who had what Boswell, in speaking of her to Johnson, called 'the insolence of wealth and the conceit of parts.'

Mrs Thrale used her brewer-husband's wealth to capture as guests the men and women of literary talent who gave her the illusion of possessing unlimited wit and social power. Johnson was almost domesticated with her; Garrick, Burke, Sheridan, and Murphy dined often at her table; she saw herself as benefactress to them all. If they smiled and bowed and talked their best, she loved them; if they resisted, she quarrelled with them and wrote harsh, almost abusive, words of them in the Journal to which her husband gave the name *Thraliana*.

Her first recorded impression of Burney was of his 'obsequiousness'; it was the behaviour of one, uncertain of his place in society, who wished to ingratiate himself with his employers. Later, she found him entertaining, and proclaimed—probably felt—genuine regard. But her best judgment was shown in the list she made in *Thraliana* of the most regular visitors to Streatham. Here marks were awarded, the maximum being twenty, for nine qualities ranging from morality to religion.

To several of her friends she gave no marks at all for certain attri- butes—Burke, for example, had no wit and no humour; Boswell a

mere five for scholarship; and Murphy only four for morality;—
but some of the others did better. Johnson was given nineteen for
scholarship, twenty. for miscellaneous knowledge, fifteen for wit,
sixteen for humour, and none for person, manners, or good humour.
Burney, on the other hand, earned only eight for scholarship, but
fifteen for miscellaneous knowledge, thirteen for person and voice,
sixteen for manners, nine for wit, no more than three for humour, but
a triumphant nineteen for that precious gift, good-humour.

This was a most perceptive estimate. If we add that Fanny described
her father as 'timid' and, as a writer, 'anxious and diffident beyond
any author that ever, I believe, existed,' and that she and her sisters
considered him 'the dearest, most amiable, best beloved, and most
worthy of men,' we shall see why he passed everywhere for a clever,
accommodating little fellow who could do no harm to anybody.
We shall also understand why he was overjoyed at Mrs Thrale's
patronage.

FIFTEEN

Evelina

SO FAR, Fanny and Susanna had been seen by great people only in the Burney home, where they were subject to Mrs Burney's 'family regulations.' Garrick was often in the house, sometimes arriving so early in the morning that he caught them before they were dressed for the day; Samuel Crisp, often a visitor in Queen Square, but latterly in seclusion at Chessington Hall, gave them well-disciplined affection when they stayed with him. Otherwise they seem to have led a chiefly domestic existence among their relatives and neighbours.

Fanny, however, transcended domesticity. She had inherited her father's busyness; and, besides helping him and reading all manner of classics and serious histories, stitching clothes, composing the Diary which is so much the best of her works, and writing long letters, full of high spirits and caustic observation, to 'Daddy' Crisp, was engaged upon another task, of which she told nobody. This was the composition of a novel.

Crisp's enthusiasm for her vivid commentaries probably encouraged her to use a well-established novel-form, story-telling by means of letters; and although the book was not the first she had written—its predecessor had been a part of the holocaust dictated by her step-mother—it was a *tour de force* which in time would startle the reading world. The very secrecy with which it had to be written heightened the author's enjoyment of stolen hours.

Sitting in a corner while other people talked and played, Fanny had mischievously noticed every affectation of manner and speech, every contradiction in thought, every betrayal of falsity or vulgarity. When free to do so, she had mimicked the affectations, evidently with great skill, and in her Diary and letters to Crisp she had already practised transcribing the vulgarities. Her experience of life was narrow—as was that of Maria Edgworth and Jane Austen—but as was the case with these others the very smallness of her world made for comprehension of it. She had the satirist's eye and ear. The self-consciousness which made her bashful, and the prudery which made one who had savoured *Pamela*, *Tom Jones*, and *A Sentimental Journey* pretend to miss the innuendoes addressed to her in a coarse age, were translated when she wrote into ruthless candour. Burney himself was immune from criticism; she passionately loved him. The rest of the world was a peepshow. Hers was the true novelist's temperament.

Evelina was written fragmentarily. 'The fear of discovery, or of suspicion in the house,' Fanny afterwards wrote, 'made the copying extremely laborious to me: for in the daytime, I could only take odd moments, so that I was obliged to sit up the greatest part of many nights, in order to get it ready.'

Like her father in so many other respects, Fanny shared his vanity, timorousness, and secret longing for fame. She was determined that, if possible, *Evelina* should be published, and when the book was only two-thirds written she could not resist the temptation to offer it to a publisher. She found difficulty in thinking of a way to do this; but at last she employed as messenger her brother Charles, who was twenty, and presumably, as he had been sent down from the University for appropriating books, was skulking at home in disgrace. Having disguised her handwriting with great care lest it should be recognized as that of Burney's amanuensis, she approached Dodsley. Dodsley; however, refused to look at the work of an anonymous author, arid she was forced to turn to another publisher (in those days 'bookseller') named Lowndes.

This second attempt also produced disappointment, for 'after all this *fagging*, Mr Lowndes sent me word, that he approved of the book; but could not think of printing it, till it was finished; that it would be a great disadvantage to it [to be published by instalments, as, for example, *Tristram Shandy* had been], and that he would wait my time.' The blow was softened by an invitation from Burney's brother Richard to stay with him in Worcester; and this visit, with some journeyings to the West of England, not only took her mind off *Evelina*, but gave her some fresh and especially lively material for the book.

It also precipitated a disclosure. 'Before I made this journey . . . I was so much penetrated by my dear father's kind parting embrace that in the fullness of my heart I could not forbear telling him, that I had sent a manuscript to Mr Lowndes; earnestly, however, beseeching him never to divulge it, nor to demand a sight of such trash as I could scribble . . . He could not help laughing; but I believe was much surprised at the communication. He desired me to acquaint him from time to time how my work went on, called himself the *Pere confident*, and kindly promised to guard my secret as cautiously as I could wish . . . I believe he is not sorry to be saved the giving me the pain of his criticism.'

The book, temporarily laid aside, was finished with gusto after Fanny's return to St Martin's Street in the summer of 1777.

She then sent her complete manuscript to Lowndes, who to her incredulous glee offered twenty pounds for the copyright. The offer, says Fanny, who had never in her life possessed so much money, 'was accepted with alacrity, and boundless surprise at its munificence.'

By now, her sisters and aunts were in the secret, as well as her artist-cousin Edward, who, assuming the name of 'Mr Grafton', took the place of Charles as negotiator. 'Mr Grafton' received proofs, which he was asked to revise and return: there was a flurry of excitement among the secret-sharers; and then, one day in January, 1778, when the author was a little less than half a year short of her twenty-sixth birthday, the still-ignorant Mrs Burney read aloud at the breakfast-table an advertisement which had caught her eye. It was of an anonymous novel called *Evelina; or a Young Lady's Entrance into the World*.

Mrs Burney was allowed to preserve her ignorance. She showed no interest in the book, which was forgotten in family concern at the serious illness, first of Burney, and immediately afterwards of Fanny, who had inflammation of the lungs. She was very ill indeed, too ill to think of herself as an author. Chessington, of course, became her refuge as danger passed; and it was while there, too weak to walk for more than three yards at a time, that she had the shock of receiving three volumes 'most elegantly bound.'

That was all. She heard no more. She knew nothing of the first favourable reviews until June, when Burney, having with unexplained suspicion read the one in *The Monthly Review* which called *Evelina* 'one of the most sprightly, entertaining, and agreeable productions' of the day, was led to buy and read the book.

His performance was described with great spirit by Susanna, who must then have been twenty-three, in a letter to the convalescent Fanny dated June 4th, 1778. She said:

'My father has at last got Evelina! . . . Yesterday morning when I was alone with him a few minutes while he dress'd—

' "Why Susan," said he to me—"I have got Fan's book."

' "Lord sir! have you?"

' "Yes—but I suppose you must not tell her—Poor Fan's *such* a prude."

' "Oh! I don't know sir, she knows *you* know of it—'tis only *others*."

' "Oh," said he, quick—"I shall keep it locked up in my Sanctum Sanctorum," pointing to his bureau—"I would not betray the poor girl for the world—but upon my soul I like it vastly—Do you know I began to read it with Lady Hales and Miss Coussmaker yesterday."

' "Lord!" cried I, a little alarm'd. "You did not tell them . . ."

' " 'Tell them,' no certainly—I said 'twas a book had been recommended to me—they'll never know, and they like it *vastly*, but upon my soul there's something in the preface and dedication vastly strong *and well written*—better than I could have expected—and yet I did not think 'twould be *trash* when I began it—" '

It was the *vastly strong* dedication which had won Burney's heart. This, as the family alone could guess, his name being indicated only by asterisks, was to himself:

> Oh, Author of my being!—far more dear
>   To me than light, than nourishment, or rest,
> Hygeia's blessings, Rapture's burning tear,
>   Or the life-blood that mantles in my breast!

Could my weak pow'rs thy num'rous virtues trace
   By filial love each fear should be repress'd;
The blush of incapacity I'd chace.
   And stand, Recorder of thy worth, confess'd;

But since my niggard stars that gift refuse,
   Concealment is the only boon I claim;
Obscure be still the unsuccessful Muse,
Who cannot raise, but would not sink, thy fame.

Here was the same daughterly love which Fanny had expressed when terrified lest she should be married, against her inclination, to Mr Barlow: 'Oh, Sir; I wish for nothing! only let me live with you!' To that appeal he had answered with the tender promise: 'My life! Thou shalt live with me for ever, if thee wilt!' This was the degree of their mutual affection. This, and the fact should be remembered in the light of after-events, was the expression of Fanny's deepest, most heartfelt desire.

Susanna's reference to 'others' from whom the secret should be kept plainly indicated Mama, who had insisted nine years earlier that Fanny must abandon scribbling, and whose 'family regulations' caused her step-daughters to hide thoughts and activities which they knew she would not approve. Burney showed that he understood the reference (perhaps he, too, concealed certain matters from his wife's knowledge) by saying that he would keep the book locked in his *sanctum sanctorum*. It was a promise of absolute secrecy.

He broke the promise. He became wild with uncontrollable excitement. He introduced *Evelina* to every household he visited, at first pretending to have heard the book recommended by others, but as intoxication seized him boasting of acquaintance with the author's identity and—although he denied having done so—of his relationship to her. Finally, supreme act of treachery, he read it aloud to his wife in the early mornings, prompting her reactions with cries of delight. 'That's excellent!' '*Isn't* that good!' '*Johnson could not have expressed himself better!*' and so on. His conclusive verdict was: 'Upon my soul, I think it is the best novel I know, excepting Fielding's—and in some respects it is better than his.'

So extreme was paternal vanity that he reported to Fanny or, in her absence from home, to Susanna, every scrap of praise he could elicit; every comment made by Lady Hales and her daughter Miss Coussmaker, to whom he insisted on reading the book aloud; the fact that Lady Radnor had bought another copy; and, at last, after fretting long for a pretext to introduce it to Mrs Thrale, recording as a miracle that the greatest critic of all had spoken of it at the Thrales' table. Peg Woffington's sister, Mrs Cholmondeley, friend of all the Wits, was determined, said this critic, to ransack London, if need be, to find the author.

' "Good God," cried Mrs Thrale—"why somebody else mentioned that book to me—Lady Westcote it was I believe—*The modest author of Evelina* she talk'd to me of."

' "Mrs Chol'meley says she never met so much modesty with so much merit before in any literary performance," said Johnson . . . "You *must* have it, Madam." '

Mrs Thrale, proud of her own fine taste and knowledge of all the latest and best in current literature, promised that she certainly would 'have it'; while Susanna, telling the story in a letter to Fanny at Chessington, added that she herself had demurely asked their father whether Fanny could possibly suffer any discredit from being known as the author of *Evelina*. ' "Discredit!" repeated my father, "no indeed,—*'t'would be a credit to her, and to me, and to you!*" '

'And to me'! He had already seen the advantage to be gained by himself from his daughter's celebrity. Fanny would be talked of everywhere in Society. He, as her father, would be exalted. The humble boy from Shrewsbury, once in servitude, and, in spite of his own publications, dependent upon the teaching of music for his income, would be recognized as the begetter of genius. Fame! Fame! The glory loomed. He would yet fulfil his lifelong dream of becoming Master of the King's Band.

SIXTEEN

Fanny as a Prodigy

THE next few months saw Fanny torn reluctantly from the routines of St Martin's Street and the enchanted ease of Chessington, where Crisp, who knew nothing of *Evelina*, treated her as a darling child, fragile beyond reason, and delicious with the wit of an unnoticed visitor from the nursery. If she had not been so small and slight, and so juvenile in face and self-betraying changes of expression, he might have noticed that her candours were sometimes unfeeling; but as it was he could give her the relief she needed when ill, and in health the sensible praise of an old man whom she revered. Crisp was now seventy, an example of what George Saintsbury once called 'the purged, considerate mind of age.' He was the wisest person she knew. His steady affection was quite different from the effusive fondness of her hitherto preoccupied father.

That father's jubilation was almost ridiculous. His idol, Johnson, had praised Fanny's book; Mrs Cholmondeley, Lady Hale, Lady Radnor, and innumerable other women of title were agog about Fanny; the rich and influential Mrs Thrale wanted to meet Fanny; at Streatham Fanny could be shown off as a prodigy and be seen by the *monde*. What might not follow? He even, in one giddy mood, perhaps prompted by the news that in this year admirers were subscribing for a bust of Gluck, wrote: 'I never heard of a novel writer's statue—yet, who knows?' And the moment he could do so he hurried to Chessington with tidings which moved him to rapture and Fanny to serious misgivings.

'In his way hither,' she wrote in her Diary, 'he had stopped at Streatham, and he settled with Mrs Thrale that he would call on her again in his way to town, and carry me with him! and Mrs Thrale said, "We all long to know her."

'I have been in a kind of twitter ever since, for there seems something very formidable in the idea of appearing as an authoress! I ever dreaded it, as it is a title which must raise more expectations than I have any chance of answering. Yet I am highly flattered by her invitation, and highly delighted in the prospect of being introduced to the Streatham society.'

She was introduced to the Streatham society. It was 'the most consequential day I have spent since my birth . . . Our journey to Streatham was the least pleasant part of the day, for the roads were dreadfully dusty, and I was really in the fidgets from thinking what my reception might be, and from fearing they would expect a less awkward and backward kind of person than I was sure they would find.'

On arrival at the house, they found Mrs Thrale strolling in the grounds. She was very kind, taking both of Fanny's hands in welcome, expressing pleasure at their meeting, and then, to give a naive child confidence, addressing all her further remarks to Burney. Presently she and Fanny explored the house together, after which Fanny, being left alone at her own suggestion in the library, had taken up a new translation of Cicero's *Laelius* when the entrance of another visitor caused her to put it down again, 'because', she noted with characteristic prudery, 'I dreaded being thought studious and affected.'

At dinner in the afternoon she sat next to Mrs Thrale, and when Johnson arrived he was put at her other side. She had seen him once before, at St Martin's Street, but without being noted by him. Now the situation was different. He was benign, complimentary; and she was filled, in spite of his almost perpetual convulsive movements, with delight and reverence for her father's hero and her own admirer. So clearly did her emotions show in her face that they moved Johnson at once to arch gallantry. As they ate, he asked Mrs Thrale what was in some little pies that were near him.

' "Mutton," answered she, "so I don't ask you to eat any, because I know you despise it."

' "No, madam, no," cried he; "I despise nothing that is good of its sort; but I am too proud now to eat of it. Sitting by Miss Burney makes me very proud today!"

' "Miss Burney," said Mrs Thrale, laughing, "you must take great care of your heart if Dr Johnson attacks it; for I assure you he is not often successless."

' "What's that you say, madam?" cried he; "are you making mischief between the young lady and me already?" '

That, in the tone of nonsensical compliment (coupled with unmistakable esteem) marking his treatment of Fanny to the last, was the beginning of a charming little friendship. The gay transcriptions of Johnson's talk which she included in a Diary meant to be seen only by Susanna and Crisp show him in moods of fun and delicacy which Boswell altogether missed. They are consummate reporting, full of wit and character. Indeed, Fanny was inspired by knowledge that what she set down would have as readers only this beloved sister and the old man who, while rejecting what he called flummery, assured her that 'I warmly interest myself in what ever concerns a Fannikin.' They were her ideal readers.

So favourable an impression did Fanny make upon the Thrales, and upon Johnson, that she was invited to stay at Streatham. Her reception there, and the happiness she felt in the praise of famous people, made the experience—in spite of all embarrassment—delightfully exciting. Mrs Thrale's aim was to encourage a modest young woman's self-confidence; and if the continual introduction of *Evelina* as a topic of conversation in the author's presence now seems ill-bred it must be remembered that the poverty of English fiction since the deaths of Fielding (1754), Richardson (1761), and Smollett (1771) made Fanny's book glitter like the rising sun.

Moreover Mrs Thrale, a collecter of human show-pieces, was not an imaginative woman. Her delicacies were superficial. Fanny was the latest fashion; her blushing *gaucherie*, and the repeated mystification of other guests, provided rich diversion. Mrs Thrale was determined to attach this curious creature to the household as Johnson was attached to that household.

Fanny had many charms. She was shy; she had written a high-spirited novel which was being talked to fame wherever, in London, books were read; and under the tender flatteries of Johnson she blossomed into repartee. Her manners, if not like her father's, obsequious, were charged with dutiful gratitude. To a woman of thirty-eight who, craving for personal distinction, had little but her table and her flatteries to attract Burke, Reynolds, and the rest, twenty-six-year-old Fanny, who looked sixteen, was as neat an additional bait to other guests as could be wished.

Fanny was given no rest. She was exhibited and taken to visit other people who wanted to see the latest prodigy. She was urged by Murphy and Mrs Thrale, even by Sheridan, to write a comedy for the stage. It was assumed that she must already have written a sequel to *Evelina*; and that her fame and success would mount higher and higher, until the great dead novelists, already equalled, were eclipsed.

Startled at her undesired reputation, and thrilled as a schoolgirl by the attention of so many of those whom she had formerly regarded almost as gods, Fanny still did not know how to behave. She ran out of the room, like a child, when *Evelina* was extolled; she was coy under her hostess's scoldings, and ridiculously upset at finding herself referred to in a pamphlet as 'dear little Burney' (which was Johnson's name for her); but in her most private letters she never failed to write of Mrs Thrale's perfections.

'I fear to say all I think at present of Mrs Thrale,' she told her confidential readers, 'lest some flaws should appear by-and-by, that may make me think differently. And yet, why should I not indulge the *now*, as well as the *then*, since it will be with so much more pleasure? In short, I do think her delightful; she has talents to create admiration, good humour to excite love, understanding to give entertainment, and a heart which, like my dear father's, seems already fitted for another world . . . Of all the people I have ever seen since I came into this "gay and gaudy world," I never before saw the person who so strongly resembles our dear father; . . . the same natural liveliness, the same general benevolence, the same union of gaiety and feeling.'

Fanny, although unusually perceptive in the matter of traits and eccentricities, was a novice. Mrs. Thrale was not. Taking a little longer to examine her new young friend, she wrote less favourably in her Journal. After a reference to Burney, she proceeded: 'His daughter is a graceful looking Girl, but 'tis the Grace of an Actress not a Woman of Fashion—how should it? her Conversation would be more pleasing if She thought less of herself; but her early reputation embarrasses her Talk and clouds her Mind with scruples about Elegancies which either come uncalled for or will not come at all. I love her more for her Father's sake than for her own, though her Merit cannot as a Writer be controverted.'

One person at least was concerned lest Fanny's head should be turned by the excitements of the Streatham scene. This was 'Daddy' Crisp, who wrote:

'When you come to know the world half as well as I do, . . . you will then be convinced that a state of independence is the only basis on which to rest your future ease and comfort. You are now young, lively, gay. You please, and the world smiles upon you—this is your time. Years and wrinkles in their due season (perhaps attended with want of health and spirits) will succeed. You will then be no longer the Fanny of 1778, feasted, caressed, admired, with all the soothing circumstances of your present situation. The Thrales, the Johnsons, the Sewards, Cholmondeleys, etc. etc, who are now so high in fashion, and might be such powerful protectors as almost to insure success to anything that is tolerable, may then themselves be moved off the stage. I will no longer dwell on so disagreeable a change of scene; let me only earnestly urge you to act vigorously (what I really believe is in your power) a distinguished part in the present one—"now while it is yet day, and before the night cometh, when no man can work." '

Still upon this same theme, he teased Fanny about her 'incessant and uncommon engagements', which he thought must be keeping her from more valuable activities. She replied with great good temper that her really incessant engagement was with her wardrobe.

' "Fact! fact!" I assure you—however paltry, ridiculous, or inconceivable, it may sound. Caps, hats, and ribbons make, indeed, no venerable appearance upon paper;—no more do eating and drinking; —yet the one can no more be worn without being made, than the other can be swallowed without being cooked; and those who can neither pay milliners nor keep scullions, must either toil themselves, or go capless and dinnerless. So, if you are for a high-polished comparison, I'm your man!

'Now, instead of furbelows and gewgaws of this sort, my dear daddy probably expected to hear of duodecimos, octavos, or quartos!—*Helas*! I am sorry that is not the case,—but not one word, not one syllable did I write to any purpose, from the time you left me at Streatham, till Christmas, when I came home.'

Not one word when she should have been deep in the sequel to *Evelina*. She had received an extra ten pounds from the publisher, making her total receipts from that book thirty pounds. Burney himself was as busy as ever; but apart from whatever income his wife brought to the common fund his earnings were all the family could count on. No wonder he had begun to fret. The result of his fretting is to be seen in Mrs Thrale's indignant Journal entry:

'What a blockhead Dr Burney is to be always sending for his daughter home so! What a monkey! Is she not better and happier with me than she can be anywhere else?... I confess myself provoked excessively, but I love the girl so dearly—and the Doctor, too, for that matter, only that he has such odd notions of superiority in his own house, and will have his children under his feet forsooth, rather than let 'em live in peace, plenty, and comfort anywhere from home. If I did not provide Fanny with every wearable—every wishable, indeed—it would not vex me to be served so; but to see the impossibility of compensating for the pleasures of St Martin's Street, makes me at once merry and mortified.'

None of these three people appreciated the fact that to Fanny, once writing had ceased to be a secret game of make-believe, another spontaneously-written novel was an impossibility. The sense that many eyes and sharp intelligences would in future scrutinize whatever she might produce paralysed her. Crisp, who had long been sterile himself, should have understood; he did not at first understand. Burney, as a traveller and compiler of history, had no notion at all of the inventive writer's problems. He could not even imagine that his own ill-advised boastfulness had created the situation whose evils he began to lament. As for Mrs Thrale, her view was that it was Fanny's duty to accept gratefully that very dependence against which Crisp's letter had been so strong a warning.

'Fanny Burney has been a long time from me; I was glad to see her again; yet she makes me miserable too in many respects, so restlessly and apparently anxious, lest I should give myself airs or load her with the shackles of dependance. I lived with her always in a degree of pain that precludes friendship—dare not ask her to buy me a ribbon—dare not desire her to touch the bell, lest she should think herself injured.'

And again, months later, after the Thrales had paid a visit to Bath which caused Fanny (as her letters to Susanna, with their constant acknowledgment of Mrs Thrale's charm and kindness, demonstrate) the most grateful delight until physical exhaustion prostrated her, we read: 'Mrs Byron, who really loves me, was disgusted at Miss Burney's carriage to me, who have been such a friend and benefactress to her; not an article of dress, not a ticket for public places, not a thing in the world that she could not command from me; yet always insolent, always pining for home, always preferring the mode of life in St Martin's Street to all I could do for her . . . I fancy she has a real regard for me, if she did not think it beneath the dignity of a wit, or of what she values more—the dignity of Dr Burney's daughter —to indulge it. Such dignity!'

So, in spite of the gaiety of her letters to Susanna, and the lively— sometimes very brilliant—presentation in these and in her Journal of such personalities as Mrs Montagu ('very flashy, and talked away all the evening'), and Mrs Cholmondeley, Fanny was in trouble with her counsellors. 'I feel very forcibly,' she wrote to Crisp, 'that I am not—that I have not been—and that I never shall be formed or fitted for any business with the public.' Fame had been thrust upon her; she was 'always pining for home.'

However, in obedience to the exhortations of Mrs Thrale, Arthur Murphy, and Sheridan, she had written a comedy (which Johnson, hearing of the project, merrily suggested should be called *Streatham: a Farce*) in snatched moments of solitude. It was called *The Witlings*, and its caricatured persons and their speeches were not inferior to those in *Evelina*. It might unquestionably, in spite of a thin fable, have been put on the stage. But Fanny would do nothing about it until her father and Crisp had pronounced approval. The approval was refused.

Burney took the greater alarm. He convinced himself that the play's failure was certain, and that it would endanger the family reputation. Crisp said *Evelina* was written 'because you could not help it', and 'it would be the best policy, but for the pecuniary advantages. . . . to write no more.' Fanny agreed. Burney could not do so. His ambition cried that she must become the most famous novelist in England. But she had written a play! He was terrified. If it publicly failed, all his blabbing and boasting would immediately become ridiculous. He himself would be made ridiculous! Stop! Stop!

Fanny read his mind, and was generous. Having received from him a letter which crushed her hopes as a dramatist, she replied:

'You, my dearest sir, who enjoyed, I really think, even more than myself, the astonishing success of my first attempt, would, I believe, even more than myself, be hurt at the failure of my second; and I am sure I speak from the bottom of a very honest heart, when I most solemnly declare, that upon your account any disgrace would mortify and afflict me more than upon my own; for whatever appears with your knowledge, will be naturally supposed to have met with your approbation, and, perhaps, your assistance; therefore, although all particular censure would fall where it ought—upon me—yet any general censure of the whole, and the plan, would cruelly, but certainly, involve you in its severity.'

The Witlings was suppressed. Fanny might be a writer of great talent, a figure tiny and fragile enough to attract the affection of Johnson and the admiration of the wits and bluestockings; but she was first of all Dr Burney's daughter. 'I *wish* for nothing!' she had told him. 'Only let me live with you.' She would have been happy at home and at Chessington, loving and being loved by her father, by 'Daddy' Crisp, by Susanna; but, being a young woman, and a bringer of lustre to the family name, she was not allowed to do as she wished.

SEVENTEEN

The Burneys Move Upward

SHE was not allowed, because they had determined otherwise. And she must hurry, lest celebrity faded. So during the first months of 1782 she was constantly at work upon a second novel, *Cecilia*, which was at least half as long again as *Evelina*, and which showed that under the pressure of reluctance, dread, and lost girlishness (for she was now in her thirtieth year) she was taking herself much too seriously as the important moral novelist of the age. Instead of spontaneous and almost headlong inventiveness, intended only for self-amusement, she was condemned to gravity and the high literary style. The high literary style of that dangerous model, *The Rambler*.

'Are you quite *enragée* with me, my dearest Susy?' she wrote to her sister. 'Indeed, I think I am with myself, for not sooner and oftener writing to you; and every night when I go to bed, and every morning when I wake, I determine shall be the last I will do either again till I have written to you. But *hélas*! my pens get so fagged, and my hands so crippled, when I have been up two or three hours, that my resolution wavers, and I sin on, till the time of rest and meditation, and then I repent again . . .

'My work is too long in all conscience for the hurry of my people to have it produced. I have a thousand million of fears for it. The mere copying, without revising and correcting, would take at least ten weeks, unless I scrawl shorthand and rough hand as badly as the original. Yet my father thinks it will be published in a month . . .

'The book . . . to my great consternation, I find is talked of and expected all the town over. My dear father himself, I do verily believe, mentions it to everybody; he is fond of it to enthusiasm, and does not foresee the danger of raising such general expectation, which fills *me* with the horrors every time I am tormented with the thought.'

Mrs Thrale, who had been widowed in the previous year, and was having to receive consolation in the form of letters and literary favours, almost equalled Burney as the arch-spreader of publicity. Both were shown the manuscript volume by volume. Both were enraptured by what they had read. 'Oh! write away, sweet Burney!' wrote Mrs Thrale. 'I think I could submit to be a printer's devil, to get a sight of the next volume, verily.' 'My notion is that I shall cry myself blind over the conclusion.' 'Oh, lovely Burney! *ma che talento mai*!' Fanny's father, 'bigoted as he was to *Evelina* . . . now says he thinks this a superior design and superior execution.'

Her kind mentor was less rapturous, and even more agitating to a writer in the very act of composition. Crisp, who had truly appreciated the particular quality of *Evelina*, now with an old man's loving concern with a favourite exaggerated every risk. He loaded Fanny with an additional anxiety to which no novelist should be subjected. 'You have so much to lose, you cannot take too much care.' A truly terrible saying for one already full of mistrust and new constraint.

Her cares increased. The hand-crippling mind-crippling labour was re-doubled. She strove, not to please herself, but to please, placate, and silence those who worried her with advice. And at last *Cecilia*, for which the publisher paid two hundred and fifty pounds, a sum large enough, it was thought, to buy Fanny an annuity, was in print. It was still the year 1782; once more she was the talk of the town; once more Burney was crazed with triumph. 'Dear soul, how he feeds upon all that brings fame to *Cecilia*! his eagerness upon this subject, and his pleasure in it, are truly enthusiastic, and, I think, rather increase by fulness than grow satiated.'

His pleasure centred upon the social advantages of his daughter's industry. He had craved all his life for two things—fame and a sinecure—and fame had been vouchsafed to him.

Both father and daughter were otherwise occupied in something less intoxicating. They had previously introduced to the Thrales an Italian friend and musician named Piozzi, who at first had so little impressed Mrs Thrale that she tried to enliven a dull party at the Burneys' by publicly mimicking his presumably florid gestures as he sang. After her husband's death, when raptures over *Cecilia* no longer satisfied her emotion, she became fantastically enamoured of the man. For his sake she was ready to abandon her children, to discard a great bear whose manners, always difficult, became suddenly intolerable, and, as it proved, to quarrel for life with the Burneys as well as with Johnson.

These wildnesses were at first held in check. She could treat them lightly in discussions with Fanny, and even when they became less controllable could still accept Fanny's disinterested hesitations and warnings. She continued to give parties at Streatham, where Fanny met Boswell's Corsican hero, Paoli, and to attend other parties at which Mrs Chapone, Horace Walpole, and such notabilities were present. Fanny attended her, and received a full volley of congratulation. But when Mrs Thrale encountered disapproval from Johnson, who was the most loyal of Thrale's executors, when she realized her daughters' implacable dislike of Piozzi as their father's supplanter, when she discovered Burney's in part religious objection to any marriage with a foreigner who was also a Roman Catholic, she was seized with fury.

This was the first time she had experienced open criticism. It was intolerable to one who had hitherto taken for granted the complaisance of all who accepted the Thralian hospitality. Her consternation was heightened by rough comment in the newspapers. Planning at first to escape censure by a stay abroad, she clung to Fanny as her one sweet sympathetic friend. She extolled Fanny. 'My beloved Fanny Burney,' she wrote in her Diary at this time, 'whose interest as well as judgment goes all against my marriage; whose skill in life and manners is superior to that of any man or woman in this age or nation; whose knowledge of the world, ingenuity of expedient, delicacy of conduct, and zeal in the cause, will make her a counsellor invaluable.'

Finally she married Piozzi, lost for life the affection of her children though not in the end their tolerance, was sternly rebuked by Johnson, and because Fanny's congratulations were less warm than she and Piozzi thought they should be, discontinued all correspondence with the paragon. From this time her comments on Fanny's character were uniformly adverse. She had previously suspected her of matrimonial designs upon Mr Crutchley, a second executor of Thrale's will whom she believed to be his natural son; and had thought the philanderer 'no match for the arts of a novel-writer'; but now she used stronger terms. Both Burneys were 'treacherous' and 'monstrously wicked'; they were, by birth, 'I believe a very low race of mortals'; Fanny's admitted charm was used entirely from 'self-interest'; and of a long-subsequent meeting she noted that her old friend's cordiality was answered 'with ease and coldness', and that their conversation 'ended, as it should do, with perfect indifference.'

Fanny for her part, much troubled by the sudden break with Mrs Piozzi, was carried—with her father—to higher fields of social contact than those of Streatham. She did not always relish her new acquaintance, of whose speech and behaviour she confided to her sister the more risible or objectionable details; he, on the contrary, saw no fault in anybody, and was all for more and ever more of the social round. Since it gave him such pleasure, it must give equal pleasure to Fanny, even if it exhausted her. Did it exhaust her? He was the last to notice the fact. But 'even my father himself, fond as he is of all this ado about *Cecilia*, was sorry for me tonight, and said I looked quite ill one time.'

He thought she looked ill; but he could not stop. When, to his joy, he could bring to her side the famous Soame Jenyns and the learned Mr Cambridge (praised equally by Johnson and Horace Walpole) he engaged them on his own account in ardent conversation. He was Burney the gay, Burney the vivacious, Burney the sire of genius, Burney the beside-himself. He was at last, as person, not as music-teacher, hobnobbing with the great.

Fanny also was proud of Cambridge's notice and personal considerateness; but she was prouder still at making acquaintance with the woman whom, above all others, she wished most to know— Mrs Delany. The meeting was arranged by Mrs Chapone, blue-stocking extraordinary, contributor to *The Rambler*, and author of a whole book of *Letters on the Improvement of the Mind*. Its consequences were momentous.

Mrs Delany, born in 1700, was a Grenville, descended from a family of renown which had produced the great admiral—'Sink me the ship, Master Gunner'—whose splendid courage and meagre carcase astounded the Spaniards in Elizabethan days, and a Royalist general of the Civil War, Sir Bevil Grenville, whom Clarendon described as a model of principle and bravery. Her parents were impoverished; she herself, expectant as a girl of becoming Maid of Honour to Queen Anne, was adopted by an aunt, wife of the Secretary to the Lord Chancellor, who lodged in Whitehall. The atmosphere in which she grew up was thus heavy, not only with distinguished ancestry, but with overwhelming reverence for the Court.

This was true, also, of Mary Grenville's two dearest friends. The first of them was the Earl of Rochester's grand-daughter Catherine ('Kitty') Hyde, celebrated in childhood by Matthew Prior, and later the bold and scandalizing Duchess of Queensberry, who was impenitent under the withdrawal of Royal favour for daring to commend John Gay. The second, with whom Mary was affectionately associated from 1734 until 1785, was the Duchess of Portland, a Harley by birth, and Prior's 'noble, lovely little Peggy.' She never at any time defied the Court. Indeed, she lived, as did Mrs Delany, on terms of respectful affability with George the Third and Queen Charlotte until the hour of her death.

Both ladies, in youth, had collected seashells; in age the Duchess passed her time in netting, while Mrs Delany copied pictures by original artists and cut out paper flowers which she then pasted into attractive patterns. Both paid and received aristocratic visits, gossiped about other great folk, continued a habit of lengthy letter-writing which Mrs Delany had formed when exiled from her family, and occasionally read carefully chosen books. As a rule these were not works of fiction; but one novel, approached unwillingly, but finally devoured with enthusiasm, was *Cecilia*. Having read it three times, according to the Duchess, they, like lesser persons, became curious to meet the author.

In view of what followed, an observation made by G. M. Trevelyan should be remembered. It was that in the eighteenth century convention aimed, not at the equality, but at the harmony of classes. Consciousness of eternal cleavage between the aristocracy and the rest of mankind was strong; and if, among the male gentry, bland with complacency, this was usually tolerant, it took a sharper edge among women.

When, for example, William Gilpin, a topographical and historical writer of eminence, ventured to express impatience at wanton delays on the part of a fashionable person, it was a woman who remarked that 'the notice and encouragement justly awarded to his talents made him sometimes forget his own position or that of those he addressed.' More strongly still, the Duchess of Buckingham, having ascertained from the Countess of Huntingdon, who favoured them, the chief doctrines of Methodism, wrote to her aristocratic correspondent that these were 'most repulsive, and strongly tinctured with impertinence and disrespect towards their superiors.' 'It is monstrous', she added, 'to be told that you have a heart as sinful as the common wretches that crawl the earth.'

'The common wretches': this was what Mrs Thrale had in mind when, having quarrelled with them, she described the Burneys as 'a very low race of mortals.' They were not gentlefolk; and they must never forget that, whatever their talents, there was no substitute for birth. As Goldsmith ironically made his bear-dancer say in *She Stoops to Conquer*: 'Oh, damn anything that's *low*, I cannot bear it!'

At the time of Fanny Burney's introduction to her, Mrs Delany was a very old woman indeed, so old, and so virtuous in every respect, that she was surrounded with an aura of saintliness. Friendship with her was a great honour for one of Fanny's upbringing; and Fanny was relieved to find that Mrs Delany, who was incomparably a greater lady than Mrs Thrale (Mrs Delany, in fact, had always avoided contact with Mrs Thrale), treated her instantly with warmth in which there was no trace of condescension. Kindness was on the one side; real, if bashful, respect on the other. An understanding creditable to both was established. Mrs Delany wrote that *Evelina* and *Cecilia*, 'excellent as they are, are her meanest praise. Her admirable understanding, tender affection, and sweetness of manners, make her invaluable to those who have the happiness to know her.'

Fanny was equally enthusiastic, and affectionate. Whatever the busily and acquisitively sociable Burney may have anticipated from this connection, Fanny had no design. She basked in Mrs Delany's sweetness. Her feeling was one of deep gratitude. She had, what her father lacked, the imagination to appreciate character for itself.

Mrs Delany's brother, a snob of the first order, who had scorned his two much more intelligent sisters for marrying persons of lower rank than their own, was dead. Her first husband, Alexander Pendarves, an ancient rake, 'fat, snuffy, sulky,' but also wealthy, to whom she had been peremptorily married when she was seventeen and he nearly sixty, had died in 1721 without making a will in her favour. She therefore, to the disappointment of her parents' expectations, remained poor.

Her second husband, a close personal friend of Swift, and like Swift a disappointed candidate for a bishopric (he was made Dean of Down), spent much of his married life in defensive and to myself incomprehensible litigation, and died in 1768, leaving her as poor as before. She owed much, therefore, to the friendship of the Duchess of Portland, after whose death King George and Queen Charlotte tactfully gave her a private annuity of three hundred pounds.

She had never been a Maid of Honour. Applications for a place about the Throne, half-heartedly made by supposed friends during her first widowhood, produced no result. Nevertheless she lived very near the Court, and her friends, besides being men and women of rank, were courtiers. For them, as for Mrs Delany, service to the Crown, with all the profit attending such service, was the highest good. Although she would have shrunk from anything so base as intrigue, Mrs Delany had been so used all her life to the pulling of strings on behalf of place-seekers that when she liked a person she saw only one way of helping that person.

She liked Fanny Burney very much. One of her earliest kindnesses, accordingly, was to ensure Fanny's presence when the King and Queen, as they often did, came to call.

EIGHTEEN

Burney Goes to Court

AT THIS time the Burneys suffered two calamities, in the deaths of Samuel Crisp and Samuel Johnson. Crisp, who was twenty years older than Burney, and had been a sage adviser to him and to Fanny and her sisters from their first acquaintance, fought a long battle with gout, and in 1783 had reached the age of seventy-six. He died in April, Fanny having hurried to his side in time to hear his last assurance that she was 'the dearest thing to him on earth.'

Burney, though quite as sincere in grief as she, was a little fine on the occasion. 'Not an hour in the day has passed,' he wrote, while Fanny was still at Chessington, 'in which I have not felt a pang for the irretrievable loss I have suffered.' But she must not let sorrow unfit her for the care of the living. 'I have lost in my time persons so dear to me, as to throw me into the utmost affliction and despondency which can be suffered without insanity; but I had claims on my life, my reason, and activity, which drew me from the pit of despair, and forced me, though with great difficulty, to rouse and exert every nerve and faculty in answering them.'

Johnson's death came in the following year, 1784; and here, too, Fanny would have been at the bedside if she had been allowed there. Burney saw Johnson a few days before the end, bringing her an apology for non-admission, and a request for her prayers. ' "I hope Fanny did not take it amiss that I did not see her? I was very bad . . . Tell Fanny to pray for me!" . . . After which, still grasping [my father's] hand, he made a prayer for himself,—the most fervent, pious, humble, eloquent, and touching, my father says, that ever was composed. Oh, would I had heard it! He ended it with Amen! in which my father joined, and was echoed by all present. And again, when my father was leaving him, he brightened up, something of his arch look returned, and he said—"I think I shall throw the ball at Fanny yet!" '

Encouraged by the message, she ventured to call again, hoping to see her gallant friend. Alas, she received only one further kind message; and in a few days Johnson, too, was gone. Taken in conjunction with the death of Crisp, this blow removed every defence she might have had against the plan preparing for her literary ruin. The impulse to write comedy for the stage had been killed. She had no hope of writing another *Evelina*; and *Cecilia* was the best she could do by conscious and laborious work. Only complete tranquillity would bring back the old fun; but her natural healer, Crisp, was no longer there to supply it. An excited and irresponsible father was in charge of her future.

Burney had now a single piece of good fortune. Burke, knowing or suspecting his friend's need, managed in one last moment of political opportunity to get him a small place. It was the post of organist to the Chapel of Chelsea Hospital. which although the salary was only fifty pounds a year carried the promise of free family accommodation in the Hospital. Burke, of course, would have preferred to give something munificent. He apologised for the smallness of the job. But it proved his good heart and his understanding. Burney was on the verge of sixty; he began to feel his age; despite good health (rheumatism apart), his expectation of life was contracting; and at present he had not attained the sinecure which was his life's ambition.

Meanwhile Fanny was sending her sister, from Mrs Delany's home, the news that she had just been kindly noticed by the King and Queen. Vivacious descriptions of the pair followed. They supplied Burney with glorious material for boasting. He carried the letters with him wherever he went; and, filled with egregious vanity, insisted upon reading them aloud to 'almost all his confidential friends.' He was frantically elated. His daughter—the famous novelist—was on chatting terms with Their Majesties! These were the joys of *Evelina* all over again.

Fanny knew what would please him: the Queen was reported to have said:

' "Do you know Dr Burney, Mrs Delany?"

' "Yes, ma'am, extremely well," answered Mrs Delany.

' "I think him," said the Queen, "a very agreeable and entertaining man."

'There, my dear father! said I not well just now, "O most penetrating Queen"?'

What exciting words for an excitable father these were! How full of promise!

This was the way in which Mrs Delany contrived that first momentous encounter. Fanny reported the affair in minute detail:

'My dear old friend, earnest I should have an honour which her grateful reverence for their Majesties makes her regard very highly, had often wished me to stay in the room when they came to see her, assuring me that though they were so circumstanced as not to send for a stranger, she knew they would be much pleased to meet with me. This, however, was more than I could assent to, without infinite pain, and that she was too kind to make a point of my enduring . . .

' "But the Queen inquires," continued Mrs Delany, "so much about you, and is so earnest that you should be with me, that I am sure she wants to see and converse with you."

'In the midst of all this the Queen came.

'I heard the thunder at the door, and, panic struck, away fled all my resolutions and agreements, and away after them flew I!

'Don't be angry, my dear father—I would have stayed if I could, and I meant to stay; but, when the moment came, neither my preparations nor intentions availed, and I arrived at my own room, and quite breathless between the race I ran with Miss Port and the joy of escaping.'

The escape was only temporary. Within a couple of days something yet more alarming occurred, and Fanny dutifully reported it.

'After dinner, while Mrs Delany was left alone, as usual, to take a little rest—for sleep it but seldom proves,—Mr B. Dewes, his little daughter, Miss Port, and myself went into the drawing-room. And here, while, to pass the time, I was amusing the little girl with teaching her some Christmas games, in which her father and cousin joined, Mrs Delany came in. We were all in the middle of the room, and in some confusion;—but she had but just come up to us to inquire what was going forward, and I was disentangling myself from Miss Dewes, to be ready to fly off if any one knocked at the street-door, when the door of the drawing-room was again opened, and a large man, in deep mourning, appeared at it, entering and shutting it himself without speaking.

'A ghost could not more have scared me, when I discovered by the glitter on the black, a star! The general disorder had prevented his being seen, except by myself, who was always on the watch, till Miss P—, turning round, exclaimed, "The King!—Aunt, the King!"

'O mercy! thought I, that I were but out of the room! which way shall I escape? and how pass him unnoticed? There is but the single door by which he entered, in the room! Everyone scampered out of the way: Miss P—, to stand next the door; Mr Bernard Dewes to a corner opposite it; his little girl clung to me; and Mrs Delany advanced to meet his Majesty, who, after quietly looking on till she saw him, approached, and inquired how she did.

'He then spoke to Mr Bernard, whom he had already met two or three times here.

'I had now retreated to the wall, and purposed gliding softly, though speedily, out of the room; but before I had taken a single step, the King, in a loud whisper to Mrs Delany, said "Is that Miss Burney?"—and on her answering, "Yes, sir," he bowed, and with a countenance of the most perfect good humour, came close up to me . . .

'When the discourse upon health and strength was over, the King went to the table, and looked at a book of prints, from Claude Lorraine, which had been brought down for Miss Dewes; but Mrs Delany, by mistake, told him they were for me. He turned over a leaf or two, and then said—

' "Pray, does Miss Burney draw, too?"

'The *too* was pronounced very civilly.

' "I believe not, sir," answered Mrs Delany; "at least she does not tell."

' "Oh!" cried he, laughing, "that's nothing! She is not apt to tell; she never does tell, you know! Her father told me that himself. He told me the whole history of her *Evelina*. And I shall never forget his face when he spoke of his feelings at first taking up the book!— he looked quite frightened, just as if he was doing it that moment! I never can forget his face while I live!"

'Then, coming up close to me, he said—

' "But what?—what?—how was it?"

' "Sir," cried I, not well understanding him.

' "How came you—how happened it?—what?—what?"

' "I—I only wrote, sir, for my own amusement—only in some odd, idle hours."

' "But your publishing—your printing—how was that?"

' "That was only, sir—only because—"

'I hesitated most abominably, not knowing how to tell him a long story, and growing terribly confused at these questions—besides, to say the truth, his own "what? what?" so reminded me of those vile Probationary Odes, that, in the midst of all my flutter, I was really hardly able to keep my countenance.

'The *What*! was then repeated with so earnest a look, that, forced to say something, I stammeringly answered—

' "I thought—sir—it would look very well in print!"

'I do really flatter myself this is the silliest speech I ever made! I am quite provoked with myself for it; but a fear of laughing made me eager to utter anything, and by no means conscious, until I had spoken, of what I was saying.

'He laughed very heartily himself—well he might—and walked away to copy it, crying out—

' "Very fair indeed! that's being very fair and honest!"

This was not the end of the King's teasing; and when, shortly afterwards, the Queen also arrived, Fanny was subjected to an even sharper ordeal. Both wanted to know if she was writing anything new and why not; the King urged her to give a performance on the harpsichord, and only ceased to tease when she made a gesture imploring mercy; while the Queen, talking easily, in very good English, with occasional slips into an idiom of her own, was impressed and cordial. Mrs Delany's delight in the encounter could not be doubted. Fanny complacently added to her recital the inquiry:

'Upon the whole, and for me, don't you think, my dear father and Susan, I comported myself mighty well in my grand interview? Indeed, except quite at first, I was infinitely more easy than I usually am with strangers; and the great reason for that was, that I had no fear of being frightened, nor shame of being ashamed; for they, I was sure, were more accustomed to see people frightened and confused, than to find them composed and undisturbed.'

Further conversations with the King and Queen followed; and Fanny received from the Royal personages some memorable remarks about writers and players which she transmitted to her correspondents. Madame de Genlis was one subject; Mrs Siddons another; but the Queen surpassed herself with the mention of a book which she had picked up on a stall, adding, 'Oh, it is amazing what good books there are on stalls.' When even the courteous Mrs Delany expressed surprise that a Queen should pick up bargains in this way, the reply was: 'Why, I don't pick them up myself; but I have a servant very clever.' The King roved farther, from Voltaire ('I think him a monster —I own it fairly') to Rousseau (about whom he told stories 'charging him with savage pride and insolent ingratitude') and from French writers to English plays, and at last to Shakespeare.

' "Was there ever," cried he, "such stuff as great part of Shakespeare? only one must not say so! But what think you?—What?—Is there not sad stuff?—What?—what?" '

To her sister Hetty, Fanny ran on in more general terms. Perhaps Mrs Delany had been prompting her to dream of a place at Court? We cannot know; but Fanny—still unaware of what lay ahead—gaily assured Hetty that she would like from the Crown, not an office involving daily work for a salary, but a handsome pension for doing nothing at all. She called this 'a young budding notice of decision,' and after further nonsense continued:

'You would never believe—you, who, distant from courts and courtiers, know nothing of their ways—the many things to be studied, for appearing with a proper propriety before crowned heads. Heads without crowns are quite other sort of rotundas . . .

'In the first place, you must not cough. If you find a cough tickling in your throat, you must arrest it from making any sound; if you find yourself choking with the forbearance, you must choke—but not cough.

'In the second place, you must not sneeze. If you have a vehement cold, you must take no notice of it; if your nose membrane feels a great irritation, you must hold your breath; if a sneeze still insists upon making its way, you must oppose it, by keeping your teeth grinding together; if the violence of the repulse breaks some blood-vessel, you must break the blood-vessel—but not sneeze.

'In the third place, you must not, upon any account, stir either hand or foot. If, by chance, a black pin runs into your head, you must not take it out. If the pain is very great, you must be sure to bear it without wincing; if it brings the tears into your eyes, you must not wipe them off; if they give you a tingling by running down your cheeks, you must look as if nothing was the matter. If the blood should gush from your head by means of the black pin, you must let it gush; if you are uneasy to think of making such a blurred appearance, you must be uneasy, but you must say nothing about it. If, however, the agony is very great, you may, privately, bite the inside of your cheek, or of your lips, for a little relief; taking care, meanwhile, to do it so cautiously as to make no apparent dent outwardly. And, with that precaution, if you even gnaw a piece out, it will not be minded, only be sure either to swallow it, or commit it to a corner of the inside of your mouth till they are gone—for you must not spit.

'I have many other directions, but no more paper.'

This light ribaldry is not that of a born, nor that of an expectant, courtier. Fanny had no serious designs upon Court employment. Her father, however, at this time saw the possibility of attaining his life's ambition. On May 20th, 1786, the blind Master of the King's Band, Mr Stanley, who in spite of illness had held on to the post for a number of years, was dead. Burney had formerly been promised, by a great man whom he supposed to be his friend, firm support for any claim to the succession; he therefore ran immediately to seek advice as to what he should do. The person he approached seems to have been a sort of Royal factotum, Mr Lemuel Smelt, whom Fanny describes in the *Memoir* as 'elegant, polished'. This was on the morning of Sunday, May 21st.

'Just as I was at the door, and going to church,' wrote Fanny, of that Sunday morning, 'my father returned, and desired me to come back, as he had something to communicate to me. Mr Smelt, he then told me, had counselled him to go instantly to Windsor, not to address the King, but to be seen by him. "Take your daughter," he said, "in your hand, and walk upon the terrace. The King's seeing you at this time he will understand, and he is more likely to be touched by a hint of that delicate sort than by any direct application."

'My father determined implicitly to follow this advice. But let me not omit a singular little circumstance, which much enlivened and encouraged our expedition. While I was changing my dress for the journey, I received a letter from Miss P—, which was sent by private hand, and ought to have arrived sooner, and which pressed my visit to my dear Mrs Delany very warmly, and told me it was by the Queen's express wish. This gave me great spirits for my dear father's enterprise, and I was able to help him on the road from so favourable a symptom.

'All the royal family were already on the terrace before we arrived. The King and Queen, and the Prince of Mechlenberg, and her Majesty's mother, walked together. Next them the Princesses and their ladies, and the young Princes, making a very gay and pleasing procession, of one of the finest families in the world. Every way they moved, the crowd retired to stand up against the wall as they passed and then closed in to follow.

'When they approached towards us, and we were retreating, Lady Louisa Clayton placed me next herself, making her daughters stand below—a politeness and attention without which I had certainly not been seen; for the moment their Majesties advanced, I involuntarily looked down, and drew my hat over my face. I could not endure to stare at them, and full of our real errand, I felt ashamed even of being seen by them. The very idea of a design, however far from illaudable, is always distressing and uncomfortable.

'Consequently I should have stood in the herd, and unregarded; but Lady Louisa's kindness and good breeding put me in a place too conspicuous to pass unnoticed. The moment the Queen had spoken to her, which she stopped to do as soon as she came up to her, she inquired in a whisper, who was with her; as I know, by hearing my own name given for the answer. The Queen then instantly stepped nearer me, and asked me how I did; and then the King came forward, and as soon as he had repeated the same question, said "Are you come to stay?"

' "No, sir, not now."

' "No; but how long shall you stay?"

' "I go tonight, sir."

' "I was sure," cried the Queen, "she was not come to stay, by seeing her father."

'I was glad by this to know my father had been observed.'

Some arch questions from the King about her literary work confused and delighted Fanny before the Royal party moved on; after which she continued:

'We stayed some time longer on the terrace, and my poor father occasionally joined me; but he looked so conscious and depressed that it pained me to see him. There is nothing that I know so very depressing as solicitation. I am sure I could never, I believe, go through a task of that sort. My dear father was not spoken to, though he had a bow every time the King passed him, and a curtsey from the Queen. But it hurt him, and he thought it a very bad prognostic; and all there was at all to build upon was the graciousness shown to me, which, indeed, in the manner I was accosted, was very flattering, and, except to high rank, I am told, very rare.

'We stayed but a short time with my sweet Mrs Delany, whose best wishes you are sure were ours. I told her our plan, and our full conviction that she could not assist in it, as the obligations she herself owes are so great and so weighty, that any request from her would be encroaching and improper.

'We did not get home till past eleven o'clock. We were then informed that Lord Brudenel had called to say Mr Parsons had a promise of the place from the Lord Chamberlain.'

NINETEEN

Servitude

BURNEY'S last hope of the coveted Mastership was gone. At his age he could not hope for another opportunity; and he must bitterly have contemplated the easy neglect of great men to keep their word. Ambitious but timid, he had suffered himself to be out-manœuvred. Mr Parsons's sponsor, losing not a moment, had approached, not the King, but the Lord Chamberlain, who had been so swift in making the appointment that the King could do nothing.

Since there was now no Samuel Crisp to offer advice and solace, the Burneys were confounded. Indeed, the loss of Crisp was a fatality. Although Fanny and her sisters could still visit Chessington, the spirit was gone. Mrs Burney, for some time addicted to valetudinarianism, absented herself from St Martin's Street for months at a time in search of health, and was no comfort to her husband; Johnson was dead; Mrs Thrale, on becoming Mrs Piozzi, had deserted them; and Burney's other friends, however cordial, lacked Crisp's wise concern with their wellbeing and Johnson's capacity for seeing events in any large perspective. Burney himself was shattered.

These doings belong to May, 1786. In June, when Fanny was visiting Mrs Delany at her home in St James's Place, another calamity occurred. The busy Mr Smelt arrived from Windsor. Having conferred with Mrs Delany he asked for a private interview with Fanny; and Fanny, who had always taken her troubles to Crisp, could do so no longer. In extremity, she ventured an appeal to the kind and learned Mr Cambridge's daughter.

'It is only by minds such as yours,' she wrote to Miss Cambridge, 'as my Susan's, Mrs Delany's, and Mrs Locke's—my four invaluable friends, that I can hope to be even understood, when I speak of difficulty and distress from a proposal apparently only advantageous. But Susan's wishes are so certainly and invariably my own that I wish to spare her from hearing of this matter till the decision is made; Mrs Delany, with all her indulgent partiality, is here too deeply interested on the other side to be consulted without paining her; and Mrs Locke has an enthusiasm in her kindness that makes every plan seem cruel to her that puts or keeps us asunder.'

Miss Cambridge, therefore, is to be the confidante. Fanny explains what has happened, tells of Mr Smelt's arrival, and says he began, 'surprising me not a little, by entreating me to suffer some very home questions from him, relative to my situation, my views, and even my wishes, with respect to my future life. At first, I only laughed; but my merriment a little failed me, when he gave me to understand he was commissioned to make these inquiries by a great personage, who had conceived so favourable an opinion of me as to be desirous of undoubted information, whether or not there was a probability she might permanently attach me to herself and her family.

'You cannot easily, my dear Miss Cambridge, picture to yourself the consternation with which I received this intimation. It was such that the good and kind Mr Smelt, perceiving it, had the indulgence instantly to offer me his services, first in forbearing to mention even to my father his commission, and next in fabricating and carrying back for me a respectful excuse. And I must always consider myself the more obliged to him, as I saw in his own face the utmost astonishment and disappointment at this reception of his embassy.

'I could not, however, reconcile to myself concealing from my dear father a matter that ought to be settled by himself; yet I frankly owned to Mr Smelt that no situation of that sort was suited to my own taste, or promising to my own happiness.

'He seemed equally sorry and surprised; he expatiated warmly upon the sweetness of character of all the royal family, and then begged me to consider the very peculiar distinction shown me, that, unsolicited, unsought, I had been marked out with such personal favour by the Queen herself, as a person with whom she had been so singularly pleased, as to wish to settle me with one of the princesses, in preference to the thousands of offered candidates, of high birth and rank, but small fortunes, who were waiting and supplicating for places in the new-forming establishment.'

Freedom was not considered. In an age when parents decided what men their daughters should marry, and when a poor young woman, daughter of a music teacher and an uneducated girl, was considered lucky to be noticed at all by the great, Fanny must do as she was told. She knew it. 'I could not reconcile to myself concealing from my dear father a matter that ought to be settled by himself.'

That girlish fling of secret independence, *Evelina*, had brought her, through Burney's officiousness, into public notice; and Burney had insisted upon the pursuit of social success. Though, when alarmed lest he should force her into marriage with Mr Barlow, she had cried 'I wish for nothing! only let me live with you!' and he had answered that she should live with him for ever, he had no realization of what that promise meant. It was inconceivable to him that her happiness depended on privacy. He had not scrupled to use her as a means of presenting himself to the King and Queen. It was now inconceivable to him that so wonderful a sinecure as was offered to her should be anything but a splendid achievement.

The Queen, learning of Fanny's unwillingness to become a Court servant, could not believe her ears. She decided to see the young woman herself. Fanny exclaimed in despair: 'I now see the end—I see it next to inevitable. I can suggest nothing upon earth that I dare say for myself, in an audience so generously meant. I cannot even to my father utter my reluctance,—I see him so much delighted at the prospect of an establishment he looks upon as so honourable.' She pictured herself as immured for ever, torn from her family and friends, torn from the quiet employments she relished, as entirely cut off from life as a nun. 'What can make *me* amends for all I shall forfeit?'

Her despair was warranted. She was a daughter; and to another daughter, her sister Charlotte, who, as one never a favourite with the second Mrs Burney, knew something of enforced obedience, she wrote: 'My dear father is in raptures; that is my first comfort. Write to wish him joy, my Charlotte, without a hint to him, or any one but Susan, of my confessions of my internal reluctance and fears.'

She continued to write to her sisters in this strain. She knew her own incapacity for Court life, as was shown by the laughing picture she had drawn for Susanna of what was now to be the reality of physical constraints and endurances. The reality was to exceed in unpleasantness what she had foreseen.

When the day came for entry upon her duties she wrote to this same sister the last cry of one sentenced to prison:

'Oh, my dear Susan! In what an agony of mind did I obey the summons! . . . I was now on the point of entering—probably for ever—into an entire new way of life, and of foregoing by it all my most favoured schemes, and every dear expectation my fancy had ever indulged of happiness to its taste—as now all was to be given up—I could disguise my trepidation no longer . . . My breath seemed gone, and I could only hasten with all my might, lest my strength should go too.'

So began five years of servitude, early in which period the fragile, sportive 'Fannikin' of Samuel Crisp's love formed a deliberate plan, she told Susanna, to lessen all her affections, curb all her wishes, deaden all her sensations:

'Such being my primitive idea, merely from my grief of separation, imagine but how it was strengthened and confirmed when the interior of my position became known to me.' She had been told she was to attend one of the princesses; now she found that she was to be in the Queen's own service. She had then assumed that she was to be the equal colleague of the Senior Keeper of the Robes: she found herself the menial subordinate of a brutal old German woman, subject to every caprice and command of a tyrant. She was horrified. So great was her distress that 'nothing but my terror of disappointing, perhaps displeasing, my dearest father, has deterred me . . . from soliciting his leave to resign.'

She did not resign. She endured. She portrayed the disagreeable Mrs Schwellenberg in terms which make that lady a character superior in verisimilitude to any in *Evelina*; but of course the exaggerative fun was gone, because Mrs Schwellenberg was her daily nightmare. Exaggeration there may be; but it is not the exaggeration of farce, and if there had been no other portraits in the Diary and Letters they would be altogether dismal reading.

The spiteful editor of Mrs Delany's autobiography claims that

Fanny made herself absurd in the eyes of more accomplished courtiers. 'Miss Burney,' says this lady, who appears to have charged Fanny with ruining her own precocious love-affair with one of them, 'was elated to such a degree by the appointment that she gradually lost all consciousness of her actual or relative position. She lived in an ideal world of which she was, in her own imagination, the centre. She believed herself possessed of a spell which fascinated those she approached. She became convinced that all the equerries were in love with her, although she was continually the object of their ridicule as they discovered her weaknesses and played upon her credulity for their own amusement . . .

'Miss Burney's situation certainly was anomalous, for although as a dresser she *had a fixed* (though subordinate) position, as a successful novel-writer she had a sort of undefined celebrity won by her talents; and though as the daughter of a music-master she had previously no *individual* position whatever, there was in her case more personal interest manifested . . . She had a *particularly* large share of *vanity*, a *particularly* lively *imagination*, and between both she made numerous mistakes in the course of her various representations of her *four characters*,—of the *timid* nobody; the wonderful *girl* who had written *Evelina*; the Queen's dresser; and the *amiable* and *devoted daughter*, "Fanny Burney." '

These strictures, whatever the personal grievance on which they are founded, are so ill-natured as to correct themselves. The writer accepted Croker's misrepresentation of Fanny's claim that *Evelina* was about a girl of seventeen (he pretended that she had said 'by'); she unwittingly represents the equerries as heartless cads; she sneers incredulously at Fanny's devotion to her father; and in the charge that Fanny had 'no individual position whatever' she reveals herself a snob. If her attitude was really that of the Court, Fanny's considerable vanity must have met with many affronts. She was not a fool, and was not so self-infatuated as to miss the signs of covert laughter. She was an unhappy prisoner, driven at times to make-believe.

There were compensations. She saw distinguished people; she was politely, even cordially, treated by her employers, who gave her tickets of admission to Handel's *Messiah* and the trial of Warren Hastings and were regaled with brilliant accounts of the trial which would have been impossible to Mrs Schwellenberg or the ribald equerries, if there were any. She was allowed to invite Burney to her apartment, and she continued to enjoy the privilege of seeing Mrs Delany. These were all exceptional favours, and were appreciated as such.

It is probably true that, owing to a small voice, her reading aloud was unsatisfactory, and that, as the Queen confided to Mrs Delany, she sometimes, through short-sightedness, tied the royal back hair into the fastening of a necklace. She was not by temperament a tidy person, nor a dresser. Perpetual standing, such as might have been tolerable to a young woman hardened at school by those eighteenth century educational horrors, the backboard, the iron collar, and the dumb-bells, produced such nausea in what Crisp had called 'that slight piece of machinery, so frail that it requires no common hand to set it right again,' as to make her constantly ill. No notice was taken of her illness, which of course she concealed.

Burney was so enchanted with the whole business that he came to Court whenever he had the opportunity to do so. There he was expected to tell the King and Queen of his unquenchable gratitude for their condescending graciousness to his daughter, and he was ready to do this with an overflowing heart.

'My Susan knows our dear father,' wrote Fanny to her sister. 'He had planned his speech, and was quite elevated with the prospect of making it, and with the pleasure of my pointing it out, and being so happy! Dearest father! how blessed is that facility of believing all people as good and as happy as he wishes them to be! Nevertheless, no sooner did the King touch upon that dangerous string, the *History of Music*, than all else was forgotten! Away flew the speech—the Queen herself was present in vain,—eagerly and warmly he began an account of his progress, and an enumeration of his materials,— and out from his pockets came a couple of dirty books, which he had lately picked up at an immense price, at a sale, and which, in showing to the King, he said were equally scarce and valuable, and added, with energy, "I would not take fifty pounds for that!" Just as if he had said—little as he meant such meaning—"Don't hope for it to your own collection!"

'Was not this a curious royal scene?'

.   .   .   .

It was a curious scene in any company; but it shows Burney's fury of enthusiasm. He saw what he wanted to see; when carried away by joy he became blind to everything else. When he visited Fanny, he would come loaded with manuscripts and proofs (for the *History* was still in progress of composition), and would quite omit to notice that from constant confinement and constant fatigue she was becoming more and more unwell. 'The health of his daughter,' writes Fanny, in the *Memoirs*, 'fell visibly into decay; her looks were alarmingly altered; her strength was daily enfeebling; and the native vivacity of her character and spirits was palpably sinking from premature internal debility.'

'Nevertheless, not the first, nor even the twentieth, was Dr Burney to remark this change.' Fanny's pleasure at sight of him; the pains she took to avert his discomfort; the triumph he enjoyed at being able to boast that his daughter was in possession of a sinecure which brought her into daily contact with his august Sovereign, was so vivid that his happiness was perfect. She could not bring herself to disturb it.

News of her state, while it passed him by, leaked to the rest of the world. 'I heard the other day,' wrote Betty Sheridan in a journal-letter to her sister during the summer of 1788, 'an account of Miss Burney which makes her rather an object of compassion than envy for having attracted Royal notice. It seems the employment she has about the Queen is litterally of that kind that requires absolute servile attendance. At Eight o'clock every morning She must be drest for the day in great form and always be within call, and so far from deriving any advantages from her litterary talents the Queen has made it a point that She shall write no more Novels. It reminds one of poor Madam de Staal's promotion to the Duchess of Maine's favour.'

Horace Walpole wrote to Fanny herself: 'I . . . would not repine, were your situation, either in point of fortune or position, equal in any degree to your merit. But were your talents given to be buried in obscurity? You have retired from the world to a closet at Court —where, indeed, you will still discover mankind, though not dis-close it . . . I will not embarrass you by saying more, nor would have you take notice of or reply to what I have said: judge, only, that feeling hearts reflect, not forget. Wishes that are empty look like vanity;—my vanity is to be thought capable of esteeming you as much as you deserve . . .'

Another protest came from William Windham. 'Charles,' wrote Fanny, naming her brother, 'told me they never met without his denouncing the whole thunder of his oratory against the confinement by which he thought my health injured'; while to Fanny's sister Charlotte he exclaimed: 'I cannot see you without recurring to that painful subject—your sister's situation,' and offered to approach Burney himself with a demand that she should be released from captivity. 'I will set the Literary Club upon him. Miss Burney has some very true admirers there, and I am sure they will all eagerly assist. We will present him a petition—an address.'

'My dear ma'am,' cried Boswell, 'why do you stay?—it won't do, ma'am! you must resign!—we can put up with it no longer . . . We shall address Dr Burney in a body; I am ready to make the harangue myself. We shall fall upon him all at once.'

No doubt all these protestations bred hope in Fanny that something would be done; but for a long time she could see no positive way of escape. And then one day she had the Royal offer of tickets for the *Messiah*, and as she knew that Burney would in any case be present she invited him to go with her. 'It gave me three hours conference with my dearest father—the only conference of that length I have had in four years.' They met; 'He was all himself; all his native self; —kind, gay, open, and full fraught with converse.' Fanny determined to risk an approach to the subject.

'Fortune again was kind; for my father began relating various attacks made upon him for procuring to sundry strangers some acquaintance with his daughter, particularly with the Duchesse de Biron, and the Mesdames de Boufflers; to whom he answered, he had no power; but was somewhat struck by a question of Madame de B. in return, who exclaimed, "Mais, monsieur, est-ce possible! Mademoiselle votre fille n'a-t-elle point de vacance?"

'This led to much interesting discussion, and to many confessions and explanations on my part, never made before; which induced him to enter more fully into the whole of the situation, and its circumstances, than he had ever yet had the leisure of the spirits to do; and he repeated sundry speeches of discontent at my seclusion from the world.

'All this encouraged me to much detail: I spoke my high and constant veneration for my Royal mistress, her merits, her virtues, her condescention, and her even peculiar kindness towards me. But I owned the species of life distasteful to me; I was lost to all private comfort, dead to all domestic endearment; I was worn with want of rest; . . . all that in life was dearest to me—my friends, my chosen society, my best affections—lived now in my mind only by recollection, and rested upon that with nothing but bitter regret . . .

'The silence of my dearest father now silencing myself, I turned to look at him; but how was I struck to see his honoured head bowed down almost into his bosom with dejection and discomfort!— We were both perfectly still a few moments; but when he raised his head I could hardly keep my seat, to see his eyes filled with tears!'

TWENTY

Liberation

To TEARS succeeded one of Burney's emotional protestations of love. 'I have long,' he said, 'been uneasy, though I have not spoken; . . . but . . . if you wish to resign—my house, my purse, my arms, shall be open to receive you back!' And when Fanny admitted that she had been about to seek the very permission he gave he replied, with the greatest self-complacency, 'But I have spoken first myself.'

What with illness and losses of courage, the letter in which Fanny petitioned the Queen for release was not presented for another six months. It was then November, 1790; and the Court had already been warned that she was consulting Charlotte's surgeon-husband, Clement Francis, about the state of her health. Francis, influenced as much by personal knowledge as by diagnosis, wrote that she 'must even be speedy in retiring, or risk the utmost danger.' The Queen, after very considerate offers of a holiday, could no longer resist; she gave her consent. Burney's thanks to her were fervid. He also sent prayers and blessings to his decayed daughter, whose frame he considered 'so nearly demolished' that nothing short of permanent resignation would prolong her life.

He hastened to take credit for this new stand, calling instantly upon 'those who had been most interested in my resignation,' from Burke to Sir Joshua Reynolds and Miss Palmer, and writing 'to Mr Walpole, Mr Seward, Mrs Crewe, Mr Windham, and my Worcester uncle.' To Fanny herself, as if expectant that, the moment she reached home, she would begin a successor to *Cecilia*, he promised 'good ink, pens in plenty, and the most pleasant and smooth paper in the world.'

> "Come, Rosalind (he quoted), oh come and see,
> What quires are in store for thee," ' etc.

Conscience had stirred. Conscience, or a wish to placate his exasperated critics.

For a time Fanny was extraordinarily happy at home, happier there than she had been since the marriages of her sisters, Susanna and Charlotte. 'My father is almost constantly within. Indeed, I now live with him wholly; he has himself appropriated me a place, a seat, a desk, a table, and every convenience and comfort, and he never seemed so earnest to keep me about him. We read together, write together, chat, compare notes, communicate projects, and diversify each other's employments. He is all goodness, gaiety, and affection; and his anxiety and kindness are more precious to me than ever.'

It is evident, from the news of Burney's being 'almost constantly within', that he was no longer careering from pupil to pupil. He had settled down in what he called 'Chelsea College,' and he was engaged in miscellaneous journalism. Fanny, 'merely scribbling what will not be repressed,' may have been elaborating the Diary she had kept while in the Queen's service; but her serious literary labours were upon tragedies intended for the London stage. These proved worthless.

Months passed. She was carried by a friend, Mrs Ord, for a long restorative trip through the West of England. She visited Charlotte in Norfolk, Susanna nearer at hand, the Lockes, and others, including the Queen, while Burney, writing garrulous accounts of current politics (like others of the time he was shocked and alarmed into vehemence by the French Revolution and the possibility that, encouraged by Fox, there might be similar trouble in England), grew testy at the unexpected silences of his daughter. 'Why, Fanny,' he began one impatient letter, 'what are you about, and where are you? I shall write *at* you, not knowing how to write *to* you, as Swift did to the flying and romantic Lord Peterborough.'

Fanny did not write to him, because she was savouring her freedom. This freedom brought her, apparently through Susanna's still greater independence, into the company of many French refugees, including the explosive Madame de Staël, with whom she formed a quick friendship. She confessed the friendship to her father, describing Madame de Staël as a captivating creature. Burney, always on the alert for signs of bad influences, especially French influences, on a child whom he had ever thought too impressionable, grew alarmed. He fed daily upon the horrors of the Revolution. He was extravagant in dislike of Fox and all who thought as Fox did on the subject of popular liberty. He itched to have Fanny safe at home, under his eye, dutifully submissive as of old.

Madame de Staël was particularly dangerous. He agreed that she must have great fascination; but her salon in Paris, surpassing that of her mother, the former sweetheart of Gibbon and now wife of the deposed financier Necker, had been a meeting—and plotting—place for intellectual revolutionaries. She was something of a libertine, 'partial' to Count Louis de Narbonne, who was supposed to be a Royal bastard. 'Unfavourable stories of her have been brought hither.' She might not be French by birth; her husband was a Swede; but she was associated with all that was horrid in France, and 'it will require ages to make the savages of that nation human creatures.'

The position, in his eyes, was desperately serious. He imagined Fanny in the midst of sin. He must rescue her, as he had rescued her from being taught by Johnson that undesirable female accomplishment, Latin. By comparison, Latin would have been venial. Madame de Staël, he indicated, was no better than she should be. In fact she was a deplorable creature. She must be dropped. 'Although I know this will make you feel uncomfortable, it seemed to me right to hint it to you. If you are not absolutely in the house of Madame de Staël ... it would perhaps be possible for you to waive the visit to her, by a compromise, of having something to do for Susy ...'

Fanny, still obedient, made the required 'compromise' with truth, and unwillingly returned home; thereupon Susanna, who had no need of compromise and who was daily meeting the refugees, reported that Madame de Staël, hurt and disappointed, was 'on the point of being offended.' 'She asked me if you would accompany Mrs Locke back into the country? I answered that my father would not wish to lose you for so long a time at once, as you had been absent from him as a nurse so many days. After a little pause, "Mais est-ce qu'une femme est en tutelle pour la vie dans se pays?" '

No doubt Susanna meant the words to sting. They stung. Fanny was in her forty-first year; life at Court had carried her from light-hearted naïveté (not quite sincere, for she was notoriously a prude)

to the edge of debilitated middle-age. Whatever the truth of Mrs
Thrale's fears for Mr Crutchley, and Lady Llanover's angry accusa-
tions of designs on the King's equerries, she had so far behaved
towards men, even if flirting a little, with exemplary discretion.
Unless Burney, hob-nobbing with her, had successfully concealed
his diminished income, she must have seen the future with concern,
perhaps with resentment at wasted years. Now, owing to her father's
already suspect management, she had just been robbed of a new and
greatly valued French friend.

'I have regretted excessively,' she told Mrs Locke, 'the finishing so
miserably an acquaintance begun with so much spirit and pleasure,
and the *dépit* I fear Madame de Staël must have experienced . . . But
there seemed an absolute resolution formed to crush this acquaintance,
and compel me to appear its wilful renouncer.'

These are the words of a rebel.

Mrs Locke, 'dearest Fredy,' was one of Fanny's truest friends,
attached during the last and best spell of social activity before the
incarceration at Windsor. She was an always welcoming hostess,
wife of a rich connoisseur, William Locke, of Norbury Park in Surrey
(very near to Chessington, which Samuel Crisp had made a haven),
whose taste was famous. It was he who brought the Discobolus of
Myron to England; it was he who, not deceived by his agent in Rome,
the nefarious Thomas Jenkins, returned to Jenkins one of the faked,
or 'restored', classical sculptures in which Jenkins traded. Locke's
house was full of beautiful things.

Moreover the household was that of a family devoid of vulgarity.
When Fanny stayed with the Lockes she never wished to leave them;
and as Susanna and her husband lived for a time in a cottage near
by the whole neighbourhood was cordial. It represented, as Chessington had done, escape from supervision. It also, at this time,
represented something more, in the shape of proximity to Juniper
Hall, which Burney described as 'the house of Madame de Staël.'

This house, a very large one, was the home not only of Madame
de Staël but of a number of interesting refugees from the Terror in
France who were settled there as a financially distressed but very
brilliant community. Susanna, referring to this band as 'our Juniper-
ians,' described a conversation which had taken place there as 'one of

the best I ever heard.' Madame de Staël's lover, Narbonne, was a member. So, although he had accommodation also in London, was Talleyrand. So, among others, was Narbonne's friend, a former adjutant-general to Lafayette, named Alexandre D'Arblay. D'Arblay and Narbonne loved each other as brothers do, and, as D'Arblay had lost all his property, shared in perfect amity whatever possessions remained to the latter.

From a first acquaintance, Susanna reported favourably to Fanny of D'Arblay. He was about forty years of age; his figure was good and his face agreeable; he was 'open, intelligent, ready, and amusing in conversation, with a great share of *gaieté de coeur*.' Fanny herself defiantly told her father that 'there can be nothing imagined more charming, more fascinating, than this colony . . . Mr de Narbonne . . . bears the highest character for goodness, parts, sweetness of manners, and ready wit. You could not keep your heart from him if you saw him only for half an hour.' As for M. D'Arblay, he 'is one of the most singularly interesting characters that can ever have been formed. He has a sincerity, a frankness, an ingenuous openness of nature, that I had been unjust enough to think could not belong to a Frenchman.'

What words to address to an already anxious father! When Burney read, among those which followed, that M. D'Arblay had 'just undertaken to become my French master for pronunciation, and he gives me long daily lessons in reading,' his forebodings became panic. His feelings towards all Frenchmen being those of detestation, the thought of his impressionable daughter actually learning a language with which he did no more than sprinkle his letters and speech was revolting. Jealousy rose. He declared, very appropriately, that Fanny was *éprise*.

She was *éprise*, and Burney, for the first time in her life, could not check her. 'The frequency and intimacy with which Miss Burney and M. D'Arblay now met,' says an editorial note to Fanny's Diary and Letters, 'ripened into attachment the high esteem which each felt for the other; and, after many struggles and scruples, occasioned by his reduced circumstances and clouded prospects, M. D'Arblay wrote her an offer of his hand; candidly acknowledging, however, the slight hope he entertained of ever recovering the fortune he had lost by the Revolution.'

Neither he nor Fanny could be dissuaded by the thought of poverty. The Queen had given Fanny a private pension of one hundred pounds a year, and 'my dearest Fredy . . . told me that Mr Locke was of opinion that the £100 per annum might do, as it does for many a curate.' 'With regard to my dear father,' she wrote disingenuously to Susanna, 'he has always left me to myself; I will not therefore speak to him while thus uncertain what to decide.'

She did not speak to him because she knew what he would reply, and her old dread of causing him pain or disappointment or displeasure was again operative. Burney, not deceived, composed a strong letter of protest and warning. He used every argument likely to reduce Fanny to tears and submission—his own 'silent gravity' which had betokened more than 'mere illness and its consequent low spirits'; D'Arblay's poverty and inability to find employment in England; his foreignness; Fanny's love for her family; even, he hinted, the probability of D'Arblay's early discontent with such a restricted life as they would be forced to live. To a daughter of forty-one, who was sick of restriction and spinsterhood, he wrote: 'For Heaven's sake, my dear Fanny, do not part with your heart too rapidly, or involve yourself in deep engagements which it will be difficult to dissolve; and to the last degree imprudent, as things are at present circumstanced, to fulfil.'

He wrote in vain. Fanny had made up her mind. She had a hundred pounds a year, and Mr Locke was giving her a patch of ground in his park for a small cottage. She was determined to take her last chance of happiness. And so she and D'Arblay were first married on July 31st, 1793, in the church nearest to Norbury Park, and on the following day they were married again, 'according to the rights of the Romish Church', in the Sardinian chapel. The Lockes, Susanna, Fanny's naval brother, and Narbonne were all present. Burney stayed away.

TWENTY-ONE

Madame D'Arblay

HE WAS ill; perhaps more than tactically so. He may have been demoralised by his daughter's firmness in marrying a penniless Frenchman; more probably he was in despair at losing for ever the first place in her affections. She was the one child who had done him public credit and brought him on terms of familiarity into the company of exalted rank; but he had relied upon her passionate love. 'I want nothing! only let me live with you!' To be cut off from her would involve much more than a diminution of reflected glory. It would leave him, since her sisters were already married, without domestic warmth.

Natural optimism returned, however, now that the marriage had taken place. When he found what esteem D'Arblay commanded among those who knew him, and learned that this penniless General had begun, like a child, to cultivate the garden about his cottage, there seemed to be compensations. Burney went so far as to send his new son-in-law a copy of Miller's *Gardeners' Dictionary*, as a help in this innocent hobby; and to Fanny, as peace-offering, he simultaneously directed an edition of Milton and a copy of Johnson's *Rasselas*. Before long, in acknowledging a gift from D'Arblay, he dropped as was his habit into familiar French, asking Fanny to 'say *mille et mille jolies choses*' on his account to her husband.

Fanny, delighted, was triumphant. 'My dearest father, whose fears and drawbacks have been my sole subject of regret, begins now to see I have not judged rashly, or with romance, in seeing my own road to my own felicity. And his restored cheerful concurrence in my constant principles, though new situation, leaves me, for myself, without a wish.'

She began to write another novel; not with the zest of girlhood—that zest was long past—but with the object of paying for the cottage which she and D'Arblay were building. It was not a novel which impressed anybody except Jane Austen, who figured in the list of subscribers and who included it by title in her famous claim for the Novel as Art; but it answered its purpose, which was to raise money, and it gave Burney an opportunity to use more French words over the reservations in a notice in *The Monthly Review*: '*J'enrage!*' he wrote. '*Morbleu!*'

Evidently he was quite reconciled to his latest son-in-law. Happiness returned. It reached a high level when he met Mrs Piozzi, who kindled in his breast something like old cordiality by exclaiming 'Why, here's Dr Burney as young as ever!' His answers to the lady were of the 'parrying' order, it seems; and the acquaintance was not actively pursued on either side. What was pursued, by Burney, was the study and translation, and a biography, of Metastasio, who quickly became so much his idol that whenever tumultuous social and apparently revived tuitional engagements allowed he was busy on the work. Youth returned to him in his seventieth year.

'What a while has our correspondence slept!' he wrote jovially to Fanny, in May, 1795. 'Let me see—where shall I begin? Why, at my resuscitation, I think. I began to stir, and rub my eyes, as I remember, ere you left these parts; and I no sooner got on my legs but it was "Mungo here and Mungo there." Engagements—scholars, —printers—proofs—revises, &c. &c . . . My hurry has been, to my present feelings and strength, greater than ever I can remember.'

His hurry embraced dazzling encounters with the leading lights of the day. One such was with Canning, whom Burney had no difficulty in confounding on the subject of electoral reform; another was with young Lady Spencer, with whom, he claimed, he had become 'very thick'; and a third was with Warren Hastings, just acquitted on charges of corruption in India. 'I had luckily left my name at his door . . . before it was generally expected that he would be acquitted.'

As Fanny wrote, 'my dearest father is made for society'; Society henceforward prolonged his life. His second wife might die; his sons and daughters might all live away from him; rheumatism might grow insupportable; and by degrees his faculties might decay; but the garrulousness encouraged by Fanny's first success increased year by year. He embarked upon a long poem dealing with astronomy; he began to gather materials for a biography of himself which Fanny was to complete in a spirit of filial piety; but it was the joy of meeting and being met by celebrities which sustained him to the end.

Fanny remained busy but uninspired. One of her tragedies, *Edwy and Elgiva*, at which Burney had always shrugged, was disastrously produced at Drury Lane. Her next novel, *Camilla*, did not please. She had a baby. And she became absorbed in pamphleteering on behalf of starving *émigrés* and refugee clerics from D'Arblay's country.

D'Arblay himself, although continuing to enjoy the idolatrous affection which she had transferred from father to husband, was a supremely unpractical man. His house-building proved much too expensive, and, while he took pride in growing vegetables, he disliked, and did not well perform, a gardener's more menial tasks, such as weeding, hedging, or ditching. Such tasks were not those appropriate to an aristocrat and a soldier.

In a state of what would nowadays be called frustration, he began to long for France. It occurred to him that with the coming of peace he could recover his French possessions and resume, always with the stipulation that he should never be called upon to fight against England, his place in the French army. He sailed for home, intending soon to return.

Unfortunately, disappointments followed. He managed to find some poorly paid work which made it impossible for him to leave his own country; and at this point he sent for his wife and child to join him. As a result, Fanny, leaving England in 1802, spent ten years of courageously-endured hardship in France, during which period, owing to censorship and a spy mania which seems to have accompanied the rise of Napoleon, correspondence with England became at times impossible. That with her father, owing to Burney's fear of bringing trouble to his daughter, perished.

When at length, in 1812, under the fear that their seventeen-year-old son, another Alexandre, would be one of Napoleon's conscripts, Fanny brought the boy to England in an American ship which was captured by the British, Burney was a very old man, broken, pensioned, and in need of constant nursing. Fanny, hastening from Deal, where she had landed, to Chelsea, was so full of excitement that she recognized none of her father's servants, and could not even remember on which floor of the College his apartment was. 'Her head was confused,' she wrote in the *Memoir*; 'her feelings were intense; her heart almost swelled from her bosom.'

The report given at the time to D'Arblay was less fervent, and more vivid. It was: 'I found him . . . in his library, by himself—but oh! my dearest, very much altered indeed—weak, weak and changed —his head almost always hanging down, and his hearing most cruelly impaired. I was terribly affected, but most grateful to God for my arrival. Our meeting, you may be sure, was very tender, though I roused myself as quickly as possible to be gay and cheering . . . In discourse he re-animated, and was, at times, all himself . . .'

Fanny was sixty, and because of ten hard years spent in France as much changed as Burney. She tried to resume her old place in his life, and for the following eighteen months, until he died on April 12th, 1814, in his eighty-eighth year, was once again his nurse. She then found thrust upon her the duty of completing or, as it proved, compiling the *Memoir* of his life which Burney had begun but never had time to write.

His activities had been miscellaneous. The scraps of information which he left were often so unenlightening, and even feeble, that she felt bound, in order to protect his reputation, to destroy many of them. He had celebrated casual meetings with famous people, without recording anything memorable about the people themselves. Even the occasional quips so much admired by his family as proof of natural vivacity were gone. All that remained was a desolating jumble of triviality.

Confronted with this dilemma, Fanny did her best. Having forgotten much that she had previously known, she stirred memory by consulting her own—then still unpublished—letters and journals, upon which she drew so heavily that exasperated reviewers accused her of intolerable egotism. She also, rather censorious in age, destroyed precious pages from her early diary for fear of giving offence to her kindred; and she inflated her narrative by using a style which was made pompous as much by subjection to French rhetoric as by the legacy of Johson's influence. The inflation is appalling.

As long as she could narrate, she narrated well: it was her gift. When she sought to do her father more than justice she became ridiculous. To her, Burney was a great man; to the rest of the world, who cared nothing for the drudgery and subservience of his early years, he was only a little busybody who had developed with age into a chattering bore.

Fanny was quite as timid and over-sensitive as her father; but not, as he was, pushful and a snob. She inspired great affection in old Crisp; she was on terms of close and playful understanding with her sister Susanna and her step-sister Maria Rishton; she most attracted those of her friends who were best qualified to judge character; and there can be no doubt that Queen Charlotte, as Mrs Piozzi angrily and jealously saw, felt genuine tenderness and loyalty to her. She had not wanted to cut a figure in the world, or to be a great writer, or to be placed about the Queen. It was Burney who, from sheer silliness, blabbed her into fame, forced her into society, and drove her into regal employment. He did all these things with good intentions; and in doing them he exposed the limitations of his mind and nearly killed her.

Much too much has been made of her swollen later style: it was laboured, because it was not spontaneous. When writing familiarly, she kept much of the old simplicity, and as a person she was loved from girlhood to old age, not alone for her quickness and acceptable manners, but for the quality noted by Crisp. 'I love Fanny', said he, 'because she is sincere.' So thought Johnson, Miss Cambridge, Mrs Delany, Mrs Locke, and, above these others, Susanna, who knew her the most closely of all.

She lived, like her father, into her eighty-eighth year, growing plump, improving (said an observer) in good looks and expression, and although losing her son in his very early manhood becoming an object of affectionate esteem to other young relatives. And towards the end of that very long life, when she continued to see the sociable men and women of a new age, she made friends with, among others, a third Samuel. This was Samuel Rogers, the banker-poet, who had once, as a boy, made a pilgrimage to see Johnson, and who, like Anna

Seward's one-time suitor, lost his courage at the door and ran off. One day, as they chatted, Rogers asked if she remembered some lines of Mrs Barbauld's which on a former occasion he had repeated to her:

> Life! we've been long together,
> Through pleasant and through cloudy weather;
> 'Tis hard to part when friends are dear;
> Perhaps 'twill cost a sigh, a tear;
> Then steal away, give little warning,
> Choose thine own time,
> Say not Good Night, but in some brighter clime
> Bid me Good Morning.

'Remember them!' said Fanny; 'I repeat them to myself every night before I go to sleep.'

The wish then implied was fulfilled. She had survived her father by twenty-six years when she died on January 6th, 1840.

TWENTY-TWO

Edgeworth of Edgeworthstown

WHEN Mrs Delany, then Mrs Pendarves, first began to visit Ireland her heart was made to ache by the sight of the poor people there. 'I never,' she wrote, 'saw greater appearence of *misery*.' The Irish— it was an observation she made more than once—'live in great extremes, either *profusely* or *wretchedly*.' Households were very large, ten being 'a *moderate family* to some in this *country*'; and the middle-class gentlefolk rode, shot, dined, gambled, and danced even more vigorously than all the aristocrats of England. Whereas, in London, the *ton* would end their dances by half an hour after midnight, or, at latest, by two o'clock in the morning, the Irish interrupted their dancing only to engage in field sports.

Many broken English merchants went to Ireland 'by way of *retrieving their affairs*'; but whether they did this successfully is not disclosed. They probably became as carefree as the native inhabitants. However, still by Mrs Delany's accounts, County Down was something of an Earthly Paradise; for 'a comfortable circumstance belonging to the county is, that the roads are *so good and free from robbers*, that we may drive safely any hour of the night.' It was not so in England, where highwaymen, not being as chivalrous as they were made to seem in nineteenth century romantic fiction, could and did rob travellers, including Horace Walpole, in the most horrid way. When caught, they were hanged; some of them seeing the error of their ways *en route* for the scaffold.

Mrs Pendarves often met Swift in Dublin, where he was the friend of her future husband Patrick Delany; and she came to have a great affection for him. He told her that he had suffered since his youth from two illnesses. The first of them, dizziness, he attributed to the eating of raw fruit; the second, the source of which he did not explain, although it may have helped to make him misanthropic, was deafness. The two generally attacked him, he said, at different times; but in 1734 they had come both together. He had 'grown sickly, weak, lean, forgetful, peevish, spiritless.'

He was then sixty-six; and he lived until the end of 1745. When the news of his death reached her, Mrs Delany described it to her sister as 'a happy release to him (I hope), for he was reduced to such a state of distress that he was a shocking object; though in his person a very venerable figure, with long silver hair and a comely counte-nance, for being grown fat the hard lines, which gave him a bleak look, were filled up.'

Swift did more for Ireland at that time than any other man; but he was not, as is often said, an Irishman. Only the chance that his widowed and destitute English mother happened to be visiting Dublin at the moment of his birth gave rise to the belief; and as he or somebody else remarked: 'because a man is born in a stable, it doesn't mean that he is a horse.'

If Swift be claimed as an Irishman, my next subject, Richard Lovell Edgeworth, most remarkable of them all, was English. True, his father owned an estate in Ireland, whereas Swift's family had been so scattered and robbed of property in England that no estate was left to it; but Edgeworth claimed association with Edgware, in Middlesex, his mother was the daughter of a Welsh judge whose father had been Recorder of London, and he was born (in May, 1744) in Bath.

In spite of these anomalies, he exhibited all his life the characteristics of an exuberant Irishman, fearless, resourceful, and talkative; and the family home, which he inherited when he was twenty-five years old, and ruled majestically until his death at the age of seventy-three in June, 1817, has only recently ceased to be named Edgeworthstown. It was in the Irish county of Longford.

He was an egotist, and probably at all times what Byron found him in old age, 'active, brisk, and endless . . . that worst of all bores, a boisterous bore.' He knew best about everything, claimed to have worsted in argument Seward's crony Dr Parr, and was always ready to lead, shout, invent, and beget and govern children.

His autobiography, if it had been published as fiction, would now be in every series of reprinted classics alongside *Roderick Random*. It is the work of one who made his friend Erasmus Darwin laugh by admitting to a love of *The Arabian Nights Entertainments*; and who was driven to self-admiration by extraordinary and well-relished triumphs in every field he entered. He was an inventor in an age of inventions. He had four wives, all of whom excepting the first, who was low-spirited, found him irresistible. He was ever surrounded by the majority of his twenty-two obedient and happy children. And it never seems to have crossed his mind that anything he did could be wrong. His conscience remained clear to the last.

As a rationalist, Edgeworth saw the world in simple, utilitarian terms; but as a romantic he exulted in family legends of ancestors tearing the very ear-rings from their wives' ears for desperate last stakes, babies saved from murderous rebels by loyal servants who half-buried them in bogs and afterwards carried them away in baskets of eggs and poultry, fraudulent witnesses confounded by the dates on coins which they claimed to have put under the seals on essential documents, and ladies sanctified for services to religion which they could not have rendered until thirty years afterwards. Lighted candles recovered in the nick of time from gunpowder stores were commonplaces in his version of the Edgeworth history, with infant marriages, love at first sight, and other oddities familiar to Mrs Radcliffe and her imitators. Nothing came amiss. He believed and repeated to his children the tallest stories ever told in Ireland.

It has been suggested that his enthusiasm waned when he came to generations nearer to his own. He did no more than step back in order to leap higher in the autobiography itself. Naturally, his father was merely 'very upright,' with an 'understanding sound and clear'; but that was because the boy saw little of him after childhood, out-argued him in their one moral discussion, and blamed him—I think properly—for putting that same boy, when still under twenty, in a situation which led directly to precocious love-making, elope-ment, and an unsatisfactory marriage. The facts that the father was a model landlord, sat for twenty-five years in the Irish Parliament, and, in true Edgeworth fashion, twice refused a baronetcy, are put to his credit. Otherwise our attention is directed to the son.

.   .   .   .   .

There is a greater, but equally significant, coolness in Richard Lovell Edgeworth's autobiography. Two cousins are not mentioned in it at all. The elder of these was at one time rector of Edgeworthstown; his second son, Richard's playmate in childhood, and of almost identical age, was Henry Essex Edgeworth, who as the Abbé de Firmont (he took that name from his Irish estate of Firmount) played an important part in French history.

Richard's silence has two aspects. The first is that the Edgeworths were a Protestant family, proud of recorded loyalty to King William the Third, while the rector, after visiting Toulouse, where there was a colony of Irish Roman Catholics, resolved to be a Protestant no longer. This was enough to divide any family; but not, one would have thought, enough to effect a complete break between affectionate cousins. Nevertheless Richard's father concerned himself with the affairs of Ireland, took the waters at Bath, and educated his son as a lawyer; while the cousin abandoned his parish, migrated to France with his family, educated his second son at the Jesuit College in Toulouse, and was never mentioned in Edgeworthstown.

Possibly Richard, being so much absorbed in his own prowess, forgot that the ex-rector's son had been his playmate in childhood. Possibly, in the absence of regular communications between the families, he knew little of what Henry was doing meanwhile in France. But the second aspect of his silence may be that there is no room in his autobiography for a second hero. If he had dwelt in admiration upon one who gave half a lifetime to service with the poorest inhabitants of Paris, who supported Louis the Sixteenth to the scaffold, was drenched with the King's blood as the guillotine fell, and eventually died of hardships endured while sharing Louis the Eighteenth's exile in bitter climates, he must have distracted attention from his own to another and nobler nature. His silence could thus be due to the selectiveness of the artist.

For us, on the other hand, some comparison of the two men and their fortunes is illuminating. Since both were Edgeworths, both had exceptional personality. But in contrast with Richard's busy, talkative, and resourceful egotism Henry's devotion to what he believed a divinely-imposed duty to his faith and his sovereign, approaches faintly monomania. We may lament the waste of too many years so a valuable life in servitude to the decayed pomp of a Bourbon; but we cannot deny Henry's selflessness, and we wonder that Richard, who so rejoiced in legendary marvels, should have spared no marvel for a story so extraordinary, and so much better worth unravelling, than those of his incredible ancestors.

It was not to be expected of Richard that he could sympathize with his cousin's devoutness. His was a practical mind, given to those personal skills in which he excelled. But he was also formed by the circumstances of his early life and an accession in childhood to the rank—for in Ireland it was esteemed no less—of heir to the estate of Edgeworthstown.

At his birth, his mother suffered a partial stroke. Like Dr Watson, whose injury from that infamous Jezail bullet moved unaccountably from the shoulder, in *A Study in Scarlet*, to the leg, in *The Sign of Four*, Mrs Edgeworth was paralysed in different parts of the body in different parts of her son's autobiography. At first it was her right side. Later, it became 'one arm and almost [the whole] of her left side'. Later still, as if the writer had grown cautious, 'she had been deprived of the use of her limbs.' As she was able to reason with her husband, and to give Richard good advice about always finishing one scheme before darting to another, her speech was apparently un-affected; but she could not chase her son when he was naughty. She was forced to rely on his obedience to threatening summons. If we knew which hand she then used for chastisement we should better understand her disability.

As the second son, Richard was not at first indulged. When he was six years of age, however, his elder brother died, and the situation changed. From that moment he became subject to princely restric-tions. He was 'obliged to take a course of physic twice a year, every Spring and Autumn, with nine days' potions of small beer and rhu-barb, to fortify my stomach, and to kill imaginary worms.' He was 'not suffered to feel the slightest inclemency in the weather'; was 'muffled up whenever I was permitted to ride a mile or less on horse-back before the coachman.' His feet 'never brushed the dew', and his head was 'never exposed to the wind or sun.'

When eight years old he passed through a religious phase, and wept because he lived in days when it was impossible to be a martyr. A little later, not in pursuit of martyrdom, but because he enjoyed the feat, he climbed a wall built by his father to protect a garden where unripe peaches were growing. Being caught and reprimanded, he philosophically turned the reprimand:

'I added, that if the garden were full of ripe peaches, it would be a much greater temptation; and that unless he should be certain that nobody *would* climb over the wall, he ought not to have peaches in the garden. After having talked to me for some time [my father] discovered that I had reasoned thus: if my father knows beforehand, that the temptation of peaches will necessarily induce me to climb over the garden wall; and that, if I do, it is more than probable that I shall break my neck, I shall not be guilty of any crime, but my father will be the cause of my breaking my neck. This I applied to Adam, without at the time being able to perceive the great difference between things human and divine.'

Whether the child's father made an adequate retort is not recorded; but precociousness in dialectic may have been one of the reasons why Richard was sent to school at a distance from home. Here, in Warwick, he had scope for further prowess. He afterwards recalled with pride that when teased about his Irish accent 'I beat one boy who was taller than myself,' and won a race 'against a boy, my superior in age, and famous for agility.' When removed from this school to one at Drogheda, where he was teased about his English accent, 'after I had once reached the head of my class, I kept my place.' He knew his lessons so well, and did them so quickly, that he was able to neglect what was taking place in class and occupy himself with the enjoyment of Pope's *Iliad* and other attractive books. Being discovered in this diversion by the master, he first boasted that he had prepared his work for a week ahead, and then proved that he had done so.

Nor was this his only triumph. 'Much more than by my scholarship I was distinguished among my companions by my activity in jumping, vaulting, and in every kind of bodily exercise.' He was also a great huntsman. 'Upon a little horse . . . I contrived to keep close to the heels of [John] Foster's excellent hunter, often to the admiration of a numerous company of sportsmen.' By the time he was sixteen, his elder sister was married, and the adult jollifications, quite remarkable for their opulence, found him, as ever, a centre of observation:

'Balls, carousings, and festivities of all kinds, followed my sister's marriage. In these I joined with transports of delight, beyond even what might have been expected from a boy of my great vivacity of temper and personal activity. Every morning I was following the hounds with my new brother-in-law, and the foremost in every desperate exploit of the chase. Every night I was the most incessant, unwearied dancer at the ball. How human nature, even the nature of a schoolboy, went through all that I did at this time, I know not. For three nights successively I was never in bed; nor was I content with all the huntings and dancings which I have described; but at every interval, when others allowed themselves some repose, or acknowledged themselves exhausted by fatigue, I was still working off my superabundant spirit of animation, and amazing my companions by some extraordinary display of activity.'

He had already shown exceptional cleverness in detecting a cause of failure in some electrical demonstrations; and had received from the inventor not only encouraging compliments but an invitation to visit a fascinating experimental laboratory. But he did not stop at electricity. His interest was directed into a new channel through the perceptiveness of Lady Longford, who lived at Pakenham Hall, near his home. When the exhibition of skill in vaulting, riding, dancing, and the chase appeared to be his one aim, she saw more deeply into his nature. She gave him a key to her husband's magnificent library.

The gift was crucial. Experimental reading of Pope's *Iliad* in lesson-time had been no more than a boy's romantic search for heroes to emulate. Romance was instantly superseded by the eager search for knowledge in books of every description. Many days spent in the library, free to range wherever he chose, opened new horizons to his mind. Never again, he assures us, did he indulge in field sports. His zest for them was at an end.

It was at Pakenham Hall, too, that he demonstrated another strength, this time a strength of character. Being given five pounds by Lord Longford with which to engage in the game of Faro, he won a hundred pounds, lost it all, remained unmoved, and refused to play further. This was the first of several displays to be recorded of his self-control at the card-table; and it greatly impressed Lord

Longford. Longford, indeed, said that it showed Richard to be 'exempt from the vice of gambling.' 'It is certain,' adds Richard himself, 'that in my subsequent life I never felt an inclination for cards, dice, or lotteries.'

He remained, however, secretly unruly, and deeply ambitious. Those early days of strict cosseting had encouraged such self-importance, and such a rebellious spirit, that when once free of restraint he took every means of establishing his own individuality. Hence the jumping and hunting, the boisterous dancing, and, a little later, defiance of his father's wish that he should become a sedate lawyer. Later still, as we shall see, he ardently embraced Rousseau's theories of education, which were opposed to everything he had known as a child; but first, upon being entered at Corpus Christi College, Oxford, he was forced, or persuaded, by his father to spend his vacations in a rural retreat. This was at Black Bourton, fourteen miles from the University, at the home of a middle-aged dreamer named Elers.

Elers not only had five daughters, whose doings he left unsupervised, but was so fascinated by Richard's mind and personality that he revealed to one who seemed like a son every ingenious speculation that danced in his airy mind. Speculations, daughters, and animal spirits combined to carry the young Richard to new heights of vainglory. He had already humbled a bully at the fencing school he attended; he had already received an apology from a Judge in the Oxford Courts who had unjustly rebuked him; he now proceeded to dazzle one of Mr Elers's daughters with his surpassing attractiveness, and to fall in love in return with the thrilled and adoring child.

TWENTY-THREE

Richard's Wife and Friends

It was natural that he should do this, so great was his animal energy; and it was natural that he should win the heart of Anna Maria Elers by that same energy and a flow of eloquence intoxicating to a young girl with no experience of the world.

Nor was this Richard's first sexual imprudence. During boyhood, at a party, he had been the bridegroom in a mock marriage-service; an adventure which so alarmed his father that legal steps were taken to annul the proceedings. Alas, in the present case there could be no annulment. Richard Edgeworth senior knew nothing of the affair until it was too late to take any action.

At least one modern writer has suggested that Anna Maria was seduced by the ardent young man, and that a runaway marriage was necessary in order to make her baby legitimate. This I think improbable. True, Richard says he was the father of a son before he was twenty; but in the eighteenth century it was easy to make mistakes of the kind. Maria Edgeworth, for example, thought she returned to Ireland from her English school when she was twelve: she was in fact fifteen. Richard says he was placed at school in Warwick in 1752; it was really 1753. Neither Maria Edgeworth nor Fanny Burney managed to give the correct age of her father at death. And as to Richard's being a father before he was twenty, he was twenty in May, 1764; and while, for his own purposes, he says the first child of his marriage was born in 1764, Maria's biographer Augustus Hare gives the year as 1765, and Emily Lawless thinks it may have been as late as 1766.

The probability, considering that Anna Maria Elers was a respectable girl, is that Richard proposed to her and was accepted by her, when both were under age and therefore subject to parental orders. He was not a libertine. Unluckily, having committed himself, he spent a holiday with his father at Bath, where he saw and danced with a splendour of young ladies whose beauty and smartness exceeded those of his sweetheart. We are not told that she was plain; she was merely unfashionable. By the time he saw her again Richard had been spoiled for simplicity by what he describes as a transcendent social success.

In the circumstances he did again what it was natural to him to do. He tried, as many another young man has done, to cry off. 'I could not find any honourable means of extrication. I have not to reproach myself with any deceit, or suppression of the truth. On my return to Black Bourton, I did not conceal the altered state of my mind, but having engaged the affections of the young lady, I married while I was yet a youth at college. I resolved to meet the disagreeable consequences of such a step with fortitude.'

He was a youth at college; he was wholly dependent on his father. Since his sweetheart, and possibly her mother, who is not mentioned, insisted that his word had been given, he was in a dilemma. Evidently Richard Edgeworth senior must be presented with a *fait accompli*, and Gretna Green is mentioned by students, though on what authority I do not know.

The *fait accompli* produced a rumpus, which was resolved by the intervention of the paralysed but speechful Mrs Edgeworth. Her husband admitted that the marriage, although by a minor, was valid (it must be remembered that the bride's father was his old friend, who had warned him of the risks involved in Richard's stay in a homeful of girls); and Richard was given an allowance. He set up a 'very moderate' establishment beside the Common at Hare Hatch, between Reading and Maidenhead, his staff consisting of but one outdoor manservant and, indoors, one man and two maids.

Here he occupied himself with scientific pursuits, including many inventions, and cultivated his mind by reading books of an educational character, which included that seminal work, Rousseau's *Emile*. *Emile*, first published in 1762, was one of the sensations of the time; its reading had been commended by Thomas Gray to all fathers; it inflamed many young spirits who were ready to rebel against pedagogy.

Richard's wife, he confesses, was 'prudent, domestic, and affectionate,' and as we hear nothing of her deficiencies in housewifery we assume that she managed very well. To a more humdrum husband her qualities would have seemed valuable; to a wild young fellow who thought himself a genius her patience was a reproach. She was not, he complains, 'of a cheerful temper.' 'She lamented about trifles; and the lamenting of a female, with whom we live, does not render home delightful.' Stoically, he 'determined to bear with firmness and temper the evil, which I had brought upon myself.'

Some society was possible to the young Edgeworths, who exchanged visits with their quiet neighbours, drank tea, talked, played cards, and were in bed by ten o'clock each night. To Richard, the constraints of such tranquillity were exasperating. He had enjoyed Bath; he was able to reach London; although now a stranger to quick spirits he needed exercise, gaiety, the talk of stimulating companions. Therefore he escaped from home whenever he could, leaving Anna Maria to bear with what firmness and temper she could command the evil which Richard had brought upon her. She lamented.

While Richard enjoyed the flattery of fellow-inventors and worldlings who encouraged and used his gifts, she was alone. He returned home at intervals, full of his own marvellousness and other great men's affairs, to beget more children. The second of these, born in 1767, afterwards gratified him by being recognized as something of a genius. Her name was Maria.

According to Richard's own account, the little scene in which he crushed a bully at their fencing school, by locking the door, removing the buttons from two foils, and challenging the wretch to mortal combat—a challenge which was 'prudently declined'—greatly impressed his fellow-students at Oxford. These fellow-students are not celebrated in his narrative, although he encountered one or two of them in later life; but he met a young Oxonian, not at the University, but during a vacation, who became his intimate companion, and remained a friend until death.

This was Thomas Day, a model eccentric in a century of eccentrics, who afterwards wrote that now-unread but lucid and long-celebrated educational classic, *Sandford and Merton*. The friendship was 'founded upon mutual esteem, between persons of tastes, habits, pursuits, manners, and connexions wholly different. A love of knowledge, and a freedom from that admiration of splendour, which dazzles and enslaves mankind, were the only essential points on which we entirely agreed. Mr Day was grave, and of a melancholy temperament: I gay and full of "constitutional joy." Mr Day was not a man of strong passions,—I was.'

Much to Richard's surprise, Anna Maria Edgeworth did not share his regard for Thomas Day. Our own surprise is less. Day, after several disappointments in what was not so much love as serious matrimonial design, considered the female sex to be incorrigibly treacherous, and ever spoke of it with cynicism. He was a high-principled pessimist, whose remarks, in spite of pomposity, could be sarcastic.

His appearance was repellent. Even Anna Seward, who for personal reasons preferred him to Richard, makes so much clear. 'Mr Day,' says Miss Seward, 'looked the philosopher. Powder and fine clothes were, at that time, the appendages of gentlemen. Mr Day wore not either. He was tall and stooped in the shoulders, full made, but not corpulent; and in his meditative and melancholy air a degree of awkwardness and dignity were blended. We found his features interesting and agreeable amidst the traces of a severe small-pox. There was a sort of weight upon the lids of his large hazel eyes.' One fact which Miss Seward does not mention, but which we owe to his friend Richard's candour, is that 'he seldom combed his raven locks.'

Pock-marked and gawky, unbrushed and unkempt, occupied exclusively (except when he was engaged in his highly theoretic schemes for matrimony which should leave all power with himself), and open in denunciation of the female sex, Mr Day disgusted young Mrs Edgeworth very much.

Perhaps because his looks were fine (he was 'of Herculean strength'), and his manners aristocratic, she felt no comparable loathing for another, decidedly corrupt, friend of Richard's, whose name, which would have suited any rake in a novel by Fanny Burney or Elizabeth Inchbald, was Sir Francis Delaval.

Sir Francis was an adventurer. Having exhausted his first wife's fortune of thirty thousand pounds, he was on the look-out for another wealthy bride. That, in an age when heiresses seem to have been acquiescent, was a common pursuit with gamesters. He was also hoping to marry his sister, who had a dying husband, to the Duke of York; and was meanwhile busy with schemes to fill his pockets with money from the pockets of comparable gamesters. He saw in Richard a convenient tool.

Acquaintance with Sir Francis began almost by chance. Richard had watched the performance of a conjuror named Comus; and having instantly grasped the secrets of parlour magic he gave displays on his own account. These delighted Sir Francis, who had a house in Downing Street, and who invited Richard to collaborate with him in the mystification of noble friends. Richard, with a secret taste for the *ton*, found himself happy in this distinguished company, and eagerly abetted one whose 'ingenuity and never failing resources made his acquaintance highly valuable to such gentlemen of the turf club, as made bets out of the common line of gambling.' The gentlemen included Lord Eglintoun, whom Boswell toadied as a young man, Lord Effingham, and Lord March, who was afterwards Duke of Queensberry.

It was Lord March who planned to receive by means of relays of fleet horses the result of a particular race at Newmarket before news of it could otherwise reach London. He would be able, he thought, then to make heavy wagers on the race in complete security. Was not that ingenious? Richard, not demurring, said that he could improve on the fleet horses. Lord March said that he could not. Richard offered to lay £500 that he could learn the result four hours earlier than his lordship; and Sir Francis immediately doubled the stake. Cool-headed Richard, however, cautioned the hotheads, explaining that he relied upon a magic invention of his own; and because of his warning all bets were gratefully cancelled. He had not been excited; his conscience was clear; his was the purely scientific mind.

He had long busied himself with the invention of a form of telegraphy; and his plan was to flash signals from point to point of the road from Newmarket to London, at a speed which should out-distance that of the fleetest horse. This telegraph was apparently not used in support of Lord March's nefarious scheme; but its inventor, with Sir Francis Delaval's energetic co-operation, was able to signal after dark, by means of lights, from Sir Francis's homes in

Downing Street and Hampstead to 'part of Piccadilly' and a house 'to which I had access' in Great Russell Street, Bloomsbury. For the present that was the extent of Richard's triumph.

Whether Sir Francis could have financed further experiments is doubtful. He did not find a second rich wife; and all hope of marrying his sister to the Duke of York was destroyed by the Duke's inconsiderateness in dying of a fever while abroad. The blow was severe. Herculean though he was, Sir Francis lacked the moral strength to endure his disappointment. He went straight into a decline; and after, under medical instruction, taking a steam bath he was seized with such remorse for the dissipations of a lifetime that in the manner of eighteenth century fiction he delivered to Richard, who was faithfully with him at the time, a long harangue. It concluded:

'If I had employed half the time and half the pains in cultivating serious knowledge, . . . I should have distinguished myself in the Senate or the Army. I should have become a USEFUL member of society, and an honour to my family. Remember my advice, young man! Pursue what is USEFUL to mankind, you will satisfy them, and, what is better, you will satisfy yourself.'

Richard was then twenty-two. When, two mornings later, he learned that Sir Francis had died in his bed, he was much impressed. This last harangue had the force of prophecy. In that moment he became a confirmed UTILITARIAN; and he remained a UTILITARIAN until the end of his days.

The propensity received further stimulus from a visit which he paid in 1765 to Chester, where for the first time he saw a planetarium. He entered eagerly into conversation with the creator of this remarkable invention, who boasted of the many distinguished people who had been to see it. One of them, he said, was the celebrated Erasmus Darwin, then living and practising as a doctor in Lichfield, Staffordshire, the birthplace of Dr Johnson and home of the Sewards. The city assumed momentous importance in Richard's life.

Darwin was not only a doctor; he had a genius for mechanical invention, and of course was the intimate friend of some of the leading scientists of the century. He had been giving thought, it appeared, to some means by which a carriage, hitherto so rigid in its frame that when reversing in a small space it was liable to overturn, could be given separately hinged or pivoted front wheels. Richard, perceiving the value of such a contrivance, set to work to invent it. His design was so successful—this was a matter of course—that it was cordially approved by the Society for the Encouragement of the Arts.

Here, then, was a chance to demonstrate his ingenuity to the learned Doctor. He wrote to Lichfield, was invited by Darwin, who supposed him to be a mere mechanic, to come and demonstrate his design, and set off at once. When he arrived, Darwin was out; but such was Richard's address that Mrs Darwin at once recognized his gentility, allotted him a bedroom superior to the one previously chosen, and gave him tea. The two were in lively converse when Darwin arrived. A happy meeting between two inventors followed.

As always happened, Richard made an easy conquest. He was urged to stay longer, was taken to the Bishop's Palace, and was introduced to Anna Seward, then 'in the height of youth and beauty, of an enthusiastic temper, a votary of the muses, and of the most eloquent and brilliant conversation.' This last was one of Richard's specialities; and if Anna Maria Edgeworth, lacking all such qualities, had been present, unseen, she might have felt alarm at the exchange of brilliancies. She knew nothing of them. Nor did Richard at first tell anybody that he was married and a father. It was left to Mrs Darwin very pointedly to reveal the fact by toasting 'Mrs Edgeworth'. Did Miss Seward, then or later, feel any serious attraction? She was no more than eighteen months his senior, and capable, as she admitted, of passionate love; her references to him, although accounted for by what she explained as another injury, were deliberately generous. I think it likely that inclination deceived her as to the purpose of his attentiveness.

TWENTY-FOUR

Philosopher Day

THIS was his first visit to Lichfield. Anna Seward in later years described him as 'the young and gay philosopher'; and expanded her description with the words: 'Then scarcely two and twenty, and with an exterior yet more juvenile, he had mathematical science, mechanic ingenuity, and a competent portion of classical learning, with the possession of the modern languages. His address was gracefully spirited, and his conversation eloquent. He danced, he fenced, and winged his arrows with more than philosophic skill; yet did not the consciousness of these lighter endowments abate his ardour in the pursuit of knowledge.'

These words give no hint of an offence to Miss Seward and the Lichfield community as a whole which lay some five years in the future. Richard passed out of that community for the present without arousing any hostility. He returned home, and to London; and in 1768 he took his friend Day to Dublin and Edgeworthstown.

Day was not pleased by what he saw in Ireland, which country, accordingly, he never re-visited. In excuse for the displeasure, Richard wrote in the year 1809 or thereabouts that Dublin 'was at that time so very different from what it is now, that it struck Mr Day with surprise and disgust. The streets were wretchedly paved, and more dirty than can be easily imagined. The poor were squalid, and their tones strangely discordant to an English ear. The hackney coaches, their horses, and still more their drivers, were so far below what were to be seen in London, and were altogether so uncouth, as to increase at every view the astonishment of my friend. As we passed through the country, the hovels in which the poor lodged, which were then far more wretched than they are at present, or than they have been for the last twenty years, the black tracts of bog, and the unusual smell of the turf fuel, were to him never-ceasing topics of reproach or lamentation. The modes of living in the houses of the gentry were much the same in Ireland as in England. This surprised my friend; he observed, that, if there was any difference, it was that people of similar fortune did not restrain themselves equally in both countries to the same prudent economy; but that every gentleman in Ireland, of two or three thousand pounds a year, lived in a certain degree of luxury and show, that would be thought presumptuous in persons of the same fortune in England.'

Whether these reflections influenced Richard, or whether, indeed, they were his own reflections, we are not told; but one of the points of agreement between the friends was indicated by his boast that 'I never was fond of money nor was I extravagant.' In boyhood he had thoughtlessly enjoyed the extravagance of his Irish neighbours; in young manhood he had basked in the comparable extravagance of his grand gambling English patrons. Now, having grown used to the narrowness of his allowance as a married man, and being on the point of inheriting Edgeworthstown, which he did in 1769, he was for the first time taking seriously the prospect of being an occasional resident there.

As for Thomas Day, he had tried England (on twelve hundred pounds a year); he had seen Ireland; he was training two young orphan girls with the object of making a wife of whichever responded more satisfactorily to his methods; and in this very year of 1768 Laurence Sterne, an Irishman who had taken orders and become a very unclerical writer, had published his *Sentimental Journey*. The book opened with significant words: 'They order, said I, these matters better in France.' It was read everywhere, and it gave its admirers a new zest for light-hearted travel. Day was not immune.

He was already a devotee of Rousseau, from whose principles of education he had learned much. Now, taking his cue from those words in *A Sentimental Journey*, he undertook the 'one and twenty miles sailing which give a man these rights,' and crossed the Channel, carrying with him the two young orphan girls who had been rather strangely entrusted to his care.

His object was to free the children from all contamination by English manners and the English tongue; but he was unsuccessful. His charges did not take to the French language, and their endless squabbles proved intolerable to a philosophic bachelor. He brought both girls back to England in 1770, and parted them. He then rented a house at Stow Hill, near Lichfield, where at Christmastide Richard paid him a visit.

This second visit of Richard's affected the whole of his later life. On the first he had made acquaintance with Erasmus Darwin and several men of science who lived in or near Birmingham. On the second he met his fate, in the person of a beautiful girl named Honora Sneyd.

He and Day visited the Bishop's Palace to renew acquaintance with the Sewards; for, says Richard, the Palace 'was the resort of every person in that neighbourhood who had any taste for letters.' Mr Seward's learning and naïveté, Mrs Seward's looks, manners, and generosity, and Anna's gracious wit were all properly savoured. More than all these, however, was the attraction of the fourth member of the household.

'Under the fond and truly maternal care of Mrs Seward was bred up Miss Honora Sneyd, daughter of Edward Sneyd . . . of Bishton, in Staffordshire. Mr Sneyd had become a widower early in life [but not before his wife had produced at least four daughters]. Honora became the more immediate pupil of Miss Seward. From her she acquired an ardent love of literature, and she afterwards formed for herself a refined and accurate taste . . .'

Daily visits followed. Both Day and Richard deeply relished 'the agreeable conversation of the whole family, and in particular the sprightliness and literary talents of Miss Seward . . . During this intercourse, I perceived the superiority of Miss Honora Sneyd's capacity, . . . her sentiments were on all subjects so just, and were delivered with such blushing modesty (though not without an air of conscious worth) as to command attention from every one capable of appreciating female excellence. Her person was graceful, her features beautiful, and their expression such as to heighten the eloquence of everything she said. I was six and twenty; and now, for the first time in my life, I saw a woman that equalled the picture of perfection, which existed in my imagination.'

Unfortunately, he had a wife. Unfortunately, too, Thomas Day, who had previously been blind to Honora's charms ('she danced too well; she had too much an air of fashion in her dress and manner; and her arm was not sufficiently round and white to please him'), suddenly became aware of them. He sought her company. He did more: while nothing should impair his feeling of friendship for Richard, he must point out, and he did point out, 'the folly and meanness of indulging a hopeless passion for any woman.' Richard was disconcerted.

He was not therefore destroyed. Having been asked by Day whether he had enough strength of mind to subdue his admitted love for Honora Sneyd, he transported his miserable wife and as yet small family to Lichfield. It was a desperate step; but it enabled him, while testing his own stoicism, to observe closely and critically the development of Day's wooing of the beauty. He insists that he did this with 'pleasure, even exultation'; but exultation may perhaps have increased when, by the chance of war, he was made the bearer of Honora's written refusal of Day's suit. Poor Day, who had drawn up a formal statement of the strict conditions under which he would require a wife to live, became so distraught after reading this refusal that he had to be bled by Dr Darwin.

He gradually recovered; and was helped in his recovery by the arrival in Lichfield of Honora's father, together with four younger daughters. The youngest of these, Elizabeth, seized Day's fancy. She was less beautiful than Honora, less light of foot, less brilliant, and less fashionable. She probably also had plumper arms; for in the course of a few weeks he entered into negotiations with her for marriage, and was so far well-received as to feel much encouraged. Elizabeth, however, had either a critical mind or an extremely mischievous humour. She drew her lover's attention to his gawkiness and slovenly dress. She could not, she said, marry a graceless man. If he wanted her to accept his conditions, which involved a secluded life devoted to intellectual effort, without society and without diversions of any kind, he must study deportment.

As was to be expected, Thomas Day took the demand very seriously. He promised to go back to France and cultivate deportment. But he was not willing, apparently, to leave his friend Richard in a state of dalliance with the highly dangerous Honora. He was full of high principles and earnest advice; even insistence upon the rigid virtue in others which he practised himself; and he produced the arguments of reason and example. Since Elizabeth was to abandon diversions and become a thinker, and Mr Day was to straighten his legs by wearing clamps upon them for hours at a time, it was only right that Richard should come away from Lichfield and learn the disciplines of renunciation.

' "They order," said I, "these matters better in France." ' To France, accordingly, Mr Day and Richard sailed forthwith; and since Mr Day did not care for the Fine Arts or sophistications of Paris, and Richard himself felt at this time no interest in public monuments, they wasted no time in the French capital. They went straight to Lyons, then the Mecca of English tourists, Richard considering as highly creditable a momentous silence to Honora regarding the cause of his flight.

TWENTY-FIVE

Richard is Free

HE LEFT Anna Maria in charge of three as yet unimportant children; but he took to Lyons his eldest boy, another Richard, for the further-ance of a vital educational experiment. This boy had been reared, with Anna Maria's consent, on the principles outlined in Rousseau's *Emile*, which were as different as possible from those applied in child-hood to Richard himself. Gone were the dosings and swaddlings intended to protect a valued child's health from worms and the inclemencies of northern weather; gone was the supervision which had developed that child's secret rebelliousness and precipitance in marriage. Instead, Richard's son was

'Dressed without stockings, with his arms bare, in a jacket and trousers . . . which were at that time novel and extraordinary. I succeeded in making him remarkably hardy; I also succeeded in making him fearless of danger, and, what is more difficult, capable of bearing privation of every sort. He had all the virtues of a child bred in the hut of a savage, and all the knowledge of *things*, which could well be acquired by a boy bred in civilized society . . . He was bold, free, fearless, generous; he had a ready and keen use of all his senses, and of his judgment.'

This was Rousseau's plan for the ideal boy. Richard's words might have been drawn directly from *Emile*. He therefore took the oppor-tunity, as he was in France, of introducing the boy to Rousseau. Alas, in spite of Richard's care, and perhaps because of his constant absences from home, errors had been allowed to creep into his son's mind. They were instantly discovered by Rousseau in the course of a two hours' walk alone with Richard junior. The boy had imbibed what the philosopher called 'party prejudice'. Whenever he saw something which he particularly admired, he exclaimed in its praise: 'That's an *English* horse!' or 'Those are *English* shoe-buckles!' Unless checked, said Rousseau, this propensity would become fixed; master Edgeworth would lose the advantage of his Spartan rearing, and become, like any common schoolboy, a slave to his associates.

Impressed by the warning, Richard was nevertheless too much engrossed in himself and his own social and scientific triumphs in Lyons to keep the boy to the true path. He engaged a tutor who stammered, a tutor who had no power at all over his pupil. The result was disastrous.

'I found myself entangled in difficulties with regard to my child's mind and temper. He was generous, brave, good-natured, and what is commonly called good-tempered; but he was scarcely to be controlled.'

Richard dismissed the tutor, and carried the boy to a Catholic seminary in Lyons. There, in spite of specific directions that nothing of the kind should be attempted, one of the teachers tried to indoctrinate him with Romish beliefs which to a Protestant were anathema; and while the boy was agile enough in mind to out-argue his preceptor (as Richard had done with his father) it became clear that this expedient also had failed. Young master Edgeworth was incorrigible. Richard was forced to admit a fallacy in Rousseau's system of education.

'I must here acknowledge, with deep regret,' he wrote, later in life, 'not only the error of a theory, which I had adopted at a very early age, when other and wiser persons than myself had been dazzled by the eloquence of Rousseau; but I must also reproach myself with not having, after my arrival in France, paid as much attention to my boy as I had done in England, or as much as was necessary to prevent the formation of those habits, which could never afterwards be eradicated.'

Experience thus caused him to lose interest in rearing the perfect savage. As far as I recall, he does not mention young Richard again in his autobiography; and we learn only from others that the boy defied all attempts to give him a conventional education, went to sea of his own accord, settled in America—a Noble Savage indeed!— and paid but one short visit to England, many years afterwards, when the Edgeworths were staying in Bristol. He had been born far from

Edgeworthstown, of an unloved English mother. He knew nothing of his sisters, who were tantalized by his almost immediate return to America. Having rejoined wife and children there, he seems no more to have been heard of. To Richard, as he represented failure, he seemed better forgotten. Preferring docility in his offspring, the father took pains to keep the remainder of them very docile indeed.

One reason for inattentiveness to his son during the long sojourn in Lyons was that he was enjoying great personal success there. This success was achieved in several ways; first at the gaming-table, where of course he won, but where his cool and exemplary determination instantly to lose his winnings earned the admiration of all; subsequently in magnificent engineering plans for changing the course of the Rhône (they were set at nought by an unexpected flood); and by a stern bogus challenge, which saved the fellow from a real and unavoidable duel, to a drunken young English milord who offended his hosts by falling asleep at a party. Courage, aplomb, a performance during the flood which risked a humble boatman's life but saved much property belonging to engineers of the district, all made him a hero.

There was nothing he could not do better than others—talk, plan, act, gamble, and invent. To the manner of an aristocrat he united the skills of a craftsman. But when he was at the height of a dazzling career, which brought him the offer—refused with truly Edgeworthian indifference to such things—of a high French decoration, news came that Anna Maria, after conscientiously bearing a fifth child, had quietly, and no doubt with characteristic 'want of cheerfulness,' left him a widower.

She had joined him for a while in Lyons, which place as a rustic and domesticated Englishwoman she did not like, and had returned to England for the birth of her baby, apparently to the home of some aunts in Great Russell Street, London, under the escort of Thomas Day, who had just completed his lessons in grace. The baby was born in Great Russell Street, and soon died; the last of her failures.

Day, having seen her safely to London, travelled on to Lichfield and Elizabeth Sneyd. To his chagrin, however, Elizabeth, 'very

pretty, very spritely, very artless, and very engaging,' as Anna Seward
tells us, was filled with horrified merriment at sight of his new, but
artificial, gainliness. It was grotesque. Bad as his former state had
been, this monstrous transformation was much worse. She summar-
arily refused to marry him.

Naturally Day was confirmed by her heartlessness in his disapproval of the female sex. He had now been rejected by both the
Sneyd sisters, and was crestfallen. A male friend was worth more to
a man than any woman on earth. His thoughts flew to Richard;
and he knew that Richard, who loved women, would not agree
with this opinion. Nevertheless, Richard was his friend, and Richard,
having loitered awhile in Paris on the urgent homeward journey,
was in England. Anna Maria was dead. Day felt that his duty was
clear. He wrote to Richard in these terms:

'While virtue and honour forbade you to think of Honora Sneyd,
I did everything in my power to separate you. But now that you
are both at liberty, I have used the utmost expedition . . . to tell
you, that she is in perfect health and beauty; improved in person
and in mind, and, although surrounded by lovers, still her own
mistress.'

Richard no longer loitered. 'At this moment I enjoyed the invaluable reward for my steady adherence to the resolution, which I
had formed on leaving England, never to keep up the slightest
intercourse with her by letter, message, or inquiry.'

He hurried to Lichfield, called first at Erasmus Darwin's house,
and by Darwin's sister was taken at once to tea with the Misses
Sneyd. This, it seems, was in March, 1773; in July Richard and
Honora were married by special licence in Lichfield Cathedral. Mr
Seward, Anna's father, while performing the ceremony, 'shed tears
of joy.'

Day, selflessly congratulating the victor in this old rivalry for
Honora's hand, added a word—a reserved word, it may seem to
us—of commendation. 'You possess,' he told the bridegroom, who
passed the praise complacently to his readers, 'an understanding
improved by observation, goodness of temper, and a variety of
literary tastes.' Not oversanguine, perhaps; but Day, as is evidenced
in the Socratic questions of Mr Barlow, in *Sandford and Merton*, was

M

a philosopher. No doubt others were more enthusiastic. The one person to strike a jarring note was Anna Seward. She never forgave Richard for stealing Honora from the Bishop's Palace and carrying her to Ireland, where she forgot the best of her old friends, who was Miss Seward herself.

Anna was inconsolable. She returned again and again to her loss in letters addressed to newer correspondents, such as the celebrated Ladies of Llangollen, who had never seen Honora. This child, whom she had tended for nearly twenty years, whom she regarded as a sister, whose prohibited but not very heartfelt romance with the Major André reluctantly hanged by Washington as a spy she celebrated in verse, and whose beauty and intelligence were the criteria by which she judged all other young women, was never seen again. Honora did not even write. She was gone. 'That form, the light of my eyes, was divided from me for life by the Irish Sea; and that heart, whose affection I prized more than life, to me became indurated.'

So much indicates Honora's infatuation with her husband. As a girl she had been courted more than once; she had borne the shock of learning through Mrs Darwin's pointed toast to the previously unmentioned Mrs Richard Lovell Edgeworth that her charmer was married, and endured separation and a silence (on which Richard congratulated himself with no thought of her feelings) of many months. Yet as soon as he reappeared, and proposed, she did not hesitate. She 'left her home and kindred,' her Lichfield friends, her benefactress Anna Seward (whom once before she had journeyed wildly through floods and across swollen rivers to rejoin), and settled in another land among people in every way strange to her. Her old and protective host, Mr Seward, had wept at the wedding. Nothing indicates that Honora wept.

What was she really like? Beyond the facts that she was blonde, with the early and fragile bloom of the consumptive, we learn only from Anna Seward that George Romney unconsciously drew her portrait, albeit 'with a ploughboy's feet,' in his picture of Serena, which proves to be that of a rather insipid young lady who sits reading a book in a conventional bower. This work, says Miss Seward, 'accidentally formed a perfect similitude of my lost Honora Sneyd's face and figure, when she was serenely pursuing the printed and unimpassioned thoughts of others. To the varying glances of her countenance when she was expressing her *own*, or listening to the effusions of genius, no pencil could do justice. But that sweet, that sacred decency, that reserved dignity of virgin grace, which characterized her look and air, when her thoughts were tranquil, live in this dear portrait, while the turn of the head and neck, and every feature, reflect hers, as in a mirror.'

Miss Seward, in this copious and highflown mood, shows none of the vivacity evidenced in her more ribald portraits. She does not bring Honora to life, as she does the several pedantic or ridiculous persons who crossed her path. Maria Edgeworth, the first daughter of Richard by the despised Anna Maria, and the only genius among Richard's twenty-two children, did better. When she was seven years old, and already as impulsive as she continued to be until she was eighty-two, she looked up at her step-mother, who sat at a dressing-table, and breathlessly exclaimed: 'How beautiful!' Thus we know why many men fell in love with Honora, and why, to Miss Seward, she represented perfection.

She is described as being possessed of much natural gaiety and a gift for mathematics which presently extended to theoretical mechanics; and Augustus Hare, the official biographer of Maria, says she gave her step-daughters 'a childhood of unclouded happiness.' This may have been true of the two youngest; it cannot be true of their elder sister, Maria. She, while Honora proceeded to bear two children of her own, was almost at once—possibly as a result of two disapproved and, by report, destructive pranks—sent away to school in Derby. She remained at this school until removal to a more advanced seminary in London, and did not return to Ireland before she was fifteen. She owed no happiness, no motherly care, to Honora, who died before the return.

Once married to his ideal woman, Richard reformed. His restlessness abated. Though still for some years a migrant, he took English servants to Edgeworthstown, corrected many things there, and even if his main efforts in that direction did not begin until 1782, showed the first signs of becoming a good-humoured landlord who felled trees, clipped hedges, and devised a new system of bog-clearance. He continued to read, invent domestic appliances, correspond with

Erasmus Darwin and other scientific friends, and in co-operation
with Honora realised Thomson's poetic vision:

> Meantime a smiling offspring rises round,
> And mingles with their graces. By degrees,
> The human blossom blows; and every day,
> Soft as it rolls along, shews some new charm,
> The father's lustre, and the mother's bloom.
> Then infant reason grows apace, and calls
> For the kind hand of an assiduous care.
> Delightful task! to rear the tender thought,
> To teach the young idea how to shoot,
> To pour the fresh instruction o'er the mind,
> To breath th' enlivening spirit, and to fix
> The generous purpose in the glowing breast . . .
> An elegant sufficiency, content,
> Retirement, rural quiet, friendship, books,
> Ease and alternate labour, useful life,
> Progressive Justice, and approving Heaven!
> These are the matchless joys of virtuous love.

TWENTY-SIX

The Edgeworth Family is Supervised

TRUE, this idyllic state lasted only briefly. In the seventh year of marriage, Honora caught cold; and the progress of her already latent disease was very rapid. Richard hurried her to Lichfield, where she was examined by Darwin, and to the celebrated Dr Heberden; but neither gave any hope. She was doomed. Richard records:

'She had long known the nature of her distemper, and that it was incurable; but never for one moment did pain, or fear, or vain regret for every enjoyment that a human creature could possess, disturb the firmness of her mind . . .

'Three days before she died, I was suddenly called up to her room. I found her in violent convulsions. Youth, beauty, grace, charms of person, accomplishments of mind, reduced to the extreme of human misery, must have wrung the most obdurate heart. What must her husband feel at such a moment? . . . When the fit ceased, she begged of me to sit down beside her bed. I took out my pencil, and determined to note whatever she said and did at this awful period, an employment that might enable me to bear with more fortitude the scene that I was to witness. She soon fell asleep, and wakened smiling. "I am smiling," said she, "at my asking you to sit beside me as a sort of protection, and at my being afraid to die in my sleep, when I never felt afraid of dying when awake." The ensuing days she talked during the intervals of dozing, about the education of her children, and about everything which concerned my happiness. She recommended it to me in the strongest manner to marry her sister Elizabeth.'

Still with these matters strongly in his mind, Richard was forced in April, 1780, to write to Maria, who was just thirteen, and was far away in London. 'My dear Daughter,' he said. 'At six o'clock on

Thursday morning your excellent mother [it was characteristic of him to ignore the unfortunate Anna Maria's right to that description] expired in my arms. She now lies dead beside me, and I know I am doing what would give her pleasure, if she were capable of feeling anything, by writing to you at this time to fix her excellent image in your mind. As you grow older and become acquainted with more of my friends, you will hear from every mouth the most exalted character of your incomparable mother. You will be convinced by your own reflections on her conduct, that she fulfilled the part of a mother towards you and towards your sisters, without partiality towards her own, or servile indulgence towards mine. Her heart, conscious of rectitude, was above fear of raising suspicions to her disadvantage in the mind of your father, or in the minds of your relations . . .

'Continue, my dear daughter, the desire which you feel of becoming amiable, prudent, and of USE . . .

'God bless you, and make you ambitious of that valuable praise which the amiable character of your dear mother forces from the virtuous and the wise. My writing to you in my present situation will, my dearest daughter, be remembered by you as the strongest proof of the love of your approving and affectionate father, RICHARD LOVELL EDGEWORTH.'

This is a very extraordinary letter to be addressed to a child of thirteen. As Maria had been banished from home, so that she had seen almost nothing of the estimable lady for at least five years, we may think it Pecksniffian. It was not. Nor should we read into it, as psychiatrists would do in the case of a modern father, the product of a guilt complex. It represented a consciously new, serious Richard, deeply shaken by Honora's death, and needing to set down what he had been able to record with pencil and paper of his wife's last injunctions. All the same, it is highly defensive.

How, otherwise, can we account for the insistance upon Honora's fulfilment of a mother's part? For the references to 'suspicions to her disadvantage' and 'servile indulgence'? Had there not been criticism in the Elers family of Maria's denial of a home at Edgeworthstown? Had the same family expressed no concern about the son who had gone to sea? Would it not be natural for Anna Maria's sisters, at least, to chat among themselves about the beauty who had so hastily supplanted Anna Maria? And do not Anna Seward's complaints that she had been summarily dropped by Honora suggest that Lichfield had felt an equal disapproval? The impression of uneasiness is heightened by Richard's emphasis in the autobiography on the presence of his first wife's brother at his third marriage.

For he did marry Honora's sister Elizabeth, only seven months after Honora's death; and the date of this third wedding was Christmas Day, 1780. Still engaged in self-justification, Richard explained his position: 'Nothing is more erroneous than the common belief that a man who has lived in the greatest happiness with one wife will be the most averse to take another. On the contrary, the loss of happiness which he feels when he loses her necessarily urges him to endeavour to be again placed in a situation which has constituted his former felicity . . .

'I felt that Honora had judged wisely, and from a knowledge of my character, when she advised me to marry again, as soon as I could meet with a woman, who would make a good mother for my children, and an agreeable companion to me. She had formed an idea that her sister Elizabeth was better suited to me than any other woman and thought that I was equally well suited to her.'

At first Elizabeth demurred, as she well might do. Her dismissal of Thomas Day had proved that she had humour and decision of character. She had not married during Honora's six years of bliss; but she had 'another attachement,' and she felt Richard to be, apart from Thomas Day, 'the last man of her acquaintance that *she* would have thought of for a husband.' She was, however, ordered to Scarborough by Darwin for sea-bathing; Richard and his younger children made the same journey; daily association brought a change in her views. The other 'attachment', if it really existed, was broken off.

Opposition to this marriage to a deceased wife's sister arose among 'certain officious friends' and spread to the local Press. Elizabeth was forced to take refuge with a friend in Cheshire, where the banns were published. Officious friends still protesting, the clergyman they had counted upon was frightened from his promise on the very day appointed for the wedding. This produced what Richard mildly calls 'unnecessary vexation'; but since he always had his way in human relations, and Elizabeth remained a young woman of spirit, they soon found a London cleric who either was not molested by the officious friends or had a stronger stomach than his brother in Cheshire.

No regrets were afterwards publicly expressed. Richard, though never lyrical over his third wife as he had been about Honora (he apostrophized her in writing as 'my dearest and kindest friend'), seems to have been content and constant. Elizabeth carried on from the point at which Honora stopped, took over Anna Maria's three daughters and Honora's son and daughter, and bore a further nine children of her own. Since Richard's eldest boy, Rousseau's failure, was safely out of the way, and a chastened Maria was presently released from school, only deaths among the offspring, and, in time, Elizabeth's inevitable death, prevented the number of eager, well-trained minds at Edgeworthstown from becoming fearsome to imagine.

Besides being a century in which men were the dominant sex and scientific discovery was a passion, the eighteenth saw a complete change in theories of education. The Lichfield set had been greatly influenced by Rousseau's *Emile*. Erasmus Darwin, less a disciple than a more moderate fellow-traveller (his original mind solved every problem by hard thought), believed previous child-training to have been mischievous. He scorned to play tricks such as Rousseau claimed to have used in teaching Emile to appreciate the rights of property or to show the dangers of walking alone in Paris. His notions were very modern indeed.

'The system of his whole life on that theme,' said Anna Seward, 'had been at war with all sort of restraint on the time, the amusements, and the diet of children. Irony was the only corrective weapon he had ever used to his own. The docility of them all, and the talents and good qualities of his three oldest sons . . . had confirmed his disdain of incessant attention to young people. He always said, "If you would not have your children arrogant, conceited, and hypocritical, do not let them perceive that you are continually watching and attending to them; nor can you keep that perpetual watch *without* their perceiving it. Inspire them with a disdain of meanness, falsehood, and promise-breaking . . . by expressed contempt of such as commit these faults." '

Now Darwin was born in 1731. He was thus thirteen years older than Richard, and seventeen years older than Thomas Day. These two, born without Darwinian irony, but full of admiration for his genius, accepted some of his ideas. Their first admiration had been for *Emile* and his hardening processes, with the result that Day, having no children of his own, tried to train his two orphans in stoicism: they became hysterical. Richard, older, and with a son, began earlier and more rationally, with his own flesh and blood. This experiment also was a failure. Day, finding imaginary characters easier to manage than 'wretched un-idea'd girls', wrote *Sandford and Merton* to show how a simple, truthful boy can triumph and a spoilt one be redeemed; Richard, deciding that those who thought Rousseau mad 'were not much mistaken,' invented his own system.

He became absorbed in the delightful task of cultivating juvenile minds; and as his family increased in number, and the juvenile minds infected each other and took pleasure in each other's society, irrespective of difference in age, he was busy and happy all day long, like Mr Robinson of the Swiss Family. No detail of the house and estate at Edgeworthstown escaped attention. He lost no opportunity of assembling the children and inviting their answers to his simplified but searching questions. Patriarchy became his goal.

Elizabeth, once a lively girl, was his chief assistant. A second assistant, more lively than Elizabeth, and a most affectionate younger friend, was his eldest daughter, Maria, who was taken all about the estate by Richard, and shown everything that was to be seen, proved not only the aptest pupil he ever had, but a superlative sister to the rest of the brood. She did not entertain them, as she had entertained companions at two English schools, with hair-raising tales of horror; both at school and in those journeys when she rode beside him on her pony 'Dapple' and kept accounts of every piece of Edgeworthstown expenditure, the lesson of DUTY had been digested. She had learned much about life; in particular she had learned to disapprove of all except moral tales.

Her schooling, unlike her brother's, had been strict. She had experienced, besides the usual tortures of establishments for young ladies, another which her father tolerantly described as 'unusual'. It consisted, as she was abnormally small, in being 'swung by the neck to draw out the muscles', and one would have expected her to look like Tenniel's picture of Alice after nibbling the magic cake which so elongated her. Maria, however, remained as small as ever.

This experience was in itself a lesson. It taught her what not to do to others. Her unstudied letters—among the most excellent ever written in English—show that she had a delicious humour as well as great intelligence, united to a simplicity of character, perhaps inherited from her unfortunate mother, which all who met her found adorable. In addition, she had a golden quality entirely lacking in her father and the other utilitarians of the eighteenth century. This was imagination, that sublimation of sympathy which gave her the power to identify herself with other persons. Besides being a wit, she was a ready and resourceful playmate who relished the experience of being a child among children.

Richard, though infatuated with his own ability as a teacher, led well. If, as I suspect, the opening words of this quotation are Maria's, even if he added the corollary, he had sense enough to leave them untouched:

'We may safely allow children to be as happy as they possibly can be without sacrificing the future to the present. Such prosperity will not enervate their minds.

'We make this assertion with some confidence, because experience has, in many cases, confirmed our opinion. Amongst a large family of children, who have never been tormented with artificial trials of temper, and who have been made as happy as it was in the power of their parents to make them, there is not one ill-tempered child. We have examples every day before us of different ages, from three years old to fifteen.'

These words are taken from a work which bears on its title page the names, as authors, of both Richard and Maria. They show how much the little brothers and sisters must have owed in happiness to their tiny and much older sister. Richard's heavy-handed revisions are evident throughout the book, and wherever 'the author' is complacently mentioned it is always 'he'; but passages of the most charming insight abound. Edgeworthstown, still a shocking ruin when the family returned to it in 1782, became a busy, cheerful place. The result of admitted collaboration between father and daughter offers advice to parents on subjects ranging from Toys to Geometry and Grammar. With a side-glance at Rousseau, the discredited theorist and philosopher, it is called, emphatically, *Practical Education*.

As to the method practised at Edgeworthstown, Maria gives important testimony. She says of her father: 'He explained and described clearly.—He knew so exactly the habits, powers, and knowledge of his pupils, that he seldom failed in estimating what each could comprehend or accomplish. He saw at once where their difficulty lay, and how far to assist, how far to urge the mind, and where to leave it entirely to its own exertions. His patience in teaching was peculiarly meritorious, I may say surprising, in a man of his vivacity.'

Not a word here about herself. We guess at her share in the proceedings only by perceiving where another hand has improved the moral by making it more explicit. Where Maria lampoons a pedantic schoolmaster watching sport with a paper kite, and remarking: 'What a pity it is, that children cannot be made to mind their grammar as well as their kites!' with some further comment on 'that pernicious love of play against which he is doomed to wage perpetual war,' Richard approves; but he feels bound to commend himself needlessly as what he calls 'a philosophic tutor.' His, I feel sure, are the words following:

'A man of sense will see the same sight with a different eye; in this *pernicious* love of play he will discern the symptoms of a love of science, and, instead of deploring the natural idleness of children, he will admire the activity which they display in the pursuit of knowledge. He will feel that it is his business to direct this activity, to furnish his pupil with materials for fresh combinations, to put him, or to let him put himself, in situations where he can make useful observations, and acquire that experience which cannot be bought, and which no masters can communicate.'

This is an echo of the letter addressed to Maria when she was thirteen—she was thirty-one when *Practical Education* appeared,— in which he urged her to be amiable, prudent, and of USE; and on another page of the book occurs a supplementary passage: 'When the powers of reason have been cultivated, and the inventive faculty exercised; when general habits of voluntary exertion and patient perseverance have been acquired, it will be easy for the pupil himself, or for his friends, to direct his abilities to whatever is necessary for his happiness. We do not use the phrase *success in the world*; because, if it conveys any distinct ideas, it implies some which are perhaps inconsistent with real happiness.'

As a consequence of the system, visitors to Edgeworthstown were astonished to find themselves amid a houseful of prodigies. Whatever their ages, the children followed useful occupations, as they would have done in one of the now disregarded Utopias of forward-looking moralists. One little boy was instructed by his father to draw a line upon a bench with only three legs, to indicate the exact point at which a man could sit without risk of falling on his back. The line was drawn. 'I give you that for a good head,' coolly remarked Richard, to his visitors; 'he will be a geometrician.'

In the same way, having learned that she had a gift for comprehension, he had encouraged his daughter Maria to write. When she was at school, he instructed her to send him a little tale, 'about the length of a *Spectator*, upon the subject of Generosity; it must be taken from history or romance, and must be sent the sennight after you receive this; and I beg you will take some pains about it.'

Evidently, Maria took the pains, and had her work corrected, and was bidden to write more; for unlike Fanny Burney, who was compelled to ruin her eyesight by sitting up o'nights to write a forbidden novel, Maria was kept busy with the pen. It is true that her first novel, *Castle Rackrent*, was composed privately and not seen by Richard until it had been published; but this, in a sense, was a private joke of Maria's. She was not afraid of her father, nor subjugated by him. She merely wanted to gratify an ambition, for the first and last time, without his oversight. The book is by common consent the best she ever wrote. All others were revised and spoiled by his determination that she should do nothing unworthy of herself and of Richard Lovell Edgeworth.

He was one of those unimaginative men—there are many of them —every novelist has known one or more—who, being unable to create fictitious characters or construct a story, cannot see a manuscript, or for that matter a printed book, without reaching for pen or pencil to change and improve it. He wrote endlessly, as the autobiography shows, just as he talked boisterously and in society snatched from Maria any story she had begun to tell; but he was no writer. He could not have created *The Absentee* or *Ormond*, but he always knew best how it should have been written, and meddled with every sentence, until every sentence was robbed of the author's own sparkle. Much later, after reading a story written when Maria was about thirty-nine years of age, he complacently and egregiously illustrated his supervisory itch:

'Your critic, partner, father, friend, has finished your *Leonora*. He has cut out a few pages; one or two letters are nearly untouched; the rest are cut, scrawled, and interlined without mercy. I make no doubt of the success of the book amongst *a certain class of readers*; PROVIDED it be polished *ad unguam*, so that neither flaw nor seam can be perceived by the utmost critical acumen . . . I advise you to revise it frequently, and look upon it as a promising infant committed to your care, which you are bound by many ties to educate, and bring out when it is fit to be presented.'

This is the same advice as that which had been given twenty-six years before.

'God bless you, and make your ambitions of that valuable praise which the amiable character of your dear mother forces from the virtuous and the wise. Continue, my dear daughter, the desire which you feel of becoming amiable, prudent, and of USE.' The key-word here is 'USE'. It is no wonder that Madame de Staël, greatly admiring Maria's work, lamented to a common friend, M. Dumont, the adroit utilitarian translator of Bentham's works into more lucid French, that 'elle se perd dans votre triste utilité'.

Maria accepted all revisions; she had a tremendous admiration for her father; and her father was used to being obeyed. A most remarkable anecdote is related by an unknown visitor to Edgeworthstown. Richard had early assimilated Rousseau's hatred of ostentation, and this hatred was one of the lessons he taught his children, who, however happy, seem to have been thankful for permitted mercies. The rector of the parish, says the unidentified memorialist, was dining with the Edgeworths in company with an officer of the British Army.

'After dinner the ladies repaired to the library, and after wine the gentlemen followed. As they entered the door of the library, the officer exclaimed, "How beautiful!" Mr Edgeworth said, haughtily and quickly, "What do you admire, sir?" He replied, "Your daughter's magnificent hair." Charlotte was standing in a becoming attitude before the bright grate, with her arms resting upon the mantelpiece. Mr Edgeworth walked across the room to the book-shelves, opened a drawer, held her head back, and cut her hair close to her head. As the golden ringlets fell into the drawer, this extraordinary father said, "Charlotte, what do you say?" She answered, "Thank you, father." Turning to his guests, he remarked, "I will not allow a daughter of mine to be vain." '

TWENTY-SEVEN

Maria

WHAT cause Richard's daughters had for vanity, apart from the fact that they were reared under his surveillance, is nowhere disclosed; but the lovely girl who lost her ringlets was described by one who should have known as 'the fairest blossom of talent'. She was a child of Elizabeth, and strongly resembled the original Honora, whose early death from the Sneyd complaint, consumption, she emulated at the age of twenty-three.

Others of the family also died untimely, nine of them before their father, while the rest, however gifted in fact, have no historic fame. Anna Maria's three daughters (for the sex of the baby who died almost at birth is unknown) were not among those who died young. Only Maria, the eldest, became famous; but the others, obviously very intelligent, married distinguished men and lived long. The husband of the second, Emmeline, was a Swiss named King, who for religious reasons sacrificed patrimony and career in his own country, found sanctuary in England, made acquaintance in Bristol with both Southey and Coleridge when they were young Pantisocrats, and, after failing as painter and engraver, became a surgeon. Anna's husband was the celebrated Dr Beddoes of Bristol who used to take cows to breathe in the bedrooms of tubercular patients, and whose son was Thomas Lovell Beddoes, author of the brilliant and 'very Gothic-styled tragedy,' *Death's Jest-Book*.

Thomas Lovell Beddoes was thought by some to resemble Keats in looks, until he grew a beard and became the image of his idol, Shakespeare. Like his father, and like his Edgeworth grandfather, he was a philosophic scientist, and he is said to have anticipated in his poetical writings the ideas of both Charles Darwin and Herbert

Spencer. He had genius and an unsettled character, and he committed suicide after parting with a young German baker whom he tried to transform into a great actor. His manuscripts eventually passed into the hands of Robert Browning, by whom their posthumous publication was arranged; and his youthful letters, penetratingly concerned with poets and German scholars, show unstrained humour and felicity of expression which his aunt Maria—to whom he was 'Tom Beddoes' and apparently less interesting than his brother Henry, who became a sailor—would greatly have relished.

According to one of these letters, he did not know, a few days before his death, who was then living at Edgeworthstown. Pride and affection were shown, however, in an earlier lively dialogue, sent from Zurich, referring to his Bristol relatives. Having spoken of a lamented silence on the part of his friend the writer Barry Cornwall (Bryan Waller Proctor) he continues:

'I shd. be extremely sorry not to enjoy his acquaintance after my return to your island: but being a great wretch, a horrid radical & a person entirely unfitted for good society, I never wonder at my acquaintances disavowing or cutting me, as the Arabs & the English say. Don't care a zephyr as long as cash, good spirits and foolery in brain.

'Capital was my first adventure in 1835 at Dover. London Coffee house, old gentleman in coffee room. Waiter says I, I wish to smoke a cigar, have you a smoking room. *W.* No occasion, sir, you can smoke here. *I.* (to O.G.) Perhaps it may be disagreeable to you, sir, in which case— *O.G.* By no means. I'm myself a smoker (laying aside specs, and looking like Cosmogony Jenkins—) *I.* I have good cigars, will you d.m.t.f. to accept one. *O.G.* Very kind. *I.* Come from Calais? *O.G.* Boulogne. Go to Bristol. *I.* Anche io sono Bristoliano. *O.G.* Know King? *I.* Wife my aunt. *O.G.* Are *YOU*? *I.* Son of well-known physician at Clifton. *O.G.* Not of Dr B? *I.* Same unworthily. *O.G.* That's curious. Your brother married my niece a fortnight ago. *I.* Happy man! Hear of it now for ye first time. Tories will never be my heirs. *O.G.* O!G—! (reassumes specs and exit).

So much for Thomas Lovell Beddoes, whose romantic verse at times has exquisite affinities, now with that of Shelley, now with that of the Coleridge who wrote *Christabel*. I return to his aunt Maria.

She, the Edgeworth daughter who gives Richard his place in this book, was as much of a genius as her nephew; but whereas he may gratify all who associate genius with morbid instability, she was normal with the normality usually dismissed as talent. Jane Austen, with more genius than either, was similarly normal.

Having been away from home for so long in childhood, Maria knew almost nothing of Edgeworthstown until her intelligence was ripe. At the age of fifteen, seeing the Irish people through her own simplicity and an alien training, she alertly seized their characteristics. Kept busy by her father with homilies in which good children were repulsively smug, and those less good, but sometimes delightful, learned the disappointments attending injudicious choice or conduct, she took it into her head to write down, unsupervised and with un-affected amusement, what she had seen of common or ridiculous Irish types. In doing this, she showed her mental health. She was not by temperament a utilitarian.

This was shown much later, when, with something of the un-quenchable fun of childhood, she played a little trick on Richard by writing, unbeknown to him, a shorter tale called *Griselda*. Perhaps wishful to repeat the surprise of *Castle Rackrent*, she had this book secretly printed by the publisher, Johnson. Then, with a dummy title-page especially provided by Johnson, she caused it to be thrust under her father's nose.

He was puzzled by what he felt to be an air of conspiracy; but at last read the book attentively and with admiration. So keen was his sense and fairness of mind that he saw it to be an Edgeworth product, and, feeling sure that Maria must have been too busy with household doings to have found time for its composition, he hit upon the idea that it had been written by her younger sister, Anna. 'She must have done it to please me!' he exclaimed; and was filled with delight. As soon as the cheat was revealed he expressed even greater delight, laughed heartily without any disapproval, and as far as we know made no attempt to re-write the story before it was seen by the rest of the world.

Also, when he decided that *The Absentee* ought to end with a letter written in the vernacular by one Larry Brady, and as an expert in the appropriate lingo prepared his own version of this letter, he at once saw the superiority of a letter written by Maria, and declared that Maria's should be used. He admired her gifts, reproached her for trusting too much to happy impressions (which he called *aperçus*), and blamed her much, as an energetic managing person was bound to do, for the artist's apparent idleness. He was incapable of such restorative quiet.

He at all times exhorted his children to effort; but he saw himself as a guiding and salutary parent, not a scold. He wanted them to do him credit in whatever he considered to be their appropriate field of action. Maria's field was that of an executant of his ideas. She, however, had given him her love and obedience, not her soul. She accepted his revisions; as a woman, when the time came, she allowed her inclination to be over-ruled by what she knew to be his need of her; but in a matter of opinion, even if it was necessary sometimes to keep it to herself, she was at all times independent.

Her final step-mother, some years her junior, recalled times when the family habit of reading books aloud was being indulged (with so large a family all at home, Richard, Mrs Edgeworth, the two sisters of Honora and Elizabeth Sneyd, Maria, Emmeline, Bessie, Charlotte, Henry, Sneyd, Honora junior, and William, it was the one way in which a new book could be instantly devored by the entire group), and dwelt upon Maria's zest for the inventions of other novelists. Once, when they were listening to a forgotten story by Lady Morgan, called *O'Donnel*, Richard protested: 'This is quite improbable!' Maria, with complete good humour, brushed the protest aside, crying: 'Never mind the improbability! Let us go on with the entertainment!'

As her fame spread, pilgrims made their way to Edgeworthstown, and she received invitations and encouragements to visit London, Paris, and Edinburgh. Richard went everywhere with her, assuming as by right the first place in any Edgeworth concern. They both fancied that the entertainments were meant for him; and when they were in company together, and other visitors were craning to see the tiny figure of his daughter, Richard did the talking. He talked tremendously, with great assurance and no tact whatever. Once, when sitting next at table to Mrs Siddons, he claimed to have seen her play the part of Millamant thirty-four years earlier. The lady bridled at this reflection upon her age: 'Pardon me, sir.' 'Oh!' said Richard;

'then it was forty years ago; I distinctly recollect it.' 'You will excuse me, sir, I never played Millamant.' 'Oh, yes, ma'am, I recollect.' 'I think,' replied Mrs Siddons, turning to her other neighbour, who was Rogers the banker-poet, 'it is time for me to change my place'; and she rose with her own peculiar dignity.

Richard probably did not understand what offence he had given. His object was innocent; he trusted his own memory; and he insisted at all times upon the accuracy and importance of his own opinions. He sometimes did this to the exasperation of those who wished to hear Maria say if need be only a few words of her own, undrowned by that loud voice and boisterous manner.

One of those who was impatient was the Scottish tragic dramatist Joanna Baillie. She, having heard beforehand of Maria's constant suppression, was determined to engage her in conversation. She took her apart, and was delighted to find that this 'frank, animated, sensible, and amusing woman,' 'entirely free from affectation of any kind,' was quiet only from modesty, and not from any undue awe of her father. Still more was she delighted to find that her new friend was capable of showing great spirit in any disagreement with him. Indeed, 'when they take up the same thing now,' Joanna reported to Walter Scott, 'they have a fine wrangle (tho' a good-humoured one) for it, and she as often gets the better as he.'

It might well be so. Maria could not be insensible to some cordial personal compliments which were clearly not intended for Richard. Richard himself, never doubting, of course, his own rightness and ability as inventor and educator, could take only partial credit for such compliments. He had not to fear a rival: he could translate the praise in any way he preferred. Furthermore, he had experienced, with the rest of the family, the thrilling surprise of coming in the final pages of *Waverley*, which they were reading aloud, upon a tribute from Sir Walter to his daughter's genius. 'It has been my object,' said Sir Walter, 'to describe these persons, not by a caricatured and exaggerated use of the national dialect, but by their habits, manners, and feelings; so as in some distant degree to emulate the admirable Irish portraits drawn by Miss Edgeworth, so different from the "Teagues" and "dear joys" who so long, with the most perfect family resemblance to each other, occupied the drama and the novel.'

Maria had been the least excited of all by this discovery. Brought up to be amiable, prudent, and useful, she thought nothing of her own capacity. Her father, she believed, was the true creator.

'Only that small circle of our friends,' she wrote, 'who saw the manuscripts before and after they were corrected by him, can know or imagine how much they were improved by his critical taste and judgment.

'Whenever I thought of writing anything, I told him . . . my first rough plan; and always, with the instinct of a good critic, he used to fix immediately upon that, which would best answer the purpose.— "Sketch that, and show it to me" . . . Sometimes, when I was fond of a particular part, I used to dilate on it in the sketch; but to this he always objected—"I don't want any of your painting—none of your drapery!—I can imagine all that—let me see the bare skeleton." . . . When he thought that there was spirit in what was written, but that it required, as it often did, great correction, he would say, "Leave that to me: it is my business to cut and correct—yours to write on" . . .

'. . . As my father remarked, the facts which strike the attention because they are out of the course of common events, are for this very reason unfit for the moral purposes as well as for the dramatic effect of fiction . . . In proportion as events are extraordinary, they are unsafe and useless as foundations for prudential reasoning.'

Unsafe, useless, prudential: what words these are to address to an original writer! *Elle se perd dans votre triste utilité*, lamented Madame de Staël, who had already made her wondering comment on the subjection of forty-year old Fanny Burney to her father's will. Maria did not lose herself: she had always been used to the discipline intended to make her amiable, prudent, and of use.

In manner and scope her fictions are quite out of present-day fashion; but nobody with any knowledge of the craft of story-telling can begin to read, for example, her second-best novel *The Absentee* without at once recognizing Maria's great natural gift for that craft. The quick gossip of worldlings is so rendered as to prepare the reader for everything that follows; and even today, when all tricks of the trade are familiar to sixth-form schoolgirls, must be seen as evidence of quality. In 1812, when it was published, *The Absentee*, however inferior to the wholly unsupervised *Castle Rackrent*, came between

Sense and Sensibility (1811) and *Pride and Prejudice* (1813), and is only made to look inferior by comparison with those two master-pieces. Left alone, it might almost have walked beside them into perpetual life.

It has not done so. It remains, with the rest of Maria's work, on shelves to which we seldom go. Richard saw to that. His 'critical taste and judgment' constituted a dead hand. Perhaps his cutting and correcting left his daughter free from an author's harassing responsi-bility for his or her final versions. It certainly taught her to avoid frippery in the novels and exaggeration of feeling and phrase in her family correspondence, which to this day can be read for its insight and fun. But it shackled her genius as any other form of censorship would have done. He was not 'Big Brother'; he was 'Big Father'.

TWENTY-EIGHT

Danger at Home

HE WAS big father, not only to his family, but to the whole district and, in one sense, to the whole of Ireland. However busy in superintending Maria's literary labours, he found time for many inventions, for designing the mechanisms needed in the family production of a play in which he and Maria had collaborated, for fighting the danger of a French invasion and an Irish rebellion, for memorializing the Lord Lieutenant on the use by Government, without charge, of his wonderful telegraphic system, for becoming a member of the Irish Parliament, and for maintaining cordial correspondence with, among others, his old friend Erasmus Darwin.

To Darwin he wrote, with customary buoyancy, at the end of 1794:

'Just recovering from the alarm occasioned by a sudden irruption of defenders [this was the name given to themselves by marauding bands of peasants, who also were known as 'heart-of-oak boys'] into this neighbourhood, *and* from the business of a county meeting, *and* the glory of commanding a squadron of horse, *and* from the exertion requisite to treat with proper indifference an anonymous letter sent by persons who have sworn to assassinate me, I received the peaceful philosophy of *Zoonomia* [Darwin's book]; and though it has been in my hands not many minutes, I found much to delight and instruct me . . .

'We were lately in a sad state here, the *sans culottes* (literally such) took a very effectual way of obtaining power; they robbed of arms all the houses in the country; thus arming themselves, and disarming their opponents. By *waking* the bodies of their friends, the human corpse not only becomes familiar to the *sans culottes* of Ireland, but is associated with pleasure in their minds, by the festivity of these nocturnal orgies. An insurrection of such people, who have been oppressed, must be infinitely more horrid than any thing that has happened in France; for no hired executioners need be sought from the prisons, or the galleys. And yet the people here are altogether better than in England; . . . the peasants, though cruel, are generally docile, and of the strongest powers, both of body and mind.'

The exertions he spoke of in this letter—of course the efforts of the *sans culottes* quickly gave way to greater danger in a subsequent year—were entirely normal. 'I never thought it wise,' he wrote to his third wife, 'to repress what little enthusiasm might remain, after what I have seen of life. I know, that without it I must necessarily cease to act; and laborious employment, tending by degrees to some object of our wish, I firmly believe to be amongst the chief pleasures of existence.'

Accordingly, 'I lay railways, and use certain carriages of my own construction upon friction-wheels, &c., upon the principle of having a number of small carriages linked together, instead of using large machines and expensive railways . . . Another more useful scheme that I have in view is, to carry marl two miles with this machinery, to improve 600 acres of coarse land, which has just, by the extinction of leases, fallen into my own hands.'

Nor was this all. He designed and erected a new tower for the Edgeworthstown church. He was at all times busy in the house, providing Maria with a little table to work on, taking advantage of his daughters' absence from home to have their rooms repainted, and putting such ingenious contrivances upon the locks of doors that some at least of his visitors felt terror lest they should never be able to get out of their bedrooms. And at one time Maria wrote to her aunt, Mrs Ruxton (Richard's sister and an early flame of Thomas Day's): 'Shall I tell you what they, my father and all of them, are doing at this moment? Sprawling on the floor, looking at a new rat-trap.' Nothing came amiss to him; his life was a series of triumphs.

'I have generally found means to execute whatever I have engaged to do,' he told Thomas Day; 'and I am, therefore, more inclined to form engagements than, I believe, on cool reflection, prudence would permit. I have also habituated my vanity to be more pleased with executing an engagement, than with doing an extempore favour.'

Maria said, of Richard's character: ' "No company or good company", was his maxim. By *good* he did not mean *fine*. Airs and conceit he despised, as much as he disliked vulgarity. Affectation was under awe before him, from an instinctive perception of his powers of ridicule. He could not endure, in favour of any pretensions of birth, fortune, or fashion, the stupidity of a formal circle or the inanity of common-place conversation. His impatience might, at the moment, be properly concealed; yet the force with which it burst out, when the pressure was taken off, gave the measure of the constraint he had endured.'

When the French fleet was operating off the Irish coast, and he had again pressed upon the Lord Lieutenant his plan for a telegraph linking various points in the threatened country, he was displeased at the indifference shown by Lord Camden. He had twice tested his system at distances of twelve and fifteen miles, and had spent five hundred pounds of his own money upon perfecting it. Nevertheless, 'my business is taken *ad referendum*, in the Dutch manner. It was expected, I suppose, that I should pay my court: no court on earth shall detain me another day from those I love, and whom I shall protect as far as my powers of mind and body will permit . . . Send the chaise to meet me on Friday.'

Now indeed events in Ireland had taken a serious turn. There were local insurrections, movements of rebellion, and it was thought clear signs of a revolutionary ferment everywhere. According to Maria, the magistracy, suffering through absenteeism from a shortage of resident gentlemen, had fallen into the hands of graziers, land-jobbers, and middle-men who lowered its whole standard. She continues:

'They bustled and bravadoed; and sometimes from mere ignorance, and sometimes in the certainty of party support of public indemnity, they overleaped the bounds of the law. Upon slight suspicion, or vague information, they took up and imprisoned many who were innocent; the relations of the innocent appealed to him who was known to be the friend of public justice . . . My father exerted himself upon all occasions to keep the law in its due course . . .

'Towards the autumn of the year 1798, this country became in such a state, that the necessity for resorting to the sword seemed imminent. Even in the county of Longford, which had so long remained quiet, alarming symptoms appeared, not immediately in our neighbourhood, but within six or seven miles of us, near Granard ... Though his own tenantry, and all in whom he put trust, were as quiet, and, as far as he could judge, well disposed, yet my father was aware, from information of too good authority to be doubted, that numbers of disaffected persons throughout Ireland were leagued in secret rebellion, and waited only for the arrival of the French to break out.'

Richard, already a Captain of Yeoman Cavalry, at length raised a corps of infantry in which both Catholics and Protestants were enlisted. His life was thereby endangered; but he was resolute, demanded a court martial on his chief assailant, and finally secured the man's aquittal as an irresponsible fanatic. During a temporary lull in such alarming manifestations he caused himself to be elected to the Irish Parliament, where he declined to 'become a commissioner of the revenue, a sinecure placeman, or a pensioner.' In fact, 'I had a charming opportunity of advancing myself and my family, but I did not think it wise to quarrel with myself, and lose my own good opinion at my time of life.'

While all these things were going on, Maria was in lively communication with her aunt, who lived some distance away, in the same region.

'We have this moment,' she wrote, 'learned from the sheriff of this county, Mr Wilder, who has been at Athlone, that the French have got to Castlebar. They changed clothes with some peasants, and so deceived our troops. They have almost entirely cut off the carbineers, the Longford militia, and a large body of yeomanry who opposed them ... My father's corps of yeomanry are extremely attached to him, and seem fully in earnest; but alas! by some strange negligence their arms have not yet arrived from Dublin. My father this morning sent a letter by an officer going to Athlone, to Lord Cornwallis, offering his services to convey intelligence or reconnoitre, as he feels himself in a most terrible situation, without arms for his men, and no power of being serviceable to his country. We who are so near the scene of action cannot by any means discover what *number* of the French actually landed; some say 800, some 1,800, some 18,000,

some 4,000. The troops march and countermarch, as they say themselves, without knowing where they are going, or for what . . .

'We are all safe and well, my dearest aunt, and have had two most
fortunate escapes from rebels and from the explosion of an ammunition cart. Yesterday we heard, about ten o'clock in the morning, that
a large body of rebels, armed with pikes, were within a few miles
of Edgeworthstown. My father's yeomanry were at this moment gone
to Longford for their arms, which Government had delayed sending.
We were ordered to decamp, each with a small bundle; the two
chaises full, and my mother and Aunt Charlotte on horseback. We
were all ready to move, when the report was contradicted: only
twenty or thirty men were now, it was said, in arms, and my father
hoped we might still hold fast to our dear home . . .'

They were to have accepted the escort of some dragoons who
were taking ammunition to the troops; but were fortunately detained
by Richard. The ammunition exploded on the road, and his foresight
saved them from almost certain death. Nevertheless they were
shortly afterwards obliged to fly, having the horror as they went of
seeing the mangled bodies of the soldiers; and just at this moment
Richard, never for one moment shaken, remembered that he had left
in his study a full list of those who formed his yeomanry corps. Discovery of it by the rebels must have produced acts of vengeance
against the members of that corps and their families. Disregarding
every danger, he galloped back, found and burned the list, and rejoined his family, who had reached what seemed to be the compara-
tive safety of an inn at Longford.

Worse followed. Richard was everywhere at once, leading his
corps, directing all as if he were actually a Commander-in-Chief;
and at one time, such were his energy and the general panic, the
Edgeworths were actually accused of making helpful signals to the
enemy. Only his stentorian cries to soldiers at dinner in the inn
averted what might have become a massacre.

Evidently some thought that this extraordinary man had gone too
far. Two hundred men, at least, had been heard to swear that they
would have his life. 'The scenes we have gone through for some days
past,' Maria told her aunt, 'have succeeded one another like the pictures
in a magic-lantern . . . It all seems like a dream, a mixture of the
ridiculous and the horrid . . . Last night my father was alarmed at

finding that both Samuel and John [two of his servants], who had
stood by him with the utmost fidelity through the Longford business,
were at length panic-stricken: they wished now to leave him.
Samuel said: "Sir, I would stay with you to the last gasp, if you were
not so foolhardy!" '

In the end, of course, everything quieted down. Edgeworthstown
House was not sacked; Samuel and John did not desert Richard; the
family, returning home, received a tumultuous welcome from their
deserted cats; the French invasion came to nothing; and Richard,
quite content to leave his family behind, went to Dublin, where he
delivered in Parliament a disappointingly temperate and temporizing
speech on the pending Union with England. Within a few weeks
the Edgeworths crossed the Irish Sea and settled for a time in Bristol.

This was the first of a series of visits paid to England, where
acquaintance was made very easily with politicians and literary men
and women. The Edgeworths visited Erasmus Darwin, then on the
point of death, Dr Beddoes, and others; they travelled to London,
where Maria formed her own opinions of great and, as she called
others, foolish personages; and as far as I can tell were never again,
while residing at Edgeworthstown, in danger or discomfort. Discomfort, and perhaps danger also, were experienced elsewhere; as
we shall see in the next chapter.

TWENTY-NINE

The Visit to France

IT IS interesting to those who have known global war, in which whole populations sheltered with varying courage from directed or haphazard bombs, to notice how free from all fears letter-writers of the eighteenth century show themselves. Horace Walpole amusingly notes the concern, but chiefly the curiosity, felt during Prince Charlie's invasion of the North; but apart from vehement debates between politicians regarding the justice or injustice of events precipitating the American War there is extraordinarily little reference to what was a major calamity to the nation. Major André's execution aroused feeling; in another war Wolfe's heroism is extolled; but until Napoleon gathered his armies at Boulogne there seems to have been no alarm whatever.

Wars were events occurring abroad. Privateers might range about the seas; men might be forcibly enlisted; no man suspected his neighbours; life continued, even on the south and east coasts, as it had done in time of peace. If it happened that English travellers were advised that it was unsafe to pass through one country on the journey home, they adopted another route and hoped to cross the Channel without mishap.

There was some change at the time of the French Revolution, when many aristocrats and priests found impoverished sanctuary in England; but even while the revolutionary government was fighting the Allies it was assumed that battles would take place in France, Flanders, or Germany. Imports were affected; the price of bread rose; it was a little dangerous to sail between England and Ireland: otherwise local affairs retained their former importance and the comfortable letter-writers could discuss books, plays, visits, their health, their rabbits or apple orchards, the price of lampreys, and their own useful inventions. Moreover, as soon as the Peace of Amiens was signed English people streamed across to France or Belgium as if nothing untoward had happened since they were last overseas.

This was the case with the Edgeworths; for Richard determined to escort his fourth wife (married very shortly after the third, Elizabeth Sneyd, had been buried), Maria, and her step-sister Charlotte to France, by way of Belgium. This latter country was visited first, in order that the less sophisticated members of the party should 'see inferior pictures before seeing those of the best masters, that we might have some points of comparison.' For the same reason, he took them to 'provincial theatres in Dunkirk and Brussels'; but unluckily Talma was playing in Brussels, so that in this respect his educational plan failed.

They set out from London in October, 1802, borne in a grand coach to which, once they were beyond the Channel, were harnessed 'by long rope traces six Flemish horses of different heights, but each large and clumsy enough to draw an English wagon. The nose of the foremost horse was thirty-five feet from the body of the coach, their hoofs all shaggy, their manes all uncombed, and their tails long enough to please Sir Charles Grandison himself. These beasts were totally disencumbered of every sort of harness except one strap which fastened the saddle on their backs; and high, high upon their backs, sat perfectly perpendicular, long-waisted postillions in jackboots, with pipes in their mouths.'

As the roads were flat and unhedged, as if 'laid by some inflexible mathematician', the Edgeworths would have slept while driving if incessant rattling and jolting had not kept them awake. They had provided themselves, however, with books which they found entertaining, including *Petits Romans*, by Madame de Genlis, which gave Maria a strong wish to meet the author; and once the tension of travel ended she had plenty of sights to rouse her novelist's memory and imagination.

'The post-houses,' she wrote to her cousin, who also felt zest for such details, 'are often lone, wretched places, one into which I peeped, a *grenier*, like that described by Smollett, in which the murdered body is concealed. At another post-house we met with a woman calling herself a *servante*, to whom we took not only aversion, but a horror; Charlotte said that she should be afraid, not of that woman's cutting her throat, but that she would take a mallet and strike her head flat at one blow. Do you remember the woman in *Caleb Williams*, when he wakens and sees her standing over him with an uplifted hatchet? Our *servante* might have stood for this picture.

'Bruges is a very old, desolate-looking town, which seems to have felt in common with its fellow-towns the effects of the Revolution. As we were charged very high at the Hôtel d'Angleterre, at Dunkirk, my father determined to go to the Hôtel de Commerce at Bruges, an old strange house which had been a monastery: the man chamber-maid led us through gallery after gallery, up stairs and down stairs, turning all manner of ways, with a bunch of keys in his hand, each key ticketed with a pewter ticket. There were twenty-eight bed-chambers: thank heaven we did not see them all! I never shall forget the feeling I had when the door of the room was thrown open in which we were to sleep. It was so large and so dark, that I could scarcely see the low bed in a recess in the wall, covered with a dark brown quilt. I am sure Mrs Radcliffe might have kept her heroine wandering about this room for six good pages . . .

'The whole road from Calais to Ghent is as flat and as straight as the road to Longford. We never knew when we came to what the innkeeper and postillions call mountains, except by the postillions getting off their horses with great deliberation and making them go a snail's walk—a snail's gallop would be much too fast. Now it is no easy thing for a French postillion to walk himself when he is in his boots: these boots are each as large and as stiff as a wooden churn, and when the man in his boots attempts to walk, he is more helpless than a child in a go-cart: he waddles on, dragging his boots after him [in a way that] would make a pig laugh.'

Once Paris was reached, they were in a whirl, meeting Madame Delessert, Madame Recamier, Madame Campan ('who keeps the greatest boarding-school in France'), Madame Suard (yet another of Thomas Day's obdurate loves), Koskiusko, and a thousand other celebrities. Richard declined being introduced to Napoleon, who was at that time First Consul, and the subject in England of many scandalous tales. 'He did not wish it.' Charlotte told her aunt, Mrs Mary

Sneyd, that when they attended a review 'we *saw* a man on a white horse ride down the ranks; we *saw* that he was a little man with a pale face, who seemed very attentive to what he was about, and this was all we *saw* of Buonaparte.'

Richard had what he considered better company. Though his knowledge of French was imperfect, he argued with a venerable French abbé about the precise meanings of the words *perfectibilité* and *perfectionnement* in such a way as to confound his opponent. He also entered into combat with two other philosophers. 'We have had,' he sent word home, 'profound metaphysical conferences in which we have avoided contest and have generally ended by being of the same opinion.' Whether those words meant that he had out-argued the philosophers (as in boyhood he had out-argued his father, and in old age professed to have set-down the acrimonious Dr Parr), or that he had merely remained, which was normal, convinced of his own rightness, the reader my decide. Richard had humour enough for either interpretation to be true.

In the midst of their engagements, and in fact when, being unwell, he was in bed, 'taking another *reef* of the blanket to keep my back warm,' Richard was waited on by an officer of the police summoning him to the Palais de Justice. There he was given a passport and ordered to leave Paris at once. No explanation was given; he was treated very rudely; and he was forced, under the advice of French friends, to withdraw from the capital. The party accordingly removed to Passy, where, after sleeping 'tolerably well', he was standing on a table pasting some paper over a broken window, when his friends came to say that there had been a mistake. It had been believed that he was brother to the Abbé Edgeworth, who was a proscribed man. As he was no more than cousin to the priest whose clothing had been soaked by Louis the Sixteenth's blood, he might stay in Paris.

He refused to stay. As Mrs Edgeworth wrote, 'rumours that war would break out with England began to be prevalent . . . Mr Edgeworth decided to set out immediately, and we began to pack up . . . M. Le Breton called, and said he was sure of knowing before that evening the truth as to Buonaparte's warlike intentions, and that if Mr Edgeworth met him at a friend's that night, he would know by his suddenly putting on his hat that war was imminent. He was unable to visit us again, and afraid if he wrote that his letter might be intercepted, and still more was he afraid of being overheard if he said anything at the party where they were to meet. Mr Edgeworth went, and saw M. Le Breton, who did suddenly put on his hat, and on Mr Edgeworth's return to us he said we must go.'

Before these unpleasantnesses arose, two events occurred, the first of which is vividly described by Maria in a letter written subsequently from Edinburgh to Mrs Mary Sneyd which I shall quote for its brilliance, and the second is an example of parental interference, common to the fathers in my Galaxy, in a daughter's love affairs. First Maria's description:

'Full of the pleasure I had received from the *Rosière de Salency*, I was impatient to pay a visit to Madame de Genlis. A few days afterwards we dined with Mr and Mrs Scotto, rather a stupid party of gentlemen. After dinner my father called me out of the room and said, "Now we will go to see Madame de Genlis." ...

'She lives—where do you think?—where Sully used to live, at the Arsenal. Buonaparte has given her apartments there. Now I do not know what you imagined in reading Sully's *Memoirs*, but I always imagined that the Arsenal was one large building, with a *façade* to it like a very large hotel or a palace, and I fancied it was somewhere in the middle of Paris. On the contrary, it is quite in the suburbs.

'We drove on and on, and at last we came to a heavy archway, like what you see at the entrance of a fortified town; we drove under it for the length of three or four yards in total darkness, and then we found ourselves, as well as we could see by the light of some dim lamps, in a large square court, surrounded by buildings: here we thought we were to alight; no such thing; the coachman drove under another thick archway, lighted at the entrance by a single lamp, we found ourselves in another court, and still we went on, archway after archway, court after court, in all which reigned desolate silence.

'I thought the archways, and the courts, and the desolate silence would never end: at last the coachman stopped, and asked for the tenth time where the lady lived ... While the coachman thus begged his way, we anxiously looking at him, from the middle of the great square were we were left, listened for the answers that were given, and which often from the distance escaped our ears.

'At last a door pretty near to us opened, and our coachman's head and hat were illuminated by the candle held by the person who opened the door, and as the two figures parted with each other we could distinctly see the expression of their countenances and their lips move: the result of this parley was successful: we were directed to the house where Madame de Genlis lived, and thought all difficulties ended. No such thing, her apartments were still to be sought for. We saw before us a large, crooked, ruinous stone staircase, lighted by a single bit of candle hanging in a vile tin lantern in an angle of the bare wall at the turn of the staircase—only just light enough to see that the walls were bare and old, and the stairs immoderately dirty. There were no signs of the place being inhabited except this lamp, which could not have been lighted without hands. I stood still in melancholy astonishment, while my father groped his way into a kind of porter's lodge, or den, at the foot of the stairs.'

The porter proved unfriendly, and sent them up the dark stairs with no effort of assistance; so that they were brought up short upon reaching 'two dirty large folding-doors,' at which they rang and thumped in vain. They pushed at one door, and found themselves in complete darkness amid what appeared to be some unrecognizable lumber. The rude porter was again appealed to. He indicated another door, 'my father had but just time to seize the handle of the bell, when we were again in darkness.' The sound of footsteps followed; they descried a very small girl with long corkscrew ringlets, who held a wavering candle; and were bidden to enter.

'She led the way with the grace of a young lady who has been taught to dance, across two ante-chambers, miserable-looking, but miserable or not, no house in Paris can be without them. The girl, or young lady, for we were still in doubt which to think her, led us into a small room, in which the candles were so well screened by a green tin screen that we could scarcely distinguish the tall form of a lady in black, who rose from her armchair by the fireside as the door opened: a great puff of smoke issuing from the huge fireplace at the same moment.'

The lady was Madame de Genlis, who remained silent until Maria addressed her in French, 'to which she replied by taking my hand and saying something·in which *charmée* was the most intelligible word. Whilst she spoke she looked over my shoulder at my father, whose bow I presume told her he was a gentleman, for she spoke to him immediately as if she wished to please, and seated us in fauteuils near the fire.

'I then had a full view of her face and figure: she looked like the full-length picture of my great-great-grandmother you may have seen in the garret, very thin and melancholy, but her face not so handsome as my great-grandmother's; dark eyes, long sallow cheeks, compressed thin lips, two or three black ringlets on a high forehead, a cap that Mrs Grier might wear,—altogether an appearance of fallen fortunes, worn-out health, and excessive, but guarded irritability . . . She seemed to me to be alive only to literary quarrels and jealousies . . .

'Forgive me, my dear Aunt Mary, you begged me to see her with favourable eyes, and I went to see her after seeing her *Rosière de Salency* with the most favourable disposition, but I could not like her; there was something of malignity in her countenance and conversation that repelled love, and of hypocrisy which annihilated esteem, and from time to time I saw, or thought I saw through the gloom of her countenance a gleam of coquetry. But my father judges much more favourably of her than I do; she evidently took pains to please him, and he says he is sure she is a person over whose mind he could gain great ascendancy . . .'

This belief on Richard's part was an instance of his exceptional vanity. He was sure of his power over women, because that power had never been challenged by any of his wives nor by any of his daughters, especially Maria. He was now to exercise it to fell purpose; and this was the second event to which I referred.

During the visit to Paris one of those with whom the Edgeworths formed social friendship was the King of Sweden's private secretary, a certain Monseiur Edelcrantz. To Richard's astonishment, and to the professed astonishment, at least, of Maria, this gentleman, who was 'of superior and mild manners,' and already a great admirer of her work, proposed marriage to Maria. There must have been considerable discussion between them; for upon Maria's mention of unwillingness to leave her country and her friends he explained that he had been all his life in the King of Sweden's service, that he should not fear blame from his fellow-countrymen if he went to live abroad, but that he felt bound in duty to finish some work he was doing 'for a large political establishment.'

Maria assured both her aunt and her cousin Sophy that she felt nothing but esteem for Edelcrantz and gratitude for his ardent proposal; but her step-mother took a different view. She knew that Richard, upon learning of the situation, experienced something like consternation. What! his obedient literary daughter forsake Edgeworthstown, her family, her fame, and in particular her father? It was impossible. She might be thirty-five, and therefore of an age to decide such a matter for herself; but he could not do without her. This, of course, was precisely Maria's dilemma. She had not, like Fanny Burney, experienced years of imprisonment at Court for which her father was responsible. She was therefore not desperate for escape, and not full of undeclared resentment towards one whom she had formerly adored. And, by comparison with Burney, Richard was a commanding personality who had never had to cringe to patrons. He was used to authority.

She was forced to admit that, as Richard several times rallyingly pointed out, Edelcrantz was extremely plain; but the same was said of herself, except when she was animated by merriment or spirit, and she was candidly informed by Richard that her own lack of beauty was likely in time to impair a husband's love. Nevertheless, according to Mrs Edgeworth, she 'liked the expression of [Edelcrantz's] countenance, the spirit and strength of his character, and his very able conversation,' and as far as we have any information, he was her first suitor. Had others been effectively dismissed?

'She was', wrote her step-mother, who saw the whole affair at close quarters, 'exceedingly in love with him. Mr Edgeworth left her to decide for herself; but she saw too plainly what it would be to us to lose her, and what she would feel at parting from us. She decided rightly for her own future happiness and for that of her family, but she suffered much at the time and long afterwards. While we were at Paris I remember that in a shop where Charlotte and I were making some purchases, Maria sat apart absorbed in thought, and so deep in reverie, that when her father came in and stood opposite to her she did not see him until he spoke to her, when she started and burst into tears . . .

'I think it right to mention these facts, because I know that the lessons of self-command which she inculcates in her works were really acted upon in her own life, and that the resolution with which she devoted herself to her father and her family, and the industry with which she laboured at the writings which she thought were for the advantage of her fellow-creatures were from the exertion of the highest principle.'

How content Richard must have been with this sequel to the early instruction written from beside his second wife's deathbed: 'Continue, my dear daughter, the desire which you feel of becoming amiable, prudent, and of USE . . . My writing to you in my present situation will, my dearest daughter, be remembered by you as the strongest proof of the love of your approving and affectionate father RICHARD LOVELL EDGEWORTH.'

THIRTY

Farewell to Richard

HAVING escaped from France, and landed safely in England, Richard and his three charges went by stages to Edinburgh, where Elizabeth Sneyd's eldest child, Henry, was at the University. He was apparently in only temporary ill-health, and Elizabeth's eldest daughter, Charlotte, who had been on the tour, was in the full bloom of loveliness; but both were already stricken with the Sneyd complaint and were to bring unaffected sorrow to the rest of this loving family.

Once back in Edgeworthstown, Richard resumed his activities as educator, supervisor, and inventor. While Maria wrote a new story with which she hoped to please her Swedish lover, the fourth Mrs Edgeworth began to make her contribution of six children to Richard's brood, which, if the nameless and sexless waif whom Anna Maria had produced just before her death be ignored, numbered twenty-two in all; and Richard himself had the joy of being allowed to erect (without remuneration) a chain of telegraph stations between Dublin and Galway.

Of the children living then, one, who was travelling in France and could not be warned, was kept a prisoner there for ten years, until, like Fanny Burney, he could return home; another was at Dublin University, where he was 'full of logic'. Maria wrote to a cousin: 'We perpetually hear the words *syllogisms*, and *predicates, majors* and *minors, universals* and *particulars*, affirmatives and negatives; . . . and we have learnt by logic that a stone is not an animal, and conversely that an animal is not a stone.' This obsession suggested to Maria a theme, or perhaps only a character, for a comedy which was to be performed domestically for Richard's birthday.

The telegraph system was finished and tested in readiness for

Napoleon's expected attack; but when Napoleon decided to look elsewhere for dominion Richard had the mortification of finding his work taken over by the military atuhorities. He was, however, appointed as unpaid member of a commission formed to study education in Ireland (his contributions to the commission's reports, naturally, were adjudged the best of all), and as member of a commission to inquire into the nature and extent of Irish bogs.

He was then sixty-five years of age, and suffering from a severe bilious fever; the district allotted to him consisted of nearly thirty-five thousand acres; and he was away from home for fifteen hours a day, in bad weather, without food, 'traversing on foot, with great bodily exertion, wet and deep bogs, scarcely passable at that season, even by the common Irish best used to them.' 'To our astonishment,' Maria confessed, 'his health not only endured these exertions, but improved under them, and was re-established.'

This activity was accompanied by experiments, continued until he was seventy, in the use of springs beneath carriages, which he showed to be productive, not only of ease to passengers and the safety of breakables carried within, but of benefit to the horses whose load was lightened by a greater mobility. It was after a visit to Dublin in connection with such experiments that he gave the first sign that a lifetime's sustained effort had begun to exhaust even his strong constitution. He was seriously ill.

'Yet there was so much animation in his manner, such firmness and strength in his voice—we saw him revive so wonderfully in every interval of sickness, and make such exertions in every intermission of pain, that we could not believe the body was failing, while the soul was so full of life and energy. But he was well aware of his imminent danger, he never deceived us or himself with false hopes. Nor did he ever for a moment repine, even when, from the loss of sight, he was deprived of all power of independent occupation.'

It was in his last months of life that Richard uttered the words—he often repeated them—which must seem a fit epitaph for this astonishing man. 'How I enjoy my existence!' he cried.

Maria hurried on with her literary work, the novel *Ormond*, which she began to read aloud to her father in the carriage taking them on the last visit he ever paid to Pakenham Hall. He was delighted with what he heard, and she was determined that, whatever the cost to herself, and the distress which Richard's failing strength caused her, the book should be finished while he was yet alive. In May, 1817, she wrote triumphantly to her cousin:

'This day, so anxiously expected—the only birthday of my father's for many, many years which has not brought unmixed feelings of pleasure. He had had a terrible night, but when I went into his room and stood at the foot of his bed, his voice was strong and cheerful, as usual. I put into his hands the hundred and sixty printed pages of *Ormond* which kind-hearted Hunter had successfully managed to get ready for this day. How my dear father can, in the midst of such sufferings, and in such an exhausted state of body, take so much pleasure in such things, is astonishing. Oh, my dear Sophy, what must be the fund of warm affection from which this springs! and what infinite, exquisite pleasure to me!

' "Call Sneyd [his second son by Elizabeth, a young man who distinguished himself by making Madame Recamier laugh] directly," and swallowed some stirabout, and said he felt renovated. Sneyd was seated at the foot of his bed. "Now, Maria, dip anywhere, read on." I began: "King Corny recovered." Then he said: "I must tell Sneyd the story up to this."

'And most eloquently, most beautifully did he tell the story. No mortal could have guessed that he was an invalid, if they had only *heard* him speak.'

He died almost exactly a fortnight later, on the 13th of June, 1817; and he left to Maria, in whose obedience he put full trust, the task of completing the story of his life, which he had carried only as far as the much publicized and, as in those days it seemed, quite scandalous marriage to his second wife's sister Elizabeth. Sudden illness at this point had interrupted him in the middle of a sentence; and although he lived for another ten years he never resumed the work. It was to be finished by Maria, who was told that she must not change a single word of his own narrative.

Maria set herself, as always, to obey. She very piously began by saying: 'I could not relinquish the hope of doing justice to the memory of my dear father; of the father who educated me; to whom, under Providence, I owe all of good or happiness I have enjoyed in life. Few, I believe, have ever enjoyed such happiness, or such advantages as I have had in the instructions, society, and unbounded confidence and affection, of such a father and such a friend. He was, in truth, ever since I could think or feel, the first object and motive of my mind.'

Her work took a couple of years to complete. When the book was published it was subjected to attack in the *Quarterly Review* from (I have always believed) the savage hand which also attacked Fanny Burney's *Memoir* of her father. The writer clamoured for an assurance from Maria that Richard had not, as he assumed, died unregenerate and ripe for eternal damnation. He did not receive this assurance. Maria, although told of the article, left it unread for fifteen years, and begged her outraged Aunt Ruxton never to 'lose another night's sleep or another moment's thought' over it. Her own feeling was 'calm of mind' a sort of 'satisfied resignation' at having done her best to produce something which Richard would have approved.

She lived for a further thirty-two happy years, chiefly at Edgeworthstown, but with visits elsewhere, some of which, eventful enough, were described with lively spirit in family letters. Many visitors waited upon her, from Sir Humphry Davy and Sir Walter Scott and his family to the American historian George Tickner. In London she met a host of society people from the nobility to Rogers and Sarah Siddons. She delighted them all. Sydney Smith said, 'She does not say witty things, but there is such a perfume of wit runs through all her conversation as makes it very brilliant.' Scott, who thought her like a fairy with a wand in her pocket, spoke of 'the *naïveté* and good-humoured ardour of mind which she unites with such fomidable powers of acute observation.'

Tickner describes Maria as she was at the time of their first meeting in August, 1835: 'A small, short, spare lady of about sixty-seven, with extremely frank and kind manners, and who always looks straight into your face with a pair of mild deep grey eyes whenever she speaks to you. Her conversation, always ready, is as full of vivacity and variety as I can imagine. It is also no less full of good-nature . . . In her intercourse with her family she is quite delightful, referring constantly to Mrs Edgeworth, who seems to be the authority for matters of fact and most kindly repeating jokes to her infirm aunt,

Miss Sneyd, who cannot hear them, and who seems to have for her the most unbounded affection and admiration.'

Books were read, and read aloud, at Edgeworthstown in profusion. She was always reading, novels, histories, scientific works, and—for example—Bentham's *Memoirs*, which proved to her that 'he could write plain English before he invented his strange lingo.' She was generous to her fellow-novelists, thinking well of Susan Ferrier, expressing enthusiasm for Fenimore Cooper's *The Pirate*, and with great pleasure reading Jane Austen's books as they appeared. Indeed, there must have been some correspondence with Jane Austen, who sent Maria a copy of *Emma*.

The comment made to her aunt by Maria on *Northanger Abbey* and *Persuasion* is particularly interesting. As a gentlewoman, she found 'that the behaviour of the General in *Northanger Abbey*, packing off the young lady without a servant or the common civilities which any bear of a man, not to say gentleman, would have shown, is quite outrageously out of drawing and out of nature.' And, as is proper to one who exclaimed 'Never mind the improbability. Let us go on with the entertainment,' '*Persuasion*—excepting the tangled, useless histories of the family in the first fifty pages—appears to me, especially in all that relates to poor Anne and her lover, to be exceedingly interesting and natural. The love and the lover admirably well drawn; don't you see Captain Wentworth, or rather in her place don't you feel him taking the boisterous child off her back as she kneels by the sick boy on the sofa? And is not the first meeting after their long separation admirably well done? . . .'

Maria's surviving step-aunt, her real aunt and cousin Sophy, her third step-mother, her brothers, sisters, nephews, and nieces were all dear to her. She enjoyed a little gossip about all sorts of people, especially the Empress Josephine and her gardening, and discreetly retailed it; she had strong feelings about Lord Byron; she was sorry when in London just to miss meeting Madam D'Arblay; and once the memoir of Richard was finished she took advantage of Napoleon's overthrow to revisit France. There she had enjoyable contact with many of those, including Madame de Staël's son and daughter (she was assured that Madame de Staël had never uttered the criticism attributed to her about 'sad utilitarianism'), and was regretful upon only one score, which unluckily was of great importance to her loving heart:

'Lyons!' she wrote to her step-sister Honora. 'Is it possible that I am really at Lyons, of which I have heard my father speak so much? Lyons! where his active spirit once reigned, and where now scarce a trace, a memory of him remains. The Perraches all gone, Carpentiers no more to be heard of, Bons a name unknown; De La Verpilliere— one descendant has a fine house here, but he is in the country.

'The look of the town and the fine *façades* of the principal buildings, and the Place de Bellecour, were the more melancholy to me from knowing them so well in the prints in the great portfolio, with such a radiance thrown over them by his descriptions. I hear his voice saying, La Place de Bellecour and L'Hotel de Ville—these remain after all the horrors of the Revolution—but human creatures, the best, the ablest, the most full of life and gaiety, all passed away.

'It is a relief to my mind to pour out all this to you. I do not repent having come to Lyons; I should not have forgiven myself if I had not.'

That was not the end of her own life; she continued very sweetly and courageously to spread delight among all she met, and to help in material ways famine-stricken inhabitants of her own land. For these poor people she worked without stint, rejoicing with deep emotion in the gifts sent for their benefit by those who loved her novels. One came from the children of Boston, with the inscription: 'To Miss Edgeworth, for her poor.' She was a good woman; and her father, vain, flamboyant, selfish, and boastful as he was, must have been a good and very upright man to inspire and keep such affection as she felt for him. He was the best of my Fathers; and he believed himself to be the best of all Fathers.

THIRTY-ONE

A Jovial Doctor

'BEFORE the eighteenth century,' wrote J. L. and Barbara Hammond in *The Village Labourer*, 'the amusement of the aristocracy was hunting the stag, and that of the county squires was of hunting the hare.' Under the Game Laws the only persons entitled to shoot game were those who possessed a freehold estate of at least one hundred pounds a year, or a leasehold estate of at least one hundred and fifty pounds a year. All others who shot or snared game were poachers; and if caught they were severely punished with imprisonment and whipping. Coursing, therefore, was a gentleman's sport; ownership of a pack of greyhounds what would now be called a 'status symbol.'

We are reminded of these facts by several episodes in the life of George Midford or Mitford (he changed the spelling in order to demonstrate his relationship to an old and wealthy family in Northumberland), who appears in this book as father of one whose best known, and indeed only now remembered, work is the collection of sketches of country life published in successive volumes under the title of *Our Village*. Walter Savage Landor, in a complimentary poem, after speaking in rapture of English rural scenes, assured Mary Russell Mitford that none could 'tell the country's purer charms so well' as she.

George Midford was what is known as a jolly man; hearty, punning, loud-voiced, coarse-grained, and a gambler. When, late in life, he was painted by John Lucas, his complexion caused the artist to run out of carmine at the first sitting. His passions were for cards, coursing, port, a seat on the bench of magistrates, and Parliamentary elections, which were associated in his mind with noise, excitement heavy drinking, and the exercise of endless shouted loquacity among his companions.

Born on November 15th, 1760, the year in which George the Third came to the throne of England, he was the second son of a Northumbrian surgeon named Francis Midford. On the death of his father he was taken care of by an uncle, and went to school in Hexham. He told his daughter in Hexham there he made friends at the age of eight with a company of strolling players who allowed him to attend the performance of at least one play because he had lent them his tame bullfinch. What happened when he left school is not recorded. Mary Russell Mitford said he studied medicine at Edinburgh University and spent three years as house-pupil to the great John Hunter; but her biographers have been unable to find any trace of attendance at Edinburgh, the Royal College of Surgeons, the Royal College of Physicians, the Royal College of Surgeons of Edinburgh, or the Royal Society of Apothecaries; and it is probable that Midford, who was a large talker and claimant to friendship with those of higher rank than his own, invented the story as part of his habitual brag. All that Miss Vera Watson, in her most admirable and scrupulous life of Mary Russell Mitford, can say on this point is that Mary's father was for two years assistant-dispenser and assistant-surgeon at the Haslar Naval Hospital in Hampshire before migrating at the age of twenty-five to Alresford in the same county.

There his attention was drawn to an unmarried woman, ten years older than himself, and no beauty, named Mary Russell. She was the daughter of a clergyman (described by Mary Russell Mitford in *Recollections of a Literary Life* as 'richly beneficed') and as far as is known lived quietly in a small unremarkable society. Midford had already jilted another young woman, to whom he behaved with impudent assurance when he met her again twenty years later at the house of William Cobbett; and the jilted girl, however charming, cannot have rivalled Mary Russell in one particular of especial interest to an adventurer. She had no fortune; whereas Mary Russell possessed nearly thirty thousand pounds in cash, together with additional property the nature of which, although it must have included her late father's house, furniture, and library, her daughter did not reveal.

George Midford was without means. He was, said Mary Russell Mitford, 'personally all that attracts the sex—clever, handsome,

young, and gay'; but he had no money. He made a feint of settling
two hundred pounds a year on his wife, 'out of his own property,
on which he insisted'; but the two hundred pounds were in the bank
of Fairyland, and it was maliciously said at the time that Mary Russell
had a set of shirts made for him, so that nobody could accuse her of
having 'married a man without a shirt to his back.'

She was so much fascinated by her suitor that she handed over to
him, without qualm, her entire fortune, excepting only a sum
variously estimated as two thousand five hundred or three thousand
five hundred pounds in the Funds which was protectively controlled
on her behalf by two clergymen, father and son, named Harness.
George Midford could never, in spite of constant effort, extract this
money from the virtuously inexorable trustees.

The pair were married at once, in October, 1785; and according to
Mary Russell Mitford they had three children, two of whom, both
boys, died in infancy. She herself, born on December 16th, 1787,
was extremely delicate—one story is that she was scrofulous, which
probably means only that she suffered from swollen glands—and in
after years she spoke of herself as having been 'a small, puny child,
looking far younger than I really was, and gifted with an affluence
of curls.'

She always adored her boisterous father ('this dear papa of mine,
whose gay and careless temper all the professional *etiquette* of the
world could never tame into the staid gravity proper to a doctor
of medicine'), and was petted by him in babyhood, taken riding on
his shoulder and allowed to pull his pigtail until the ribbon loosened
and powder showered upon them both; taken riding behind him on
the docile blood mare—it had to be a blood mare—which he used in
paying professional visits; and being made much of at all times in a
way to give her a sense of great importance.

She was then, as she became very differently as a grown-up person,
exceedingly important to her father and mother. As the only surviving
child in a family profuse in caress and endearment she was regarded
by them as unique, a prodigy of beauty, wit, and intelligence.

The house in which her first years were spent was ever afterwards
seen in a radiance of sentimental memory. It was, she said, 'a large
house in a little town of the North of Hampshire—a town, so small

that but for an ancient market, very slenderly attended, nobody would have dreamt of calling it anything but a village. The breakfast-room . . . was a lofty old spacious apartment, literally lined with books, which, with its Turkey carpet, its glowing fire, its sofas and its easy chairs, seemed, what indeed it was, a very nest of English comfort. The windows opened on a large, old-fashioned garden, full of old-fashioned flowers—stocks, roses, honeysuckles, and pinks; and that again led into a grassy orchard, abounding with fruit-trees, a picturesque country church with its yews and lindens on one side, and beyond, a down as smooth as velvet, dotted with rich islands of coppice, hazel, woodbine, hawthorn, and holly reaching up into the the young yaks, and overhanging flowery patches of primroses, wood-sorrel, wild hyacinths, and wild strawberries . . .'

Every memory she reproduced in her published works or correspondence with strangers was tinged with similar prettification. There had always been sunshine and flowers; discomforts were minimized, poverty not admitted, her father's habits glossed over. Knowing his true character quite well, she described him in *Our Village* as if he were a delicious morsel:

'The master of this land of plenty was well fitted to preside over it; a thick, stout man, of middle height, . . . with a healthy, ruddy, square face, all alive with intelligence and good humour. There was a lurking jest in his eye, and a smile about the corners of his firmly closed lips that gave assurance of good fellowship. His voice was loud enough to have hailed a ship at sea, without the assistance of a speaking-trumpet, wonderfully rich and round in its tones, and harmonizing admirably with his bluff, jovial visage. He wore his dark shining hair combed straight over his forehead, and had a trick, when particularly merry, of stroking it down with his hand. The moment his hand approached his head, out flew a jest.'

Less sentimental commentators, William Harness and Henry Chorley, gave a different turn to this agreeable portrait. Harness alluded to him as 'that old humbug,' and Chorley as 'utterly worth-less. . . . a robust, showy, wasteful profligate—a man whose life was a shame; whose talk was too often an offence, not to be tolerated.'

As for the wonderful house and garden, they had soon to be vacated; for the Doctor quickly spent a great deal of his wife's fortune, if not all of it; and his violently Whig or Radical opinions, presumably expressed with the noisiness of a bottle-lover, so much offended his neighbours and patients that he lost their esteem. He decided to move to Reading, a much bigger town in Berkshire, where politics were as exciting as he could wish, and coursing and high play at cards were common enjoyments.

The change was not satisfactory. In politics he quarrelled with the town's Corporation; at coursing he greatly enjoyed himself with greyhounds but wasted his time; and from cards he was led to ruinous extravagance by a French *émigré* schoolmaster who signed his letters 'De St Quentin'. With St Quentin he entered into speculations through which he lost thousands of pounds; and although for a time he tried to practise as a Doctor, and was credited by his daughter with one extraordinary cure, he soon abandoned the uncongenial effort. His great vanity was social position. Aspiring to the amusements of an aristocratic landowner, he had neither land nor birth, and was forced into ludicrous ostentation. His wife and daughter loved the ostentation; both, encouraged by his example, pretended a little in their turn.

Reading became uncomfortable as the Doctor's means declined and his debts and borrowings—for he is said to have borrowed far and wide—grew conspicuous. Even Mary Russell Mitford, always ambiguous about her father's monetary affairs, admitted in her *Recollections of a Literary Life* that by now his wife's money was gone and he was in serious trouble with creditors. He could not retrench; that was not his nature. He was committed to what Mary calls 'his own large-hearted hospitality.' Therefore, 'with characteristic sanguineness' (her phrase again), he thought he had better try his luck in a different neighbourhood, and when his daughter was eight years old she was again uprooted, this time to a large house in Lyme Regis.

Here, according to the rosy account given to Elizabeth Barrett, the garden was a paradise and the house a palace, with marble hall, long galleries and corridors, and noble staircases; and here Midford entertained *en prince*. Nevertheless within a year of the first display of grandeur in Lyme his fortunes had sunk so low that he had once again to escape his creditors by flight. Sending his wife and daughter before him, he went to London, too late for complete salvation; for it was now that he spent some time 'within the rules of the King's

Bench' or what St Quentin, reminding him of certain favours done, called 'in durance vile'. St Quentin asserted that he had used great address in raising money 'to get you out immediately.'

They were still in London upon Mary's tenth birthday. Midford, experiencing the familiar urge to become rich at a single throw, resolved on that day to buy a ticket for an Irish lottery. He thought the day propitious. He took his daughter for a walk which brought them to 'a not very tempting-looking place,' and there he invited her to choose from among the lottery tickets displayed whatever number she fancied. She fancied number 2224.

There was some haggling, because other people had already bought shares in the ticket; but she reminded Midford of his promise to buy whatever number she chose, and pointed out that the four figures added up to ten, which was her age that very day. Firmness, probably assisted by superstition, had its reward. The whole ticket was bought. It won the prize of £20,000. And Dr Midford was rich again. The family could return in safety, not to Lyme, but to Reading.

During these years of prosperity and collapse, the prodigy child received her father's haphazard attention. He was often away from home, gaming; but he received a prodigal's welcome when he returned, and having so much of the spoilt baby in his own temperament he was at his most jovial—with a tippler's ingratiatingness—in her company. Moreover, he took a boastful pride in displaying her precociousness to others.

At the age of three she was made to stand on the breakfast-table and read aloud from the day's newspaper. When she was six he took her to London by herself and treated her to a round of sight-seeing and theatre-going which she never forgot. As soon as she went to school he decided that she was to be a brilliant pianist; and teacher after teacher was blamed for her complete incompetence in piano-playing. At last he made up his mind that the instrument must have been wrongly chosen. It should have been the harp. It must now be the harp.

The harp, too, was a failure. Mary had almost as little ear for music as her father, who 'never knew the tune of *God Save the King*, from that of the other national air *Rule, Britannia*'. Since she was left alone to practise the harp in a room full of books, she delightedly examined those books. They fascinated her. Forsaking the harp, she read dramatic works by Molière and Voltaire, of which her father, who could not distinguish between 'oui' and 'non', knew nothing. They gave her already existing taste for old English ballads a new direction. Drama, especially poetic drama, and drama opening a whole new world of action and character to her limited vision, was an enchantment. Not yet essaying tragedy, she began to write poetry.

Meanwhile, making a fresh start in Reading, Midford bought with his lottery-winnings an old farmhouse, about three miles from the town, demolished it, and built on the site an imposing new residence. In compliment to Bertram Mitford, head of the Northumbrian family to which, stretching a local elasticity of cousinship, he claimed to belong, he gave it the name of Bertram House. At the same time he changed the spelling of his name to Mitford, so that he and his wife and daughter could refer, in a way reminiscent of Sir Walter Elliott's boastings about the Dalrymples, to 'my cousin of Mitford,' and 'my cousin Mitford of Mitford.'

The newly affluent Doctor saw himself as not only, like the Duke of Plaza-Toro, 'blazing in the lustre of unaccustomed pocket-money', but at last what he had pretended to be, a man of family, a landed proprietor, a gentleman farmer, and, very soon afterwards, a magistrate. He was able to hobnob with Shaw Lefevre, the Member of Parliament for Reading; he assumed a not quite genuine familiarity with political leaders in London; he talked loud and big, laughed, carried his daughter's poems to show to anybody whom he thought likely to advance her fame as a writer; and at last he took her to Northumberland as an exhibit and perhaps to open doors there which had never been opened to him before.

THIRTY-TWO

Wolf at the Door

AT the height of this northern triumph, as it seemed to a delighted girl of nineteen, Mitford (for in future we shall adopt his revised spelling) showed the appalling irresponsibility of his nature. He also allowed us a first glimpse of Mary's harsher side, a side never revealed in the idyllic writings by which she is remembered. Suddenly, in the midst of festivities, when he had arranged to spend two days with a former acquaintance, he heard that an election was to be held in Reading. Instantly abandoning his hosts and his daughter, he hurried south for the fray.

The hosts were naturally outraged, and Mary was deeply mortified. She wrote demanding his immediate return to Northumberland. 'Little did I suspect,' she said in a bitter letter, 'that my father, my dear beloved father, would desert me in this manner, at this distance from home.' And to her mother: 'You have no notion how very much I am offended with Papa for leaving me without even waiting a few hours to inform me of his intentions in person. I shall never again go such a distance from my Mama . . . for I perceive that on him I can place no reliance.'

Nor did she go again to Northumberland; but that was because the object of Mitford's excursion had been achieved and because his difficulties grew ever more acute, so that long journeys were impossible. He drove to London, he played cards at Graham's Club, in St James's Street, and less reputable places at which he thought himself swindled; he attended local race-meetings; he kept champion greyhounds; he insisted on bringing other carousers home for merry feasts; but if he promised, as he did, to carry his wife and daughter to any distance greater than Southampton they did not believe him.

Mary wrote to a correspondent: 'Papa has promised . . . that we shall all go to Devonshire this summer [to visit Sir William Elford]; he has likewise promised that we shall go to Paris. How he will settle this affair I cannot tell. He may perhaps satisfy his conscience by breaking both promises.'

The practice of card-playing, whatever objection may be made to its uncertain returns, develops in the player some skill, at least, in chicane. Mitford was full of deceptions, believing strongly in his gambler's power to deal with any situation requiring finesse. He was also vain of his business ability; and as soon as Mary began to think of making money by her pen he took a masterful hand in her concerns.

This was the male prerogative. Mary and her mother, being eighteenth century women, had no knowledge whatever of business. Mrs Mitford was a simpleton who never forgot to be grateful to her husband for marrying her; Mary was a dumpling entirely inexperienced, whatever omniscience she might assume in writing to female correspondents, in affairs outside her garden and the local countryside. She read prodigiously and uncritically, with a sense of refinement which caused her to refer to Jane Austen's lack of 'grace' and 'entire want of taste', to *Jane Eyre* as a 'coarse book', and Charles Lamb's Letters as 'not elegant enough'; but her notions were always restricted and restrictive, and her judgment did not equal her enthusiasm for expressing it.

Although never a poet, she turned with facility to verse. By the age of twenty-three she had ready for the Press a collection, largely consisting of tributes to Whig leaders such as Samuel Whitbread, which she bravely called *Miscellaneous Poems*; and the Mitfords, jubilant over this performance, which might help the Doctor into political circles, decided to have the book printed. They had some acquaintance with the celebrated Dr Valpy, head of one of the many schools in Reading, and this led them to Valpy's son, who had just set up in London as a publisher. Young Valpy agreed to print five hundred copies at their expense. Publication occurred in 1810.

Mary was afterwards much shocked by Valpy's bill; but Mitford, with his 'characteristic sanguineness,' brushed dismay aside. He busied himself, or pretended to busy himself, with the task of getting the book reviewed in as many journals as possible. 'Ten thousand thanks,' wrote Mary, who was convinced of his power to win friends and influence people, 'for your management of the Reviews.'

Had he been as successful a manager as he claimed to be? I think not. He certainly knew James Perry, of *The Morning Chronicle*—the Perry who found Hazlett's dramatic criticism for his paper such 'damned stuff'—and he told Mary that Perry had promised to make him acquainted with Brougham, afterwards Lord Chancellor, but then associated with *The Edinburgh Review*. This was news worth sending; and Mary was impressed by what looked like a *coup*.

'It is very kind of Mr Perry,' she wrote, 'to invite you to meet Mr Brougham, and I am sure it will be greatly in my favour. You advertize my poems *viva voce*, you know, my dearest, and your manners and conversation are the greatest recommendation. He will overlook the daughter's defects in the father's excellence.'

No review appeared in the *Edinburgh*. No account of any meeting with Brougham is extant. Probably it never took place. Nevertheless Mitford persisted in other directions. He and Mrs Mitford sent the poems to every great man they could think of, and Mrs Mitford, at least, was thrilled at receiving a polite but perfunctory acknowledgment from Lord Holland. She wrote a pompous notification of it to her husband, as if to show that she, too, had magnificent strings to her bow. But she and Mary were both quite in the dark about Mitford's doings. They supposed him to be living among the rich and mighty, and carrying all before him.

This was a misunderstanding, which he fostered. He had no such triumphs. All that happened was that his present efforts, like all subsequent negotiations with publishers, editors, and theatrical producers, took him an inordinate time, and enabled him to escape the unpleasantnesses which were gathering at home.

The unpleasantnesses were greater than they had been since 1797, the year in which Mary's choice of a lottery-ticket had brought blessed relief to the family. William Harness asserts that within six years of building Bertram House the owner's splendour had faded. By 1808 'the servant out of livery had been dispensed with. There had ceased to be any lady's maid. The footmen had degenerated into an awkward lad, who was not only expected to wait at table and go out with the carriage, but to make himself useful in the stable or the garden. The carriage horses were employed on the work of the farm, and it was not every day of the week on which Mrs and Miss Mitford could command the use of them. In a year or two the chariot disappeared. It was out of repair, and its place was never supplied. Afterwards the pictures were sent up to town in a hurry and sold at Robins's. By-and-by Mrs Mitford is harassed by difficulties in obtaining remittances for the moderate expenses of her diminished household. She thanks her husband for sending her ten pounds, and tells him, with a grateful sense of relief, how she will go to Reading and pay the butcher and baker on the morrow. Taxes fall into arrears, and are only extorted by threatening notices from the collector. Tradesmen refuse to serve the house with the common requirements of the family till previous accounts are settled. On several occasions they are at a loss whence to procure food for the greyhounds, and once Mrs Mitford writes imploringly to the Doctor, with the greatest earnestness, but without the slightest intimation of reproach, requesting him to send her *a one pound note* by return of post, as they are actually in want of bread.'

Harness's account appears in a note to *The Life of Mary Russell Mitford*, edited by the Rev. A. G. L'Estrange, and published in 1870. It summarizes events covering a number of years subsequent to that in which the *Miscellaneous Poems* were published; but it is made quite clear that by 1811 Mitford was in a considerable mess. Having become full of schemes for farming, he had arranged, although insolvent, to buy land for this purpose from Lord Shrewsbury. He had lent or invested money which he would never see again. His genius for whist, at which Mary said he was one of the six best players in England, produced no gains but only losses. He was at the end of everything.

As a last resort (Harness's note refers to this) he sold whatever pictures remained in the house. Cheated, by his own account, by Lord Shrewsbury and Lord Shrewsbury's agent, cheated by a cousin to whom he had lent money and the French *émigrés* who had induced him to put it into bubble companies, cheated again over the sale of the pictures, he was forced to admit to Mary, then twenty-four and the brains of the family, that things were not all they might be.

When Harness came to edit Mary's letters in conjunction with

L'Estrange he told his friend that some of her terms of endearment needed to be pruned before publication. 'Some of her "dearest loves" to that humbug, her father, must be slightly mitigated; its exuberance must be a little repressed.' He was wise, no doubt, to make this recommendation; but Mary was only following family custom, for the George Mitfords were much given to flummery. They all used terms of endearment; they all boasted of 'our chief, Bertram Mitford, of Mitford' (whom Mary claimed as her godfather); Mrs Mitford spoke in writing to her husband of 'my illustrious relation, Lord William Russell'; and Mary herself referred to 'our dear friend, the member for Reading . . . Monck, a collateral branch of the great Duke of Albemarle's family.' Among other curious insincerities to correspondents, there is one, written in 1830, which asserts that she had been 'born and reared in affluence, being the child of very rich parents,' and adds: 'About fifteen years ago a most expensive chancery suit and other misfortunes too long to detail, reduced my dear father from opulence to poverty.'

This florid habit was used only with strangers. It is absent from letters to Harness, and in those to Mitford there is sometimes plain-speaking which approaches rudeness. Once, in acknowledging some gloves, Mary said: 'You never could mean those machines you sent me for gloves. You fitted them on the shopman, did you? I really should have thought you had tried them upon an elephant.' So, in 1811, she wrote:

'The distressing intelligence conveyed in your letter, my best-beloved darling, was not totally unexpected. From the unpleasant reports respecting your affairs I was prepared to fear it. When did a ruined man (and the belief is as bad as the reality) ever get half the value of the property which he is obliged to sell? Would that Monck had bought this place last autumn! At present, the best we can do seems to me to be, to relinquish the purchase of Lord Shrewsbury's land, and (if it will be sufficient to clear us, mortgage and all) to sell all we have out of the funds, and with that, and Lord Bolton's legacy, and the money in Lord Shrewsbury's hands, and the sale of the books and furniture, clear off our debts and endeavour to let this house.

'If this can be done, and we can get from three to four hundred a year for it, we may live very comfortably; not in a public place, indeed, but in a Welsh or Cumberland cottage, or in small London lodgings. Where is the place in which, whilst we are all spared to each other, we should not be happy? . . . This scheme is the result of my deliberations. Tell me if you approve of it, and tell me, I implore you, my most beloved father, the full extent of your embarrassments. This is no time for false delicacy on either side.'

The letter filled Mitford with indignation. It was such an unexpected affront that she was forced to apologize for having written her 'most beloved ittey boy . . . one word that could by any possibility vex him whom she loves better than all the world.' What! Live in rural obscurity, or cheap London lodgings! Abandon coursing, cards, his dogcart, his carousals, his magistracy! He was a Mitford, a man of standing. The suggestion that he would make any sacrifice in order to pay his debts was an outrage. It filled him with horrified anger.

He did not reveal the full extent of his embarrassments. Mary never knew what they were. She knew only that Bertram House, together with the land half-bought from Lord Shrewsbury, was sold at auction, that the purchase was repudiated by the buyer on the ostensible ground that Mitford had no power to sell Lord Shrewsbury's land, and that the Doctor began that interminable action in the High Court to which Mary attributed his fall from opulence to poverty.

It is not known how the family managed to go on living in the house, as they did until 1820; but Mitford constantly absented himself from home on the pretence of having much business on his hands, and Mary and her mother bore alone the frightening calls of duns. Mary told her father what was happening. He did not stir, but lived from week to week in town, playing with energy, but otherwise showing supreme carelessness of events at Reading. At last she said that unless he immediately answered urgent demands for the payment of taxes, 'the things will certainly be sold . . . There is nothing but resolution and activity that can make amends for the time that has been wasted.'

In another letter she adds to the story. 'I am sorry to tell you, my dearest father, that Mr Riley's clerk has just been here with a law paper utterly incomprehensible, but of which the intention is to inform you that, if the mortgage and interest be not paid before *next Monday*, a foreclosure and ejectment will immediately take place; indeed I am not sure whether this paper of jargon is not a sort of ejectment. We should have sent it to you but for the unfortunate circumstance of not knowing where you are . . . No time must be lost in doing something, as next Monday someone will be put in possession.'

In spite of worry, Mary was getting fat. With exquisite pleasantry Mitford, when he saw this, talked of taking down the doors of the house, widening the chairs, and new-hanging the five-barred gates in order to accommodate her increased girth. It was characteristic of his levity. He ignored the fact that his house and garden were falling into visible decay. 'The gravel is covered with moss—the turf turned into pasture—the shrubberies into thickets.'

Mitford now tried very hard to get hold of that small and inalienable Trust of Mrs Mitford's. It would save him. He could pay a few debts, stake the money, be a rich man again. Harness, however, obdurate in duty, and disliking and distrusting the man he had to deal with, would not part with Mary's one asset. He refused again and again. Mitford, almost crazy to get his fingers on the money, was baffled. He had nothing but the interest on its investment in the Funds, which was pledged to the creditors. Maddening! Maddening! No wonder Mary besought her own dear love to take care of himself in every way, and to keep up his spirits.

THIRTY-THREE

A Writer is Made

SHE still had occasional triumphs with her verses, as when a poem on the British and Foreign Bible Society was read aloud at a great dinner and her health was drunk by those present. She also stayed at the home of James Perry in London, where she was introduced to Thomas Moore and Thomas Campbell; and she wrote a play called *The King of Poland* which was not produced. From her accounts of these doings one might be led to suppose that she had the reception of a new literary lioness; but she made the most of casual encounters with well-known people who were met at large parties; and her familiar references to them are not to be compared in authenticity with comparable references in the letters and diaries of Maria Edgeworth or Fanny Burney.

Here is the explanation. Maria was a gentlewoman, whose father frequented the most distinguished company of his day as one assured of respect because of his character and intelligence; Fanny, however doubtful of her own quality, did really receive the arch flattery of such men as Johnson, Cambridge, Burke and Horace Walpole because her father was known and liked, if not always deeply respected, as an active, modest, and amusing personality. Mary Russell Mitford alone had a father on whose word and reputation neither she nor anybody else could rely.

Whatever show he and his wife might make of social distinction (the latter characteristically told her daughter that before marriage she had known Jane Austen as 'the prettiest, silliest, most affected, husband-hunting butterfly,' when in fact Jane Austen was only ten years old at the time, and neither Mary nor Harness knew of any continuing acquaintance), Mitford was a virtually bankrupt opportunist who drove his daughter into perpetual struggle to keep up appearances. She told the world of his medical degree, his splendid character, his greyhounds, and his magistracy; but she had met the duns, she knew some of the truth about his gambling, and she lacked all sense of fundamental security. She therefore prized and magnified every contact and every compliment paid to her. It was precious in itself; the magnification was a part of the family *rococo*.

By the end of March, 1820, when she was thirty-two, the Mitfords had been forced at length to vacate Bertram House ('it nearly broke my heart') and go to live a mile away in a dilapidated cottage at Three Mile Cross, on the Turnpike Road between Reading and Basingstoke. This hovel filled Mary with dismay. To a familiar correspondent, already doing her best to smile, she supplied a rueful picture of the place:

'Our residence,' she said, 'is a cottage—no, not a cottage—it does not deserve the name—a messuage or tenement, such as a little farmer who had made twelve or fourteen hundred pounds might retire to when he left off business to live on his means. It consists of a series of closets, the largest of which may be eight feet square, which they call parlours and kitchens and pantries; some of them minus a corner, which has been unnaturally filched for a chimney; others deficient in half a side, which has been truncated by the shelving roof. Behind is a garden about the size of a good drawing-room, with an arbour which is a complete sentry-box of privet. On one side a public-house, on the other a village shop, and right opposite a cobbler's stall.'

Such was the report to a friend. Observe how the miserable dwelling was transformed in the idyllic pages of *Our Village*:

'Divided from the shop by a narrow yard, and opposite the shoemaker's, is a habitation of whose inmates I shall say nothing. A cottage—no—a miniature house, with many additions, little odds and ends of places, pantries, and what not; all angles, and of a charming in-and-outness; a little bricked court before one half, and a little flower-yard before the other; the walls, old and weather-stained, covered with hollyhocks, roses, honeysuckles, and a great apricot-tree; the casements full of geraniums (ah, there is our superb white cat peeping out from amongst them); the closets (our landlord has the assurance to call them rooms) full of contrivances and corner-cupboards; and the little garden behind full of common flowers, tulips, pinks, larkspurs, peonies, stocks, and carnations, with an arbour of privet, not unlike a sentry-box, where one lives in a delicious green light, and looks out on the gayest of all gay flower-beds. That house was built on purpose to show in what an exceedingly small compass comfort may be packed.'

The difference between private view, glossed as it was, and the pretty sketch offered to the public is full of interest. It shows, I think, the defensive veneer of kindness, happiness, and sweetness with which it had become natural to her to cover all unpleasant reality. That there was such a veneer, and that it was known to be a veneer, is indicated by a brief note, written in 1819, to a novelist named Barbara Hofland:

'My Miss J— always speaks of her mother with a respect and affection which does great credit to herself, but I have no doubt that she can be disagreeable enough. I only wish she may take it into her head to give me a scolding. I have a snug little taste for impertinence, which I make it a point of conscience not to indulge unprovoked, but which it quite does me good to let loose when I see occasion; so that those who, presuming on a very undeserved character for gentleness and so forth, which I have got . . . sometimes find themselves turned round in a very unexpected manner.'

After the move to Three Mile Cross, Mary was led by the desperate fortunes of this contracted household to consider what she herself could do to earn money. A Mitford of Mitford obviously could not engage in work which would lower the family socially. She had already, however, used her pen to some purpose. Could she not turn it to even greater advantage?

She had written narrative poems which made no serious impression on critical taste—the very name of one of them, *Blanche of Castile*, gave her father, he said, the vapours;—but there were other and more remunerative kinds of writing. She remembered how much she had enjoyed her early adventures with Molière and Voltaire; and while the comedy of Molière was not within her compass the tragedies of Voltaire, from *Mérope* to *Mahomet* and *Iréne*, suggested possible themes. Why not emulate Voltaire?

It seemed a possibility. All the poetasters of her time were writing for stage performance blank-verse tragedies about foreign tyrants or heroes or upstarts. They may have been led to do this by naural relief at the defeat and exile of Napoleon, or by the general ferment of ideas on the Continent, or by certain political constraints nearer home; but the grandiose figure, from Tamerlane to Louis the Four-teenth of France, offered material, not merely for the printed play, but for the stage, where Kemble, Kean, and Macready were either rivalling each other, or forming coalitions, or quarrelling, and ex-pressing hunger for splendid parts.

The authors may also have been influenced by a contemporary rediscovery of the Elizabethans. German metaphysical writers discussed them in terms which Coleridge found worthy of adoption; Schiller and Goethe, leading a romantic reaction from rigid French classicism, delighted in reviving German legends and portraying German heroes; Charles Lamb published his great anthology, *Specimens of the English Dramatic Poets who lived about the Time of Shakespeare*; and from reprints of contemporary writings on the theatre it would seem that Shakespeare was constantly performed in London.

Since the Elizabethans, for reasons of personal safety, had often laid the scenes of their plays in Italy, Italy was a happy hunting ground for modern copyists who sought practicable tyrants, heroes, and upstarts. Shakespeare and Ben Jonson had found such men in Rome; two hundred years later the city states of as yet un-unified Italy repre-sented twenty Romes. Italy was especially a land, as Verdi showed when he wrote tragic opera in the mid-century, where violent action was both natural and exciting.

Mary, having read continuously since publication of *Miscellaneous Poems* and composition of the unperformed *King of Poland*, saw the scenic attractiveness of Italy. She had never been there; but this was of no account. Hers was no such high line as conscious genius would dictate; she was too modest for that. She aimed, in need, at financial returns. She wrote with particular actors or managements in view, and cut out characters, or put in characters, re-wrote acts, and re-wrote leading parts, in order that Macready or Charles Kemble or Young, or some other jealous performer, should be induced to include the play in his repertory. Alterations were endless, first this person, and then that other person, offering advice or instruction which she tried to follow; and after all changes had been made and high hopes had been roused by the reported enthusiasm of some fidgety star the plays were ignominiously rejected.

Her disappointments were heart-rending. She faltered often; she endured many humiliations, including contemptuous comments from her father and one or two superior-minded judges like Thomas Noon Talfound, who had associations with Reading; she gave everybody leave to meddle with what she had written; and she waited upon the whims of famous actors with truly touching humility; only desperate resolve to earn money by the stage supporting her courage for months on end.

Mitford was galvanized into activity by the prospect of a new source of money for use at the card-table. He waited upon the managers; he undertook to supervise his daughter's contracts; and when, over a period of years, *Julian, Foscari* (about a Doge of Venice), *Rienzi* (about a medieval Roman revolutionary and dictator), and other plays had been written, he and Mary had the satisfaction of finding the family benefited by sums ranging from one to five hundred pounds at a time. The encouragement was tremendous.

Nor did plays represent the whole of Mary's output. She became a very hard-working professional author, writing incessantly for magazines and the popular 'annuals' and 'almanacs', and trying later on to hit public taste with a novel; but in chief, and to her continuing fame, beginning and selling the series of widely charming country sketches known when collected into volume form as *Our Village*. Nothing else she wrote was quite as successful as *Our Village*, which when the sketches appeared in five series between the years 1824 and 1832 made friends everywhere in England and abroad. These books were humane, sentimental, and quite her own. They most creditably helped to keep the Mitfords alive, and would have done more if there had not been one constant extra-domestic strain upon them.

Mitford was always sure that with a little luck he could gain more in a single night than his daughter could do in a year. Sometimes, hopeful of using her earnings for this purpose, he made good contracts for her; sometimes he was either over-reached by publishers or so sceptical of the prospects of what he offered that he suffered himself to be beaten down. Once Mary angrily sent him back to

Bentley; once she wrote that she was 'determined never again to trust my father with any matter of business'; but I do not think she kept her word. He was probably by that time getting old and mentally feeble; and her vehemence against him was gone as soon as it had been expressed.

The strain caused by all this overwork was too much for Mary. As early as 1823 she wrote to a friend: 'My father has resolved—partly, I believe, instigated by the effect which the terrible feeling of responsibility and want of power has had on my health and spirits—to try if he can himself obtain any employment that may lighten the burden. He is, as you know, active, healthy, and intelligent, and with a strong sense of duty and of right. I am sure that he would fulfil to the utmost any charge that might be confided to him; and if it were one in which my mother and I could assist, you may be assured that he would have zealous and faithful coadjutors. For the management of estates or any country affairs he is particularly well qualified; or any work of superintendance which requires integrity and attention.'

This appeal produced no response from the person to whom it was addressed. He was personally acquainted with Mitford, whom he had first met at the card-table. It was followed, three months later, by a second: 'My dear father, relying with a blessed sanguineness on my poor endeavours, has not, I believe, even inquired for a situation; and I do not press the matter . . . Pray, my dear friend if you should hear of any situation that would suit my dear father, do not fail to let me know, for that would be the real comfort, to be rid of the theatre and all its troubles. Anything in the medical line, provided the income, however small, were certain, he would be well qualified to undertake. I hope there is no want of duty in my wishing him to contribute his effort with mine to our support.'

Still there was no response and no paternal effort. To Harness, the only person with whom she was entirely candid, she wrote two years later: 'You cannot imagine how perplexed I am. There are points in my domestic situation too long and too painful to write about . . . The terrible improvidence of one dear parent—the failure of memory and decay of faculty in that other who is still dearer, cast on me a weight of care and of fear that I can hardly bear up against.'

Finally, on this point and one other of much importance, she wrote to an old friend in 1829: 'My father—very kind to me in many respects, very attentive if I am ill, very solicitous that my garden should be nicely kept, that I should go out with him, and be amused —is yet, so far as art, literature, and the drama are concerned, of a temper infinitely difficult to deal with. He hates and despises them, and their professors—looks on them with hatred and scorn; and is constantly taunting me with my "friends" and my "people" (as he calls them), reproaching me if I hold the slightest intercourse with author, editor, artist, or actor, and treating with frank contempt every one not of a certain station in the county.'

Any other course would have been unbecoming in a father claiming close kinship with landed gentry in the North, in a magistrate, in one who, like his daughter, combined radical views with an aristocratic outlook.

THIRTY-FOUR

The Last Flickers

GEORGE MITFORD, like Charles Burney, Thomas Seward, George Crabbe, and Richard Lovell Edgeworth, was a robust and inexhaustible man. Like them, he lived long; and his strength lay in the almost mesmeric power he enjoyed over one devoted, hard-working daughter who was nurse, housekeeper, and breadwinner for so long that she was ultimately exhausted. She herself could have lived on almost nothing at all, as she was forced to do in old age; but while Mitford was sponging on her this was not possible. Owing to 'the absolute inertness of my father in such matters—an obstinacy of going on in the same way which I cannot describe—I find myself compelled to acquiesce in a way of living which, however inexpensive, is still more so than we can afford.'

She was offered a home with people whom she described as rich cousins named Raggett; 'it was, however, clear that my father's comfort would have been destroyed by such an arrangement. To have left him *here* would have been impossible; and if Mr Raggett had (as I believe he would have done) given him a home at Odiam the sacrifice of his old habits—his old friends—the blameless self-importance which results from his station as Chairman of the Reading Bench —and his really influential position in this county, where we are much respected in spite of our poverty, would have been far too much to ask or to permit.'

Those words were written two years after the death of Mrs Mitford, whose mind had faded long before her fatal seizure on Boxing Day, 1829. The Doctor was then seventy, and apparently in excellent health; Mary, besides writing hard, was tending a garden which became famous, keeping house and entertaining her father, and—once again—being deeply agitated by his efforts to gain possession of the small Trust to which he had no right. She appealed, in the midst of this agitation, to her true protector, William Harness:

'My dear Friend, I write in great haste, just to caution you in case you should receive any authority, or pretended authority, from any quarter, to sell out our money in the funds, not to do so without communicating with me. I have no doubt of my father's integrity, but I think him likely to be imposed upon . . .'

Harness's reply is noteworthy:

'Depend upon it the money shall *never* be touched with my consent. It was consideration for your future welfare which prevented my father's consenting to its being sold some years ago, when you had been persuaded, and wished to persuade him, to your own utter ruin. That £3,000 I consider as the sheet anchor of your independence, if age should ever render literature irksome to you, or infirmity incapacitate you for exertion; and, while your father lives, it shall never stir from its present post in the funds . . . I do not doubt Dr Mitford's integrity but I have not the slightest confidence in his prudence; and I am fully satisfied that, if these three thousand and odd pounds were placed at his disposal today, they would fly the way so many other thousands have gone before them, tomorrow. Excuse me saying this; but I cannot help it.'

Mitford was foiled. His next step was to take one of Mary's manuscript plays to London, in order to sell it. According to Harness, he was away from home on his mission from early May until the end of June; but what he did while in London, and how he managed to live without remittances from his daughter, is not known. He certainly was producing no income at all; for in his absence Mary wrote to a friend: 'I must trust in Providence to have sufficient strength of mind and body to support us by my own efforts.'

The father's strength of mind and body had hitherto been model. He now began to suffer from lameness. He also fell mysteriously and broke an arm and two ribs, while severe attacks of what Mary calls English cholera considerably reduced his vitality. She told her new friend Elizabeth Barrett (who also had father-trouble, of a different variety) that she was 'now sitting on the ground outside his door, with my paper on my knee, watching to hear whether he sleeps . . . For the last two years I have not had a week without anxiety and alarm, so that fear seems now to be a part of my very self . . . I hardly dare leave him for half an hour.'

Illness grew upon the Doctor. His eyesight began to fail. 'He could read, I think; but, somehow, to read to himself seems to give him no pleasure; and if anyone else is so kind as to offer to read to him, *that* does not do . . . I have been obliged to resume my old habits, and to read to him and play cribbage with him, during more hours of each day (every day, except Sundays) than you could well believe.'

'He is sadly out of spirits, and very feeble, and his eyesight fails him so much that I read to him during many, many hours of every day and all the evening; but his want of spirits renders it most difficult. During our cribbage-playing, my reading, my talking, he often moans for hours together. Mr May [the surgeon] comforts me by saying, that there is more of habit than of suffering; but what a trial it is to hear, and how difficult to bear up with undiminished cheerfulness, I leave you to imagine . . . Not a day passes now without his saying, and repeating perhaps a hundred times, that he has but very few days to live. Only yesterday he came into my room to take leave of it, and blessed me at night, "for", he said, "the last time." '

He was too pessimistic. There was still life in the old dog. As late as January, 1841, when Mitford was eighty, Mary wrote to Elizabeth Barrett:

'I write, my beloved friend, by my dear father's bedside; for he is again very ill. Last Tuesday was the Quarter Sessions, and he *would* go, and he seemed so well that Mr May thought it best to indulge him. Accordingly he went at 9 a.m. to open the Court, sat all day next the chairman in Court, and afterwards at dinner, returning at two o'clock a.m. in the highest spirits—not tired at all, and setting forth the next day for a similar eighteen hours of business and pleasure. Again he came home delighted and unwearied. He had seen many old and dear friends, and had received (to use his own words) the attentions which do an old man's heart good; and these, joined to his original vigour of constitution and his high animal spirits, had enabled him to do that which to those who saw him at home infirm and feeble, requiring three persons to help him from his chair, and many minutes before he could even move—would seem as impossible as a fall of snow between the tropics, or the ripening of pineapples in Nova Zembla.

'All this he had done, but not with impunity. He had caught a severe cold, and having on Saturday taken nearly the same liberties at Reading, and not suffering me to send for Dr May, until rendered bold by fear I did send last night—he is now seriously ill . . . He is so restless, too—so very, very restless—and everything depends upon quiet, upon sleep, and upon perspiration; and yet, for the last twelve hours I am sure that he has not been two minutes without his getting out of bed, or up in bed, or something as bad.'

This was almost Mitford's last frolic. In September, 1842, he was hoisted into a carriage by four persons to attend the laying of the first stone of the Reading reading-room; and this was his very last public appearance. He lived until the end of the year after having been able in sunny weather to 'sleep all the afternoon in the garden, and . . . sit up all night to be read to.' Seeing that Mary was 'greatly fatigued—much worn—losing my voice even in common conversation' he attributed her state 'to the last drive or walk—the only thing that keeps me alive—and tells everybody he sees that I am killing myself by walking or driving; and he hopes that I shall at last take some little care of myself and not stir beyond the garden. Is not this the perfection of self-deception? And yet I would not awaken him from this dream—no, not for all the world—so strong a hold sometimes does a light word take of his memory and his heart—he broods over it—cries over it!'

His tears lapsed. He was protected from anything which could cause them to flow. Mary even persuaded Harnett to relinquish some small part of the Trust, so that certain debts could be paid and his gloom and irritability allayed. Having been relieved of every earthly distress, he sank into a state of near-senility, repeating prayers and hymns and listening to the gospels; and at length, on December 11th, 1842, he died without a sign or a struggle. Mary could not account for the fact that as soon as he was dead she was seized with terrible and continuous shivering.

'I have just strewn flowers over him (the lovely chrysanthemums that he loved so well, that he helped me to strew over my dear mother), and he looks with a heavenly composure, and almost with his own beautiful colour, the exquisite vermilion for which he was so famous, on his sweet serene countenance. I could not touch him. Mr May desired me not. He said that there was danger in renewing the chill, which has now passed away. I mean the shiverings.'

Psychologists will explain those shiverings. To myself they indicate, besides an overwhelming reaction from the strain of many months, the awakening of long-suppressed aversion. Mary could not bear to touch the old man. He was dead; the falsity of all her encomiums upon him was recoiling. Too strong to be dismissed at once it appears in this account of his funeral:

'My great grief for my dear, dear father has been much soothed by the singular respect shown to his memory. The chief gentry of the county sent to request to follow his remains to the grave; the six principal farmers of the parish begged to officiate as bearers; they came in new suits of morning and were so deeply affected that they could hardly lift the coffin. Every house in our village street was shut up; the highway was lined with farmers and tradesmen, in deep mourning, on horseback and in phaetons, who followed the procession; they again were followed by poor people on foot. The church and churchyard were crowded, and the building resounded with tears and sobs when the coffin was lowered into the vault . . . Everybody loved him.'

Two comments may be permitted. The first is from Elizabeth Barrett, who wrote: 'I feel grateful to all the dear people . . . for their dissuading you from attendance at the funeral.' The second is a footnote to this description by Henry Chorley, who said: 'Of the sincerity of Miss Mitford's feelings expressed in this letter, there can be no question; as little the extent of her hallucination; merciful, as rescuing her from bitter thoughts and retrospects, but utterly baseless as anything like fact, or the feelings of those who knew the whole story. Dr Mitford was tolerated because she was beloved. The respect paid to his remains was not so much to them as to her . . . From none of the many survivors of both, with whom I have spoken, have I heard any other than one and the same judgment.'

Epilogue

THE severity of every posthumous condemnation of George Mitford arises from the fact that he lived on into the Age of Queen Victoria. The large tolerance of the eighteenth century, and the aristocratic tradition from which that tolerance drew its strength, had passed or was passing. A censorious parochialism was taking its place; parents were to be, not grossly and thoughtlessly, but by system, harsh with their children, from rectitude and a zeal for punishment.

> Speak roughly to your little boy,
>   And beat him when he sneezes;
> He only does it to annoy,
>   Because he knows it teases.

Mitford was as far as possible from the Victorian ideal. By 1842 he was as much of an anachronism as Seward, who could have lived in no other century than the eighteenth. Mr Barrett, that more notorious father (I sometimes feel that he has been unjustly abused, since his daughter, upon whom he had lavished so much care, was not really the little dove of sentimentalists), was a real Victorian. He could be adamant when his daughter offended his *amour propre*. He cast her off. But in doing this he was forced to *insist* upon his mastership of the house, as other Victorian fathers were forced to insist that they were the masters, because there was a great rumbling of revolution out of doors and a first bright-eyed questioning of authority within. Politics were running to liberty; only in Church and home was there a stiffening of control.

None of the daughters I have described in this book ever questioned her father's right to do what he pleased with her life and her fortune. Edgeworth himself, the model father, ruled by kindness and encouragement; Burney, less model, meant only to be kind, although he lived a helter-skelter life of no great sagacity. Neither had any jealousy of his daughter's literary skill. The one capered with excitement over it; the other turned it to sound educational or utilitarian purposes. Only Mitford, loving the outward show of rank, was aristocratically amused by his daughter's literary fame and aristocratically contemptuous of all literary fame.

According to our views, he was a silly and reckless man, who threw away two fortunes—his wife's and his lottery prize—from sheer love of excitement. But by eighteenth-century notions, which embraced gambling as one of the truly aristocratic sports, he was blameworthy solely because he had no great estate on which he could draw to make good his speculative losses.

We have seen how Edgeworth proved immune in boyhood to the temptations of the card-table, and how he was warned by the dying gambler, Sir Francis Delaval, against the life of dissipation which was being led by all the high-wagering gentlemen of the day. We have seen how young Charles Burney was amusedly exposed by Greville to the excitement of seeing gamblers win and lose fortunes in a night. We know that Greville himself, rich as he was, suffered deeply in the end as a result of this passion for gaming. Such glimpses reveal the commonness of ruin.

Nor were men of intelligence immune. Horace Walpole, who contented himself with modest games of loo and quadrille with countesses, makes merry over Charles James Fox's immense losses, and tells one shocking story of seeing Fox's belongings piled in the street as a consequence of seizure for debt. But Fox had a rich father; Mitford had no father, no landed estate, and, once he had run through his two bonanzas, no resource but his daughter's pen. That pen did not earn enough to justify his way of life; but he could not bear to change his way of life. To do so would be to wake from a dream.

Therefore he died owing what in those days and in rural circumstances was the considerable sum of nine hundred pounds, which Mary's friends clubbed together to pay. Mary herself, after great hardship, was granted a Government annuity. In this respect she resembled Burney, but not Madame D'Arblay. As for the

Edgeworths, Richard was never at any time short of money, but when he died the son who inherited Edgeworthstown had to accept so much help from Maria that the estate belonged to him in name only.

These instabilities were natural in the eighteenth century with its overlap into the early years of the nineteenth. The only solid values lay in the ownership of land, the possession of one or more sinecures, investment in the Funds, or successful trade. Since trade rose every year to greater importance the social atmosphere changed. It is still changing. No father of the present century dominates a daughter as those old fathers, Edgeworth, Burney, or Mitford, did. If he were to try to do so he would hear something to his disadvantage.

Index

ADDISON, Joseph, 62

Aldeburgh, Suffolk (birthplace of George Crabbe), 49, 50

Allen, Maria, 80, 82

Allen, Mrs (second wife of Charles Burney), 80 ff., 88, 105–6, 107

André, Major John, 40, 204

Aram, Eugene, 75

Armstrong, Dr (medical adviser to Charles Burney), 73

Arne, Thomas, 62, 67, 69

Aston, the Misses, 76

Aston, Sir Willoughby, 76

Austen, Capt. Francis (brother of Jane Austen), 23

Austen, the Rev. George (father of Jane Austen), 19–20, 33

Austen, Jane, 19–20, 104, 149, 193, 217, 227, 233

BAC, Godwin, 73

Bach, Johann Sebastian, 62

Baillie, Joanna, 195

Barbauld, Mrs (poet), 153

Barber, John (printer), 88

Baretti, Giuseppe (of the Thrale household), 100

Barlow, Thomas, 93–8, 107

Barrett, Edward Moulton, 245

Barrett, Elizabeth, 241, 242, 244

Barry, James (painter), 50

Barry, the Misses, 76

Beattie, Dr James (poet), 100

Beckford, William, 87

Beddoes, Thomas Lovell, 191–2, 203

Beerbohm, Max, 14

Belvoir Castle, George Crabbe at, 50, 52–3

Benet, the Rev. James (Rector of Aldeburgh), 50

Benson, A. C., 14

Benson, Edward White (Archbishop of Canterbury), 14–15

Benson, Robert Hugh, 14

Bentham, Jeremy, 21, 217

Bertram House (home of the Mitfords), 225, 228–9, 234

Biron, Duchesse de, 140

Black Bourton, Oxon (home of the Elers family), 161

Bolingbroke, Henry St John, first Viscount, 22, 69

Boswell, James, 27, 31, 36, 37, 101–2

Bouffleurs, the Mesdames de, 140

Brady, Larry, 193

Bridges, Lady Augusta, 76

Bristol, the Edgeworths at, 203

Brown, 'Capability', 60

Browne, Sir Thomas, 59

Browning, Robert, 192

Brudenel, Lord, 132

Bruges, Maria Edgeworth at, 206

Buckingham, Duchess of, 122

Burke, Edmund, 22, 28, 37, 50, 62, 66, 100, 101, 125

Burney, Charles, 19, 28, 65–97, 100–10 passim, 114, 115–16, 118, 124–53 passim, 162, 245, 246: for his wives, see Sleepe, Esther; Allen, Mrs

Burney, Charles, junior (son of Charles Burney), 78, 104

Burney, Charles Rousseau (cousin and husband of Hetty Burney), 82

Burney, Charlotte (sister of Fanny Burney), 62, 78, 82, 135, 140–3 passim

Burney, Fanny (Frances), 28, 33, 61, 67–9, 73, 74, 78, 79, 81, 82, 86–9, 91–9 passim, 102–16, 119–23 passim, 124–5, 130–53 passim, 162, 216, 217

Burney, Frances: see Burney, Fanny

Burney, Hetty (sister of Fanny Burney), 73, 77, 78, 79, 81, 82, 88, 94, 96, 99, 129

Burney, James (later Rear-Admiral; son of Charles Burney), 74, 75, 78, 82, 147

Burney, Richard (brother of Charles Burney), 104–5

Burney, Susanna (Susan; sister of Fanny Burney), 78, 82, 103, 107, 108, 111, 115, 117, 118, 134, 135–6, 143, 145

Burns, Robert, 56

Butler, Samuel (1835–1902), 15

Buxton, Thomas Seward at, 41

Byng, John, fifth earl of Torrington, 23, 24, 30

Byron, Lord, 56, 217

CAMBRIDGE, Miss (friend of Fanny Burney), 133–4, 152

Camden, Lord, 200

Campan, Madame, 206

Campbell, Thomas, 56

Canning, George, 149

Carlyle, Thomas, 16

Cary, Henry (translator of Dante), 40

Chandos, Duke of, 76

Chapone, Mrs, 119, 120

Charlotte, Queen (wife of George III), 121, 123, 125–6, 128–9, 131–2, 134, 135, 142, 147, 152

'Cherokee King', the, 76

Chessington, Surrey (home of Samuel Crisp), 82, 88–92 passim, 105–6, 109, 124, 133

Cholmondeley, Mrs, 108, 109, 113

Chorley, Henry, 222, 244

Churchill, Lord Randolph, 28

Churchill, Winston, 28

Cibber, Colley, 61

Cibber, Mrs Colley, 67

Clayton, Lady Louisa, 131

Cobbett, William, 21, 220

Coleridge, Samuel Taylor, 191, 192, 236

Congreve, William, 59
Cooper, Fenimore, 217
Corelli, Arcangelo (Italian composer), 69
Cornwall, Barry, 192
Cornwallis, Lord, 201
Coussmaker, Miss, 106, 108
Cowper, William, 51, 56
Crabbe, George, junior, 16, 28, 48–9, 50, 53–5, 57–8
Crabbe, George, senior, 16, 48–58, 61–2
Crabbe, John, 57
Crisp, Samuel, 76, 79, 82, 88–92, 103, 104, 109, 111, 113, 114, 115, 124, 125, 138
Crutchley, Mr (executor of Thrale's will), 119–20, 145

D'ARBLAY, Mrs: see Burney, Fanny
D'Arblay, Alexandre (husband of Fanny Burney), 146–7, 148, 150, 151
D'Arblay, Alexandre, junior (son of Fanny Burney), 150–1
Darwin, Erasmus, 24, 25, 35, 37, 38, 73, 167–8, 171, 180, 185, 198–9, 203
Davy, Sir Humphry, 216
Day, Thomas, 164–5, 169–72, 176–8, 185, 199, 206
Defoe, Daniel, 21, 24, 29
Delany, Mrs Mary (earlier, Mrs Pendarves), 18–19, 25, 35, 63, 79, 120–1, 122–3, 125, 126–7, 132, 133, 136, 138, 149, 152, 154–5
Delany, Dr Patrick, 64, 123, 154–5
Delaval, Sir Francis, 165–7, 246
De Quincey, Thomas, 37

Dewes, Bernard, 126–7
Dickens, Charles, 15
Dodsley, James (publisher), 38, 50, 74, 104
Drury Lane Theatre, Charles Burney at, 67
Dryden, John, 59
Dublin, R. L. Edgeworth in, 169–70

EDELCRANTZ, Monsieur (King of Sweden's secretary), 210–11
Edgeworth, Abbé, 207
Edgeworth, Bessie: see Edgeworth, Elizabeth (daughter of Richard Lovell Edgeworth)
Edgeworth, Charlotte (daughter of Richard Lovell Edgeworth), 190, 194, 205, 206
Edgeworth, Elizabeth (daughter of Richard Lovell Edgeworth), 185, 194
Edgeworth, Emmeline (daughter of Richard Lovell Edgeworth), 191, 194
Edgeworth, Henry (son of Richard Lovell Edgeworth), 194, 213
Edgeworth, Henry Essex (brother of Richard Lovell Edgeworth), 157–8
Edgeworth, Honora (daughter of Richard Lovell Edgeworth), 194, 218
Edgeworth, Maria, 104, 179, 181–2, 184, 185, 186–90, 192–218, 247
Edgeworth, Richard (father of Richard Lovell Edgeworth), 162, 163
Edgeworth, Richard (son of Richard Lovell Edgeworth), 174–6

Edgeworth, Mrs Richard (mother of Richard Lovell Edgeworth), 158, 163

Edgeworth, Mrs Richard (fourth wife of Richard Lovell Edgeworth), 207, 211, 213

Edgeworth, Richard Lovell, 19, 24, 155–60, 174–90 passim, 193–210 passim, 246; for his wives, see Elers, Anna Maria; Sneyd, Honora; Sneyd, Elizabeth; Edgeworth, Mrs Richard (fourth wife)

Edgeworth, Sneyd (son of Richard Lovell Edgeworth), 194, 215

Edgeworth, William (son of Richard Lovell Edgeworth), 194

Edgeworthstown House (home of Richard Lovell Edgeworth), 169, 179–80, 186, 192, 203, 213

Effingham, Lord, 166

Eglinton, Lord, 166

Elers, Anna Maria (first wife of Richard Lovell Edgeworth), 162–3, 164, 174, 176

Elers, John (father-in-law of Richard Lovell Edgeworth), 161

Elers, Mrs John (mother-in-law of Richard Lovell Edgeworth), 161

Elmy, Sarah, 49, 52

Evelyn, John, 60

FERRIER, Susan (novelist), 217

FitzGerald, Edward, 49, 52

Fitzroy, Lord Charles, 36

Forster, John, 15, 16

Fox, Charles James, 22, 50, 62, 246

Francis, Clement (husband of Charlotte Burney), 141

Froude, James Anthony, 15–16

GARRICK, David, 61–2, 66, 67, 86, 90, 99, 100, 101, 103

Gay, John, 121

Geminiani, Francesco, 68

Genlis, Madame de, 205, 208, 209–10

George III (King of England), 65, 121, 123, 125, 127–9, 131–2, 138

George IV (King of England), 28

Gilpin, William, 121–2

Gluck, Christoph, 90, 109

Goethe, Johann, 236

Goldsmith, Oliver, 32, 122

Gosse, Edmund, 15

Grafton, Duke of, 36, 85

'Grafton, Mr' (Fanny Burney's cousin), 105

Gray, Thomas, 62, 63, 77, 85, 87, 163

Grenville, Sir Bevil, 120–1

Grenville, Sir Richard, 120

Grétry, André (French composer), 63

Greville, Fulke, 68–74, 87, 99, 246

Greville, Mrs Fulke, 74, 85, 99

HALES, Lady, 106, 108, 109

Hammond, Barbara, 29, 219

Hammond, J. L., 29, 30, 219

Handel, George Frederic, 62, 65, 75

Hare, Augustus, 14, 162, 179

Hare Hatch (home of Richard Lovell Edgeworth), 163

Harley, Robert (first Earl of Oxford and Mortimer), 21

Harness, William, 221, 222, 228–30, 231, 232, 238, 241·

Hastings, Warren, 22, 137, 149

Hawkins, Sir John, 64, 92
Hawkins, Laetitia, 64
Haydn, Franz Joseph, 71
Hayley, William, 40
Hazlitt, William, 56, 60
Heberden, Dr, 181
Herbert, George, 59
Herbert of Cherbury, Lord, 68
Hertford, Lady, 41
Hogarth, William, 60
Holdernesse, Earl of, 85, 90
Holkham House, Norfolk, 75
Holland, Lord and Lady, 57, 228
Houghton House (home of the Walpoles), 75
Hudson, Thomas (painter), 60
Hunter, Mr (headmaster of Lichfield free-school), 37
Huntingdon, Countess of, 122
Hyde, Catherine ('Kitty'), 121

INCHBALD, Elizabeth, 51, 165
Ireland, 154, 169–70

JENKINS, Thomas, 145
Jenyns, Soame, 120
Johnson, Dr Samuel, 27, 28, 35, 36, 37, 41, 50, 60, 61, 62, 64, 65, 66, 75–6, 80, 86, 99, 100, 101, 102, 108, 109, 110–11, 112, 115, 119, 120, 124–5, 152, 167
Jonson, Ben, 59
Josephine, Empress (wife of Napoleon), 217

KEAN, Edmund, 236
Kemble, Charles, 236
Ketton-Cremer, R. W., 27

King's Lynn, the Burney family at, 74–5
Kirkman (Kirchman), Jacob, 67, 68, 90

LAMB, Lady Caroline, 57
Lamb, Charles, 236
Landor, Walter Savage, 15, 16, 219
Langton, Bennet, 100
Le Breton, Richard, 207–8
Lefevre, Shaw, 225
L'Estrange, the Rev. A. G., 229, 230
Lichfield, Staffordshire, 36, 37, 38, 41, 167–8, 169, 184
Linton, Mrs Lynn, 13, 16
Liston, John, 56
Lluellyn, the Rev. George, 67
Locke, William, 21, 145, 147
Locke, Mrs William, 144, 145, 147, 152
Lockhart, John Gibson, 15, 16, 49
Longford, Lord and Lady, 160–1
Louis XVI (King of France), 157
Louis XVIII (King of France), 157
Lowndes, Mr (publisher), 104, 105
Lucas, John (painter), 219
Lyme Regis, Mitford family at, 223
Lyons, Maria Edgeworth in, 218
Lyttelton, Lord, 41

MACAULAY, Thomas Babington, first Baron, 88
Macready, William Charles, 236
Marcello, Benedetto, 62
March, Lord (later Duke of Queensberry), 166
Marlborough, John Churchill, first Duke of, 22

Mason, William (writer), 67, 90

Mecklenburg, Prince of, 131

Meriden, John Byng at, 30

Metastasio, Pietro, 90, 149

Midford, Francis (father of George Mitford), 220, 221

Midford, George: *see* Mitford, George

Mitford, George, 219–46 *passim*

Mitford, Mary Russell, 37, 219–47 *passim*

Mitford, Dr William, 19, 24

Monboddo, James Burnet, Lord, 37

Montague, George, 41

Moor Park (home of Sir W. Temple), 23

Moore, Tom (writer), 49

Morgan, Lady (novelist), 194

Mozart, Wolfgang Amadeus, 87

Murphy, Arthur (author and dramatist), 80, 100, 101, 102, 112

NAMIER, Sir Lewis, 22

Napoleon, 204, 206–7, 208, 214

Narbonne, Louis (lover of Madame de Stael), 146, 147

Newton, Sir Isaac, 99

Nollekens, Joseph, 61, 99

Norbury Park, Surrey (home of William Locke), 145, 147

North, Lord, 50

Northcote, James, 60

Northumberland, Mitford family in, 225

ORD, Mrs, 143

PAKENHAM HALL (home of Lady Longford), 160, 214

Palestrina, Giovanni, 62

Paoli, Pasquale, 119

Paris

Charles Burney and his daughters in, 78–9; Maria Edgeworth in, 206, 211

Parr, Dr Samuel, 37, 38, 155, 207

Pendarves, Alexander, 122–3

Pendarves, Mrs Alexander: *see* Delany, Mrs Mary

Pergolesi, Giovanni, 62

Perry, James (of the *Morning Chronicle*), 228, 233

Piozzi, Mrs: *see* Thrale, Mrs

Piozzi, Gabriel (second husband of Mrs Thrale), 118–19

Pitt, William (the elder; first Earl of Chatham), 22, 62

Poland Street, London, the Burney family's home in, 76–87

Portland, Duchess of, 121, 123

Prior, James (biographer of Edmund Burke), 62

Prior, Matthew, 121

Procter, Bryan Walter: *see* Cornwall, Barry

QUEEN SQUARE, Bloomsbury, Charles Burney's family at, 87 ff.

Queensberry, Duchess of, 121

Quin, James (actor), 67

RADCLIFFE, Mrs, 156

Radnor, Lady, 108, 109

Reading, the Mitford family at, 223

Récamier, Madame Jeanne, 206, 215

Reynolds, Sir Joshua, 37, 50, 60-1, 99, 142

Richardson, Jonathan, 60, 111

Rishton, Maria, 152

Rogers, Samuel, 44, 57, 152-3, 195

Roubiliac, Louis François, 61

Rousseau, Jean Jacques, 64, 87, 161, 163, 170, 174-5, 184, 185, 187

Russell, Mary (wife of George Mitford), 220, 221, 227-30 *passim*, 232, 240

Rutland, Duchess of, 28

Rutland, Duke of, 28, 50, 53

Ruxton, Mrs (sister of Richard Lovell Edgeworth,), 199

Ruxton, Sophy, 211, 213, 215

St Martin's Street, Leicester Fields, London: the Burney family at, 99 ff.

Saintsbury, George, 22, 109

Scarlatti, Alessandro, 69

Schiller, Johann, 236

Scholes, Percy, 73

Schwellenberg, Mrs, 136, 137

Scott, Sir Walter, 15, 16, 28, 40, 56, 195, 216

Selwyn, George, 30

Seward, Anna ('Nancy'), 35, 36, 37-47, 100, 165, 168, 169, 171, 177-9, 183

Seward, Thomas, 19, 35-47, 113, 142, 171, 178

Seward, Mrs Thomas, 37, 171

Shaw, George Bernard, 59

Shelburne, Lord, 50

Sheridan, Betty, 139

Sheridan, Richard Brinsley, 67, 74, 101, 112

Shrewsbury, Lord, 229, 230

Siddons, Mrs Sarah, 56, 194-5, 216

Sitwell, Sir George, 16

Sitwell, Osbert, 16

Sleepe, Esther (first wife of Charles Burney), 70-2, 73, 74, 77, 80

Smelt, Lemuel, 130-1, 133, 134

Smollett, Tobias George, 205

Snetzler, John (German organ-builder), 75, 90

Sneyd, Elizabeth (third wife of Richard Lovell Edgeworth), 172-3, 176-7, 178-9, 183, 184, 194, 205, 215

Sneyd, Honora (second wife of Richard Lovell Edgeworth), 40, 171-3, 178, 179, 180, 181-2

Sneyd, Mrs Mary (aunt of Charlotte Edgeworth), 207, 208

Southey, Robert, 40, 191

Spencer, Lady, 149

Staël, Madame de, 143-5, 146, 189, 196, 217-18

Sterne, Laurence, 61, 85, 170

Stevenson, Robert Louis, 59

Stow Hill, Lichfield (home of Thomas Day), 171

Strachey, Lytton, 15

Streatham, the Thrale family at, 100 ff., *passim*

Stuart, Charles Edward (Prince Charlie, the 'Young Pretender'), 204

Stuart, Christopher, 67

Suard, Madame, 206

'Swan of Lichfield', the: *see* Seward, Anna

Swift, Jonathan, 23, 59, 123, 155

Talfourd, Sir Thomas Noon, 237
Talma, François Joseph, 205
Tartini, Giuseppe, 69
Temple, Sir William, 60
Thomson, James (poet), 67
Thornhill, Sir James (painter), 60
Thornhill, Jane (wife of William Hogarth), 60
Thrale, Henry, 100
Thrale, Mrs (later Mrs Piozzi), 40, 79, 100–2, 108, 109, 110–15, 118–20, 122, 149
Thrale, Queeney, 100
Three Mile Cross (home of George Mitford), 234–5
Thurlow, Lord, 50, 55
Tickner, George (American historian), 216
Traherne, Thomas, 59
Trevelyan, G. M., 21, 121

Vaughan, Henry, 59
Verdi, Giuseppe, 236

Voltaire, François, 87, 235

Walpole, Horace, 22, 27, 36, 41, 63, 87, 119, 120, 139–40, 142, 154, 204, 246
Walpole, Sir Robert, 22, 60
Watson, Vera, 220
Wells, H. G., 15
Wesley, John, 22, 23, 24, 31, 64, 75
Whitbread, Samuel, 227
Wilbury House, Wiltshire (home of Fulke Greville), 70, 74
Windham, William, 140, 141
Woodforde, the Rev. James, 23, 24, 25, 33
Woodforde, John, 25
Woodforde, Nancy, 24, 34
Wordsworth, William, 57

York, Duke of, 166, 167
Young, Arthur (brother-in-law of the second Mrs Charles Burney), 83–5
Young, Mrs Arthur, 83
Young, Charles Mayne, 236
Young, Dolly, 80